This book is dedicated to the mothers and fathers whose sons and daughters willingly set off on a strange and dangerous road and never found their way home.

Published by John Thomas Ambrosi

ISBN-13: 978-0615572451

ISBN-10: 0615572456

Certain persons appearing in this book are provided pseudonyms to protect their privacy.

Cover: Hancock Monument, Gettysburg National Military Park, Photographs in the Carol M. Highsmith Archive, Library of Congress

Dedication: Union Soldier Reloading by Randy Steele

ROUTE 15

TO

GETTYSBURG

✳ ✳ ✳ ✳

A JOURNEY

BY

JOHN THOMAS AMBROSI

CONTENTS

CONTENTS

CONTENTS

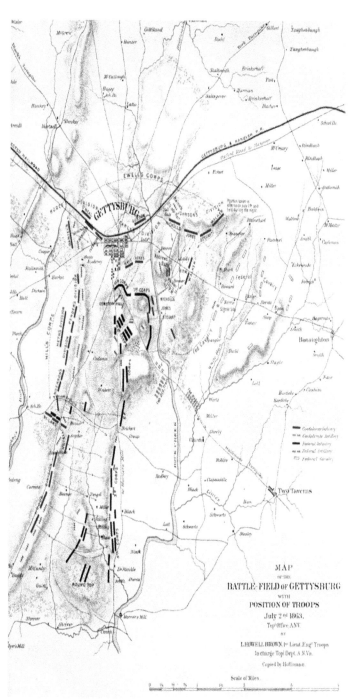

(Map of the Battlefield at Gettysburg, Library of Congress)

"Our battered suitcases were piled on the sidewalk again; we had longer ways to go. But no matter, the road is life."

- Jack Kerouac –

✳ ✳ ✳ ✳

My Familiar Place

COLLEGE, that final fling, the last carefree period of forgivable immaturity, faded in my mind and in my rear view mirror as I drove down winding Route 15 through the northern hills of Pennsylvania.   It was June of 1984 and the unseasonably early spring heat was my sole companion as I sped south to my journey's end in northern Virginia.

I had recently graduated from the University of Rochester, an institution with some esteem in the college ranks. The campus boasts an attractive quadrangle, a Greek Revival styled library and brick dormitories perched on a wide bend of the Genesee River on the southern edge of the city from which it took its name.   My undergraduate years there were pleasurable and, by choice, unchallenging since I pursued a major in which most of my young life I had remained deeply immersed.

The hospital where I was born and the house in which I spent my first year were just a stone's throw across the river from Rochester's ivy covered walls. The Bull's Head section of the city, taking its moniker from a long demolished nineteenth century tavern, had seen better times. It had declined to a level of sorry repute and was eyed by the city's gendarmerie as one of the most violent and crime ridden neighborhoods in Rochester. Quite a few illuminati at the university considered it a fortunate circumstance that the Genesee flowed where it does. Its log choked, silted waters provided a natural moat, shielding academia's erudite peninsula from urban reality.

The campus was also only a few miles from my parents' house in suburban Penfield. I was a homeboy, far too comfortable in my surroundings and inexplicably reluctant to pick up stakes and leave the nest as most did at my age. So I chose to stay in Rochester and, for the next four years, was never more than minutes from a home cooked meal and my mother's washer and dryer.

Hard work in high school had won me a scholarship to Rochester and the honor of membership in its blue jacketed and gold buttoned Naval Reserve Officer Training Corps Battalion. Originally hoping to be an officer in the navy, a change of heart after a summer midshipman cruise on a destroyer drove me towards the Marines instead. That long ago decision put me on the road on this hot June day to Quantico, the crossroads of the Marine Corps.

Parting with family and good friends saddened me while at the same time filling my mind with fresh and satisfying memories. My father once told me that college is the best four years of one's life. I was probably in the midst of a semester's final exams and wouldn't have believed him even if I had been paying attention. With the benefit of hindsight, dear old Dad hit the nail squarely on the head. For those lucky enough to attend, college is the last chance in life to be as free with such limited responsibility. In my case, its end meant a much delayed but permanent cutting of the umbilical cord that connected me to home.

I pondered all of this as I navigated the downslope off the Allegheny Plateau and slowed through the depressed towns decaying along the shores of the Susquehanna River. Farther on, I weaved back and forth on the perpetually potholed and congested stretches of road that plague Harrisburg area drivers. Pushing past the commercial strip at Camp Hill and out of stop-and-go traffic there, I accelerated up to highway speed as Route 15 transitions into a four-lane divided freeway outside Harrisburg's southern suburbs. Approaching the Maryland border, I sighted the first of six exits to Gettysburg and its resident National Military Park. On a whim and with some time on my hands, I decided to stop in for some lunch and a brief visit to a battlefield I had not set foot on in over eight years.

Arriving in town, I dawdled a bit, finally pulling into the parking lot of a fast food joint on Steinwehr Avenue. The air here felt like a summer afternoon in a Miami laundromat. My new truck had no air conditioning so the chill in the crowded restaurant felt good. I took a comfort break and grabbed a bite to eat. After a half an hour and an unremarkable burger and fries, I hopped back in my truck and proceeded south on the Emmitsburg Road. Turning left just before the Peach Orchard, I drove east on the much quieter United States Avenue towards Plum Run. There I bent left on Hancock Avenue which points back north, paralleling the crest of Cemetery Ridge. Out the passenger window, the colossal monument to Pennsylvania's contribution here lorded over all the others. I approached a mass of people and vehicles gathered ahead. Coincidentally, I noticed a car leaving and jumped into the just vacated parking rectangle on the right side of the broad pavement.

I stepped from my pick-up, dressed for the tropics in shorts, a t-shirt and sandals. Slamming the door, I shuffled across the park road to the large, bronze opened book set on a stone pedestal. Its raised letter pages shone dully in the high June sun. The tome was flanked by two cannons, each with an ornamental pyramid of round shot stacked at the ready. A clump of trees provided a background to the sober monument to the blue and gray divisions, brigades and regiments that clashed here during General James Longstreet's failed assault on the Federal center on Cemetery Ridge. Reverently, I silently ticked off the emblazoned manifests of both Union defenders and their Confederate counterparts who had washed up on this northern shore. The tide of rebellion had lapped at this symbolic high water mark and, exhausting itself, had receded.

Well, not really. In actuality, Confederate infantry had run rampant all over southern and central Pennsylvania during the last days of June

1863.   Stunned Pennsylvanians, not at all expecting an invading army on their doorsteps, stared in disbelief and fascination as the scruffy, seasoned ranks of the Army of Northern Virginia marched by.   In skirmishes wide and far, the distant shots of what was to become the battle of Gettysburg were fired long before the opposing armies clashed at Herr Ridge and McPherson's farm on the outskirts of the town. But, it was here, at this legendary grove, that fortune finally turned against Robert E. Lee's magnificent band of warriors.

To the right of where I stood, a few brave souls formed a seated crescent, wiping glistening brows or waving park information brochures back and forth in front of their reddening faces. A bony, perspiring battlefield guide with a half empty plastic water bottle hanging from his belt, pointed out the nuances of the defensive tactics of a long dead army along the same ridgeline on which they now sweltered. Puffy cumulus clouds bubbled up on the western horizon, fattening in the heat of the day. Thunder would arrive later for sure. The inert leaves buzzed with invisible hordes of cicadas. The small group, gathered in the insufficient shade, strained to hear the guide's voice. I moved closer and sat down cross-legged with them, inviting myself to join the presentation.

The tall grass in the vast expanse sandwiched between similar sounding ridges, Cemetery and Seminary, browned in front of us. The much farther trace of South Mountain combined with a washed out sky. Both waved and warped in the moist air. As the guide droned on, I surveyed the fields in front of me. I looked past the rail fences, running parallel down both sides of the Emmitsburg Road, off to the purplish tinted stand of maples and oaks marking the low hump of Seminary Ridge. The trees danced in the mirage rippling up from the undulating grassland spread like a carpet before them. The light hurt. I closed my eyes for a moment. Specks wandered in the fluid behind my shuttered lids and played their tricks. Those oddly dancing shapes that drift in a darkened field of view turned at once to marching figures, brown and gray.

They were desperate men, arrayed on farmers' ethereal fields. The guide still talked and the cicadas sang but I couldn't hear them. I was in my own world, visualizing how it must have been on that summery, seismic day.

THE heat drained the bodies and spirits of the men as they lay waiting in the trees. Alabamians, Mississippians, Virginians, North Carolinians; all strangers on this rolling farmland. They marked time in nervous conversation or fearful silence while their artillery boomed ahead of them. Then, it suddenly ceased. The shouts of solid fellows relayed orders the anxious men did not want to hear. "Move out!" Hearts and stomachs sank. "Form up and prepare to attack."

Exquisite ranks of petrified boys emerge from the woods. First a jumble, they are aligned neatly and stepping forward, revealed only from the waist up in the tall grass. Aware of their fate, the men hesitate. They are shoved forward by the barks of sergeants growling at their heels. Left oblique! Now, guide to the center! Forward! Their pace is steady, not quite a charge, more of a brisk walk. For too short a time, precious swales all but hide the men, protecting them from what was to come.

The thump of the big guns begins again but this time from the other side. Get out of the kill zone! Yankee artillery, to the right and left, on the high ground, black and staring. The cannon crews serve their pieces like ants swarming a dropped morsel of food. Foreboding iron tubes with gaping dark maws are laid hub-to-hub in front of Farmer Ziegler's woody grove, on the rock bound Round Tops and amidst the broken grave markers on Cemetery Hill.

Expanding puffs of white obscure the gun line. The smoke is caught up in what little breeze exists and then, drifting away, reveals the spoked wheels, detached limbers, caissons and maddened, frothing horse teams barely controlled.

The thunderclaps of the guns, delayed only an instant, reverberate in the ears of the butternut shapes as the shells crash near, fuzes detonating, metal shards blasting cavernous fractures in collapsing formations, taking out ten men at a time. Yankee cannoneers revel in their power. As the enemy's grim faces reveal themselves, they switch to shotgun-like canister. Uniform tops stripped in the torrid tropical air, they fiendishly swab sizzling barrels and ram home fresh loads run up from the fast depleting ammunition lockers. An officer's sword is raised, glinting bright. Lanyards tense, the sword falls in a command to fire. The rows of deadly black mouths erupt in smoke as one, pulverizing shot casings, releasing tiny lead bees that rip the brown ranks, effortlessly punching bloody holes.

Heaps of torn and wasted bodies lie in the brittle grass. The dead mix with the writhing injured whose agonized sobs are masked by the din. The untouched persist, filling in holes in the broken rows, reacting now purely through animal instinct. Nearer they come, far fewer than the full strength divisions that leapt to the charge a half mile away in the shade and security of the woods.

Rifled muskets are lifted as clubs. Intermingled, countless red and blue crossed banners waggle above the hordes. Those flags, pockmarked and torn by shot and shell, are stitched proudly with yellowing letters telling of past engagements at far off places: Manassas, on the Peninsula and in a sunken road at Fredericksburg. Underneath, the hunched figures lurch up a matted incline towards the objective; still breathing, still able to scream.

Behind the low stone angled wall and all along the ridge, the defenders, the blue veterans of Fredericksburg's slaughter, contemplate savage revenge. Federal officers, gloriously mounted, nod and grin from behind. Those wonderful men, their boys, the cream of the Army of the Potomac, sight down an impossibly long, silver line of primed rifles; hammers cocked and waiting for the word. It comes. Fire is unleashed and ripples up and down the blue human chain, stabbing out from their prone, impenetrable fortress.

Thirsty, filthy, stained mouths with blackened teeth tear furiously at paper cartridges. Swallowing and spitting loose powder grains, quivering hands pour remnants in the blistering barrels. Ramrods clang as they are drawn from the ground in front, spun in hand and thrust down, jamming home the round. Percussion caps scatter from waist boxes; one is somehow placed securely on a nipple. Rifles are thrown to shoulders and fired again and again without aim.

A dismounted, hatless company grade officer shouts. The soldiers are deaf from the roar around them. The firing continues unabated but their lead strikes at nothing. The officer sprints down the line pounding soldiers on the back commanding they cease fire. The ripping of musket fire slows. It turns to a crack, crack here and there and then fades. As the last of the battle smoke dissipates, the enemy is gone, fleeing *across the fenced road and out of sight, escaping to the trees beyond.*

The trampled grass reveals the dead, the dying, the garbage and waste of war. Only hours later, trapped in July's relentless oven, the bodies stiffen and bloat, covered with flies and other creatures who know not of humanity but only the selfish sake of their next generations. The sun broils the bodies to black. It contorts faces into unrecognizable beasts; the rebel yell long expired from their silent throats and empty lungs.

I opened my eyes. The fields and ridges of modern Gettysburg were again before me, baking, wilted and empty. A chugging, diesel duel-wheeled truck, towing a camper, roared by on the Emmitsburg Road. The guide finished and answered a few questions from the few of the fly swatting and melting tourists that still cared. That task completed, he begged his pardon and departed leaving the group to wander back to cars or hike down the asphalt park road back towards town.

Tired and hot, the tour group dispersed, escaping to comfortable hotels, restaurants or quirky old museums where air conditioners hum, up and down the length of the streets, on the very same ground, that a century and more ago saw only misery and death.

THE Emmitsburg Road, today's Business Route 15, and the hard surfaced park roads were once dirt and dust. Carrying cars and recreational vehicles now, they once bore the feet of soldiers, shod hooves of horses and the wheeled commissary and artillery wagons of armies. Though asphalt better facilitates vehicular travel, paved roads don't blend seamlessly with the past. Nevertheless, hard and mostly unseen work of conservators has allowed us to glimpse what the blue and gray suited masses saw during the Gettysburg campaign. Forested areas that stood then and subsequently fell are being replanted. The overgrowth that an 1863 soldier would find strange is being cut back in order to restore landscapes familiar to him. The rocks, fields, barns, houses, ridges and hills are watched and maintained so as to better bring the visitor back to what the combatants saw on those three fateful days. And most who come appreciate the effort.

Drawn to the majesty of the battle, the characters that fought it, the noise and the smoke of what must have been a terrifying display; I too am appreciative of those whose stewardship keeps the field as it was. I can stand exactly where generals deployed brigades in echelon across a no man's land to meet an opposing line of infantry. I yearn to study in detail a commander's decisions in light of the tactical situation and the orders of those senior to him. I revel in the bravery of the smaller unit leaders and individual fighters who captured the hearts of Americans, both northerners and southerners alike. Reciting the acts of valor the soldiers routinely and repeatedly performed on this soil is as exciting now as it was the very first time I read about Gettysburg and the very first time I set eyes on its grand scenery.

OUTSIDE of the tourist traps and chintzy commercial fronts, the modern borough is a typical American place. Its ordinary people possess stories of their own; mostly involving how they cope with a couple million transients each year to their very backyards. For me, to visit dozens of times as I have to date not only sheds brand new light on a previously unknown aspect of the battle, it gives me a chance to say hello again to familiar faces.

In all but a couple of my journeys to Gettysburg, the friends and family who have accompanied me are enthralled with the park and enamored of the people as well. Most have only a faint memory from a long ago high school lecture about the battle or, more likely, Abraham Lincoln's acclaimed speech of dedication at the Soldiers' National Cemetery. Visiting the Military Park, they inevitably gain new appreciation and pleasure at reinvesting personal time and energy in relearning their own heritage. One can literally see their eyes light up with interest as the story of the battle fought here is told. Each promising, whenever the chance arises, to take their kids or parents or some other family member or friend they know to Gettysburg and invest in them the same knowledge they feel fortunate to possess.

My mania for history and the respect and admiration I have for those who have served and fought in defense of our country is enhanced here. My own military experience, and the successes and failures I have had in life, develop new meaning when placed in perspective against the battle's lessons of dedication to a cause or selfishness; heroism or cowardice; triumph or disaster. I never tire of this place. Gettysburg has become as familiar to me as any place in which I have lived.

So too has the road that connects my hometown of Rochester to Gettysburg. If it weren't for the pervasive construction and inescapable rerouting of Route 15, I could almost drive it blind. Like some of the banal interstate highways over which I pounded out miles crossing the country, moving from one Marine Corps duty station to another, Route 15 was once just another road. It facilitated the quickest way to get from point A to point B. But, as I began to use it to guide me on my ever more frequent trips to Gettysburg, I began to take note of the people and places seen along the way. As I dug around, I made some observations about locations and people on or near Route 15. I confirmed suspicions that large parts of New York and Pennsylvania are sadly representative of the not so optimistically changing face of America. They hold towns and cities that will never be as they once were. Quite a few are rotting places where the young grow up and leave and never come back.

That did not dissuade me. I began to look forward just as much to the journey as I did visiting the battlefield. Not because Route 15 has mile upon mile of spectacular views, great sightseeing, glamorous faces or five star restaurants all along its course. Those it surely does not. I was attracted to it because, like the home I was reluctant to leave, it had become routine. It was comfortable and familiar. The road was now a friend that never let me down. Without fail, it was Route 15 that carried me and those who traveled with me to Gettysburg; the place I love to go.

Chapter 1

SCHOOL DAYS

"I never let my school interfere with my education."

- Mark Twain –

✳ ✳ ✳ ✳

On the Straight and Narrow

GEORGE Hinkel welcomed me into his world of the Civil War. We had met in kindergarten at Atlantic Avenue Elementary School and become fast friends after a terrifying near death experience. It was late spring and we had both been invited to a birthday party of a mutual friend. The friend's house, a rickety old place, sat at the top a very steep hill overlooking a busy road. Blind curves blocked the view as drivers approached from both directions.

After pin the tail on the donkey, cake and opening presents inside, a passel of kids burst through the front screen door to play in the yard. There, overturned in the grass, lay a wagon begging for attention. Thinking the sloping driveway would provide a memorable ride, I turned the wagon over, pulled it on to the driveway near the garage, jumped in and headed down. Accelerating quickly, I shot into the street. With brakes squealing and rubber burning, a car narrowly missed me. The driver adroitly swerved, avoiding me as well as an injurious plunge over the embankment on the opposite side of the road. After spewing a critique on the merits of my action, the driver sped away. Humbled but alive, I meekly towed the wagon to the top of the driveway barely noticing the shocked looks of the other party goers watching the drama unfold before them. George Hinkel was right there to comfort me and help me forget my tears.

AS chance would have it that good friend of mine was a devotee of the Civil War and the battle of Gettysburg. Of any influence in my young life, he was instrumental in triggering my zeal for both. George was a physical giant among the urchins. Towering above everyone for as long as I can remember, this greasy blonde headed, deep voiced, pensive young man was enamored with America's deadliest war and, in particular, his hero Abraham Lincoln. From the first day I met him in elementary school until the last day we parted upon graduation from high school, George effusively shared his dedication to studying Mr. Lincoln and Mr. Lincoln's war. I can't say George was a stellar academic. He certainly didn't impress me as someone with a natural ability to crack the code to succeeding in high school. It came down to studying the material that would appear on the state Regents Examinations and also preparing for the college entrance Scholastic

Aptitude Test. George was not prepared for either. His gift was an incredible ability to draw and he spent most of his time doing it. It was unexpected not to see him, head down, glasses focused, one long lock of hair occasionally dropping down to block his vision, scratching away at a pad of paper or in the margins of a book. That's why his studies suffered. Note taking and listening to lectures took a back seat to penciling battle scenes. Rare was the time seeing him lumbering down the school hallway without drawing materials in hand. He, like a lot of bored kids, liked to draw imaginary conflicts between idealized armies. He also was quite good at sketching soldiers dressed in Union blue or Confederate gray, rifled-muskets at their sides and grim determination set on their faces. All who knew him, though, were familiar with and envious of his most elegant and talented work: *Gettysburg Lincoln.*

ALEXANDER Gardner framed that stunning portrait of Abraham Lincoln on November 8, 1863. That Sunday fell a few days before the president's train trip north to deliver his famous address at the dedication of the Soldiers' National Cemetery at Gettysburg. Gardner's portrait of Lincoln is brilliant. I can stare at it for hours. It becomes almost a game to me to pick out details one would never expect to be so clear in a print of a negative exposed 150 years ago.

Devotees of Civil War photography have discovered that, in many instances, the Scotsman's work was not pure. He didn't take unadulterated photographs of battlefields and dead bodies but, rather, moved the bodies or weapons in an attempt to create a more dramatic exposure. Further, there remains some doubt as to who actually took some of the photographs attributed to him. Gardner was a protégé of the well known Matthew Brady and, for a time, worked under him and for his company. He later split amicably from Brady to do his own work. But, both employed competent assistants. It is possible the fingers of several of either studio's unknown attendants may have triggered camera shutters in the numerous outdoor scenes attributed to either Brady or Gardner. Sadly, for those anonymous few, the true artists' identities are lost to us and will probably stay that way.

Despite the validity of criticism of Gardner's staged battlefield photographs, he does have to his credit a number of portraits in his portfolio. Historians agree, they were all made by him and those connoisseurs of his art are unanimously admiring of his superior skill.

ABRAHAM Lincoln was a man reinvigorated by the Union victories at Gettysburg and Vicksburg in the summer of 1863. Although he was painfully aware that the war was far from over, Federal forces had gained the irreversible initiative. Gardner, whom Lincoln knew and had sat for in the past, asked the president to do so again. Lincoln accepted Gardner's invitation to his studio that November. He didn't come alone. The president was accompanied by his secretaries, John Nicolay and John Hay.

The place to sit, the pose, the focus and the light allowed for the portrait were all choreographed by a master artist without an agenda. Unlike modern paparazzi interested only in capturing the subject for monetary gain,

Gardner intended to capture the soul of the man for posterity. Gardner took a few photographs that day including a group shot of Lincoln with his two faithful assistants. Armed only with the cumbersome photographic technology available to him, there was a lot of work to be done. Gardner certainly must have known that Lincoln had very little time to spare and was, accordingly, the consummate professional. After the niceties were dispensed, he was on to the business at hand.

Gettysburg Lincoln is without doubt the most beloved and reproduced photo of Lincoln. It mesmerizes. In it, Lincoln stares confidently into the lens. He appears wind burned, tanned and healthy. A few wisps of gray hair streak his temple and the tuft above his ample forehead. He is unsmiling but clearly a man in control. He is tired though. He has suffered both personal and public grief. His eyes tell the tale. If the photo is enlarged on a computer screen, one can see that his left eye is bloodshot. The vessels are large and dilated. Both eyes are surrounded by the halos of darkness that are typical of a countenance and a body short on rest. No wonder knowing what we know about the burden he bore. Despite his apparent weariness, he is much less pale, wrinkled and aged as he appears in later photographs.

Gardner's less well known 1865 "cracked glass plate" portrait of Lincoln, once believed to be the last photograph of him alive, is a case in point. In that melancholy shot, Lincoln leans forward. He is old and frail. His is a tortured body and mind. Gray hair takes charge of his beard and receding hairline. His eyes disappear in the recesses of darkened caves. Heavy bags droop under those onyx slits, surrounded by fields of wrinkles. Yet, despite his personal torment, a faint hint of a smile crosses his face. The biggest crisis ever to face the Union was near an end.

Many who study Lincoln and the possible diseases from which he is believed to have suffered think he would have died soon of natural causes. His assassination at Ford's Theater a few weeks after the portrait was taken prevent that theory from being proved. However, our last image of the man tends to make one think he did not have long to live.

But not in *Gettysburg Lincoln*. From that photograph, there is no doubt that, even if one had never set eyes on the man, leadership is in his blood. This man controls armies. The pursed lips belie his legendary, and sometimes ribald, sense of humor. His high white collar hides his wrinkled, bronzed neck.

I have always been fascinated by this photo for its one queer detail. The iris of Lincoln's left eye is distinctly raised higher than that of his right eye. Only a still camera could catch the oddity of Lincoln's lazy eye. It's almost as if Gardner's wet plate exposure captured it to tantalize historians.

The portrait is so beautiful it brings to mind the flawless majesty of the statue of Lincoln seated at the memorial to him on the Mall in Washington. The similarity is not at all coincidental. The sculptor, Daniel Chester French, used the Gardner *Gettysburg Lincoln* as a guide for his brooding work. Like the statuary handicraft of the ancient Greeks, the stone representation of Lincoln is impeccable. In Gardner's portrait, though, imperfection mars America's perfect man.

GEORGE loved to draw this visage from memory. He was particularly diligent about this photo and worked to get it just right. From the famous Lincoln mole to the bow tie, angled and slightly left of center. Pencil and pen were the instruments he used to put his visual images on paper. With those tools in his capable hands he proved talent is much deeper than the simpler acts of taking lecture notes or passing standardized tests. He seemed to have reached, early on, a higher state of sophistication. Taking a cue from him, I began to plumb the depths of my ignorance of the Civil War. The curious nature in me was aroused. I became somewhat obsessed in learning more about America's most fractious era and high school was the place I chose to expand my knowledge.

In doing so my routine was unchanging. The bus pulled into the school's traffic circle promptly at 7:35 A.M. and dropped us off at the front doors of Penfield High. The school was located on the southern fringe of the town of the same name and an inner ring suburb adjacent to the industrial city of Rochester. In the 1960s, Penfield was the new Valhalla for whites fleeing the city and seeking extra-urban bliss on quarter acre home lots, trimmed lawns and split-level homes. These perks were the sought after rewards for hard working baby boomers.

Penfield is a hilly and wooded place and around the time my family moved there was considered a suburban frontier. It, like Gettysburg, consisted mostly of large plots of apple orchards, cornfields and other agricultural interests. Penfield's rough handed farmers soon found out they were sitting on gold mines. They jumped at the chance to park their tractors and sell to flush developers motivated to bulldoze fields and chainsaw orchards. Soon replacing them would be neat, carbon copy housing demanded by the newly mobile middle-class. Before too long, the town's population soared past 25,000 and kept growing. Elementary and middle schools were sketched and blueprinted by the town planning board and then cobbled together to provide sanctuaries to educate the kids of a burgeoning population. The high school, at the time I wandered its halls later in the 1970s, reflected the town's expansion and boasted an enrolled student body of approximately 1,600.

DISEMBARKING from the buses, we scurried inside to our lockers, dropped off coats and books and then I, without fail, paced down the bustling hall to the Earth Sciences classroom. It was the homeroom of two of our close knit group and the morning gathering place I and those few friends chose to meet every morning for twenty minutes or so prior to the start of the day's classes.

We were an odd bunch. Most of the kids chased a ball on the lacrosse or baseball fields or orbited around the cool kids' lockers and tittered over social events of the weekend past. Parties were the main topic of conversation. But, the little band I hung out with stayed away from high school binge drinking and casual drug use. Our abstinence was difficult to maintain. Beer and marijuana were inexpensive and readily available. I don't remember seeing much of the harder stuff like heroin or cocaine, but pot was all over the place. One could smell it on the kids coming in from recess. In full view of everyone, they marched to the tree line behind the school and lit up a pipe or passed around a joint. Some even boldly tried it in the restrooms and those who did inevitably got away with it. The kids who routinely smoked and got high were not at all disruptive in class. The offenders were from both sexes. They sat quietly, relaxed and slumped in their chairs. The only bother to other students was that the faded denim jackets they wore held a faint whiff of smoke. Occasionally, they'd muster enough energy to brush shoulder length bangs out of their eyes but otherwise remained immobile and happily compliant.

The dealers were easy to pick out. They hung by lockers that remained open far too long to justify the simple task of grabbing books or a backpack. They shopped out their dime bagged wares brazenly under the noses of teachers and administrators strolling by. Who knows how many adults bought and used? Quite a few I bet, but not from students and not on school grounds. Back then I naïvely thought that everybody with enough sense to know better followed the law to the letter. Through most of high school and college life, though, it was a rare social event where the burned grass smell of weed wasn't drifting about.

AS the wall clock ticked towards the eight o'clock homeroom bell, our sober cohort solved the world's woes sitting around a boxed air system under the room's wall high windows. There we chatted about current events, major league sports and, uniquely, history.

There was no one source for my growing joy at the chance to learn about American history. It did not come over me at once but rather it grew in dribs and drabs. Logically, I gravitated to those with the same interests. They, as I was, were mostly self-taught. I immersed myself in Americana. Instead of posters of Aerosmith or the big hair heavy metal bands popular in that era, I chose to plaster my bedroom walls with romanticized events of America's past. My brother, who shared my bedroom with me, suffered quietly through it all. As the older sibling, I relegated his stuff to a few scant square feet of shelving and wall space. The rest I took for mine in my little version of suburban Manifest Destiny.

If a stranger had visited our bedroom during those years, she would have been greeted with pictures of dirty colonials tossing shovelfuls of dirt as they entrenched at the crest of Breed's Hill in Charlestown, Massachusetts the eve before General Howe's bearskin topped, red coated British grenadiers tramped up the gentle slope to disaster. Nearby, tanned and buckskinned Corps of Discovery adventurers cast off in a flatboat out of St. Louis towards an ascent of the Missouri River and glory. Sprinkled throughout the book lined shelves, and on any unused flat surface, perched memorabilia of the War Between the States including a Confederate battle flag, miniature soldiers in blue and gray and brass toy field artillery and naval cannons.

My parents and grandparents fed my growing addiction with ever more sophisticated reading material. As I matured, so too did my literary tastes. I tired of the colorful but elementary American History or National Geographic series, picture heavy story books of the Revolutionary and Civil Wars. Hungry for more substantive reading, I moved on to the more subtle and introspective work of Carl Sandburg and Bruce Catton and even the entertaining historical fiction of Gore Vidal and MacKinlay Kantor.

Flush with money I earned from a paper route, snow shoveling and lawn mowing, I purchased replica period firearms, cartridge boxes, canteens and uniforms. My main source of armaments was a gun shop run by a snaggle-toothed, oily man with a shaved head who sold his wares on the ground floor of an old house in nearby East Rochester. It always looked to me like the place was just barely solvent. The proprietor was never without a bag filled with french fries and, in between puffs on a cigarette, drained a coke through a straw. The informal way in which sales transactions were conducted would raise the eyebrows of an adult but didn't seem at all strange to a teenager. There was no register and receipts were hand written but I got what I wanted having paid in cold, hard cash. Not surprisingly, the gun shop is long gone. The doors were closed permanently some years back. The house was abandoned and lay empty for a time. Eventually, it was bulldozed. The cellar was filled in and on the lot where I purchased so many replica historical weapons and accessories stands a hometown sub and sandwich franchise.

NOTHING kindles the love of studying history like touching antique objects and walking in the footsteps of the men and women who made it. My interest in the past was further kindled on a tour I took when my mother surprised me with plane tickets for both of us to accompany my father on a day long business trip to Philadelphia. That city is a place that prides itself in showing off its historical sites to out of towners. Precocious and wide-eyed, I couldn't get enough of the place. We took the easy way out and signed up for one of those city-wide bus junkets. Stopping at various points of interest, I was that kid that shot his hand up every time a tour guide asked a question. At lunch, I even bagged an autograph of Philadelphia's controversial mayor Frank Rizzo. He was gracious enough to sign my souvenir rotating Wheel of Presidents when, egged on by a waitress, I bothered him at a restaurant at which he and his staff were holding court.

Catching the travel bug then and there, I set off on more journeys, no longer in the company of adults. Those included a trip with George Hinkel to Boston where, after landing at Logan Airport at sunrise, we sprinted the entire red-lined Freedom Trail in order to take it all in and catch a late afternoon flight back home. I also took advantage of the sites within a relatively short driving distance of Rochester including Forts Niagara, Stanwix and Ticonderoga and other less well known historical venues closer to home.

MANY who graduate from high school fondly remember a guidance counselor or teacher that mentored them in an area of interest. I was fortunate to have enjoyed the tutelage of Penfield High's Don Stewart as he graced us with his thorough recitation of two centuries of our fascinating past in Advanced Placement American History. Woven throughout was his wonderful and ideologically unbiased view of the events that brought America into the present. Don encouraged us to read on our own. Naturally, what he said was important but he urged us to make it a practice to keep an open mind and judge for ourselves.

His favorite author was the social and political commentator Richard Hofstadter whose work influenced Don's AP class syllabus. Rather than American wars, Don emphasized presidential politics, elections and the influence of key administrations on the economic and social growth of America. Analyzing and interpreting other experts' recitations of history rather than reading one dull text book made us far better and well rounded students. I was hooked and began to read whatever I could get my hands on. The words of brilliant writers like Shelby Foote, Bruce Catton, Edwin Coddington and Oliver Norton and hundreds of others found their way on to my bookshelves. Their work captivated me. They remain valuable references to which I continually refer to this day.

NO book, no story, no historical drama on the flat screen, no interpretation penned by another could replace the thrill of actually being at Gettysburg. That experience did not come for me until the eighth grade when I first gazed on the battlefield during a greatly anticipated field trip to Washington, D.C.

Early on a Saturday, we tossed our duffel bags and suitcases into the filthy storage compartments sandwiched between the wheel wells of three silver chartered tour buses. We tramped onto the idling monsters and settled in to the high backed seats for the most exciting trip of our young lives.

The buses turned out of the high school parking lot and rumbled through the eastern Rochester suburbs to Route 15. We had our sights set on the nation's capital so we sailed by

Gettysburg this time by. Out the right hand windows we strained our eyes to see something of the battlefield as we passed. There! Was that the east side of the Round Tops? Through bare February trees whizzing past, the top of the steel structure of the Gettysburg National Tower loomed. The 307 foot tall spidery and steel contraption built on private land adjacent to the battlefield dominated the landscape for miles. It, like so many impetuously built, misplaced structures on or near the battlefield, was designed for commercial benefit. Eventually, preservationists and advocates of returning the field to its 1863 state won eminent domain lawsuits against the tower's owners. In 2000, the now former owners, fairly compensated, watched alongside spectators and news media as the tower was dynamited and crumbled to the ground. But, in 1975, it was still there and beckoned Route 15 travelers to turn in and see the sights.

Returning north from that field trip to D.C. on a crisp, sunlit, late winter weekday, we briefly stepped off our tour buses in front of the old Gettysburg Visitors Center and Museum on Taneytown Road adjacent to the National Military Cemetery. While most of the larger class treated this stop as academic corporal punishment, a few of the ecstatic among us swore Christmas had come again in February.

Like the tower, the museum was out of place in its surroundings. It also encroached on a key portion of the battlefield at Cemetery Hill. After years of legal wrangling, it was finally condemned and torn down. The wrecker also set its sights on the Cyclorama building. Not so fast. While the ugly tower held no aesthetic value, preservations and historians have thought the opposite of the post-modern, ridged, circular structure that formerly housed the Gettysburg Cyclorama. Turning it into dust is being held up by lawsuits filed by people who believe the building is of historical significance. I am sure some of the millions who passed through it over the course of decades would agree. But, it sits right on land occupied by a good part of the Union army during the battle. If keeping to the fidelity of the original battlefield is the ultimate goal, move it or down it must come. Regardless of the outcome of that real estate skirmish, while the bunker-like Cyclorama building sits empty, tourists now flood to the expansive and modern building just down the Baltimore Pike.

ANYONE who visited the old battlefield museum in years past was missing something special if they did not drop in and take the brief course: The Battle of Gettysburg 101. The classroom was the Electric Map set in the center of a square, gymnasium-like arena. Patrons sat in backed seats stepped upward in five or so rows surrounding the low-tech topographical map display. After the lights were dimmed, a taped narrator walked the crowds through the three day battle. The presentation was enhanced by blinking lights on the map tracing out a line of troops or prominent terrain. The hushed audience learned of the famous Union defensive "fish hook" bending from Culp's and Cemetery hills south on Cemetery Ridge and terminating at the Round Tops. Most became aware how very large the battlefield actually is. They learned that its scope overwhelmed the ability of the two men in charge of their respective armies to control events.

Today's technologically adept and discerning crowds, raised on smart phones, live streaming movies and virtual reality game consoles would yawn at the rendition. But, in 1975, it was the thing to see.

At the end of the Electric Map show, we were chaperoned over to the planetarium-like mausoleum that held the Gettysburg Cyclorama. This splendid late nineteenth century canvas depicts the curtain call of the battle as long butternut lines sweep across the fields in an attempt to take the Union position on Cemetery Ridge. After ninety years, the painting had frayed and faded. It was peeling in certain places, suffering from water stains and cast in less than favorable lighting. In spite of its dark and shabby appearance, the Cyclorama retained the power to amaze.

The center of the action in the 360 degree painting depicts the Confederate high water mark at the Bloody Angle and the famous Copse of Trees. Rebel formations are shattered by flanking Union artillery fire as the cringing troops cross the open terrain between Seminary Ridge and the Emmitsburg Road. The survivors mix with desperate defenders all along the Union front. An artillery caisson explodes in a cloud of smoke and flame. Men grunt and scream. Shouts are drowned by the bang of artillery and the unceasing crackle of musket fire. Harnessed horse teams drag cannons and limbers to the action. In and about Ziegler's Grove, Union cannoneers blast away. To the rear, reinforcements hustle to the front and makeshift field hospitals tend to the wounded.

Our young eyes were careless; too unsophisticated to differentiate between superbly detailed accuracy and historical error. The artist, Frenchman Paul Philippoteaux, with several assistants dabbing along, oddly brushed Union soldiers in white trousers and introduced European style haystacks to Pennsylvania farm country. Confederate General Armistead is shown falling wounded, tumbling back off his horse. In actuality, the general strictly obeyed orders. He was not mounted at that moment in the attack. He had walked in with his men, hat hanging on upraised sword, leading from the front. Follow me! And his men, those few survivors that remained, were energized by his example. That is until three Federal minie balls found purchase in Armistead's body. Amazingly, he survived, albeit temporarily. Not believed to be mortally wounded, he died a couple of days later in a Yankee hospital.

Naturally, being a group of teenagers, more than just this display of history before us occupied our time. There was no shortage of immature behavior mostly consisting of plenty of friendly pushing and shoving. Keeping our mouths shut was impossible. Not a moment passed without a scatological comment or some inane banter slipping past our lips.

The three hours we were scheduled to be at Gettysburg sped by and soon we were back on the buses as the low midwinter sun dipped over the line of South Mountain to the west. We pulled back out on to the road out of Gettysburg and on to Route 15. Most of us, and especially me, came away with a fond affection for the National Park and what we had seen there. We chatted and horse played until the thrum of the big diesel engine lulled us into a thoughtful quiet. In the dark of the trip north to Rochester we fell off to sleep, giving parent and teacher chaperones sweet respite for the remainder of the journey home.

After that visit, I didn't return to Gettysburg for almost a decade. The next time I would wander on the park paths, I would be a college graduate with a military career ahead of me. But, each time I go back, my thoughts return to that archetypical, exceptionally rewarding few hours on the battlefield. I have never forgotten that virgin trip. Experiencing it as I did, with close friends by my side, was sheer joy. Those precious moments cemented that wondrous place in my mind. Gettysburg had captivated me and secured its significant role in my life to come.

* * * *

A *Well Regulated Militia* . . .

I was in a hurry. A very big hurry. I flew off the school bus barely clearing the swinging doors, crossed recklessly in front and then up my driveway into the open garage. It was a brilliant western New York October afternoon and the early fall sun enhanced the reds, yellows, oranges and rusts blazing from the countless trees in the suburban middle-class neighborhood in Penfield. Our split level early 1960s house was comfortably set alongside others on a circular drive. The red shingle-sided, white shuttered domicile sat on top of a sand and gravel glacially deposited hill overlooking Irondequoit Creek, Irondequoit Bay and the great blue mass of Lake Ontario beyond.

In our 2,200 square feet of space I, my four siblings and our infinitely patient mom and dad, made a home. Mom, a night nurse at a retirement home for Catholic nuns, was napping. There was no eight hours of sleep for this woman. Her brief afternoon snoozes had to suffice for what was to come. Awakened now at the end of the school day, she jumped into dinner preparation for seven, brought order to domestic and extra-curricular confusion and refereed fights between the five of us. I don't know how the heck she did it. Tending to food baking in the oven or on the stovetop, doing laundry or cleaning she hustled around responding to our annoying demands with justifiably limited patience. "I guess I could stick a broom up my butt and sweep the floor while I am waiting on you damn kids hand and foot," was a classic response to our pestering.

Dad, as was common in the business world of the time, was at work and released promptly at five in the afternoon without fail. He would pull into the driveway, stride in the house from the garage and get the "Where have you been all day?" look from my mother. He stood there in the doorway with his coat unbuttoned and a dumb look on his face, getting an earful and shaking his head the whole time. After dinner, Mom was off to work for the night shift and we became Dad's problem.

Our evolutionary leap to middle and high schools was welcomed by our parents as they assumed we could now mostly manage on our own. After classes were done for the day, either we'd grab a snack, hit the books or head out into the neighborhood to hang out with friends. On some nights my siblings stayed late at school for sports or clubs and didn't get home until dinner.

I routinely came home, as I did on this spectacular fall day, to deliver the evening edition of the local newspaper. My boss was the Gannett Rochester *Times Union,* a publication with a profitable circulation in the waning years of the 1970s. Then, people still watched the nightly news and read the evening newspaper. Cable broadcasts were just coming on line and the Internet was years in the future so the evening fish wrapper was a prime source for news events of the day.

The newspaper distributor had not arrived with my papers yet, so I popped into the house and dropped my school stuff off in the carpeted and paneled downstairs storage space which served as a bedroom I shared with my younger brother. I ran back upstairs to the kitchen to raid the "goodies" cupboard next to the stove. Jamming a few pecan sandies in my mouth, I heard the loud muffler of the rusted hatchback, carrying that afternoon's quota of newspapers, as it backed into the driveway. The driver's door opened and the thump of a bundle of papers hitting the garage floor followed. I went into the garage, waved to the distributor as she departed and pulled my bike out into the driveway. Back in the garage, I snapped open the plastic band that bound the bundle and threw the loose newspapers into a dirty, yellow canvas delivery bag with the words *Times Union* emblazoned in navy blue on the side. On top, I gently lowered a towel wrapped octagonal flintlock pistol barrel in the bag alongside the newspapers. Looping the bag's straps around the handlebars of my single speed Huffy, I mounted the banana seat and raced down the driveway. Today, my previous record for delivery would be shattered.

Just yesterday, the barrel I now carried had arrived in the mail as part of a replica flintlock pistol kit. A gregarious neighbor at the far end of my route had offered to help me put the thing together. He was an inveterate tinkerer and possessed a garage full of machines and tools. I had dropped the kit off that same day at his house but the barrel needed some preparatory work.

Bluing the barrel the previous evening in my mother's oven caused some commotion. In order to protect a gun barrel from rusting, a chemical solution is applied to its surface. The best way to get that solution to adhere is to heat the solution, and the surface on which it is to be applied, to about 300 degrees. I determined our oven would do the trick. In the midst of the "hot bluing" process, an unpleasant, burning smell had wafted throughout the house. It was luckily completed before Dad sprinted upstairs to the kitchen to shut down the project. The barrel came out perfectly. I set it to cool overnight in the garage. The remaining assembly required drills, sanders and other implements we did not own. Thus, my neighbor's offer to help was warmly welcomed.

I sped along the route never sacrificing precision; placing each paper exactly where a respective customer wanted it: front door, garage door, mailbox. The destinations were committed to memory. Around the Woodhaven Drive circle, down the gentle slope of Parkview Drive, up past the "blind curve" and then down the last stretch of Parkview to where it joined with Old Browncroft Boulevard. All the while the solid mass of the flintlock barrel lying at the bottom of the delivery bag banged against my shin.

Old Browncroft, now a very quiet residential street, once served as the main route connecting the farms dotting the east side of the county to the city. It was long ago replaced by a four-lane highway which dipped down into the valley of Irondequoit Creek and back up again eventually dumping commuters on to busy city streets or on to interstate freeway ramps of Rochester's inner beltway. Except for the faint hum of traffic down below, all was peaceful now on Old Browncroft. It ran along a glacial ridgeline and offered a clear view of the skyline of Rochester on the western horizon. The street was lined with maples and oaks and acorns cracked and popped as they fell under my speeding tires. My destination was near its dead end at a brown Cape Cod style house with a lower stone face and a large garage all neatly set back off the street on the ridge's southern facing slope.

Mr. Parson, the owner and my woodworking mentor, was waiting for me. His tartan flannel was tucked neatly into suspendered khakis as he stood in the garage surrounded by a cloud of smoke from his unfiltered cigarette. He snuffed it out in an ashtray perched on top of an ancient band saw, picked a fleck of milled tobacco from his tongue and gave me a wave and a big hello. I shook his hand, sidestepped him, entered the screen door that separated the garage from the house and placed his afternoon newspaper on the kitchen table. Mrs. Parson was at the sink tending to dirty dishes. My nose caught a whiff of a strange odor. Mr. Parson loved limburger cheese sandwiches and it was evident he had just cooked, assembled and eaten one. The odor of the cheese combined with the stale stench of countless smoked cigarettes left a very musty and unpleasant smell in the house. Yuck! I hated cigarettes.

My mom had smoked since her teens and I constantly berated her for her bad habit. But, over time, I came to understand why she had relied on cigarettes. Her father and her brother had smoked and it was a far more common practice when she was growing up. She was addicted. Having to work nights, raise five kids and deal with the rigors of life smothered any desire she may have had to quit. She needed some sort of drug to get her through the long days and even longer nights. To her, smokes and strong coffee were the answer.

Mr. Parson was an ardent conversationalist, an avid reader and expert on local history and the weather. He liked talking to me and clearly enjoyed my company with or without a woodworking or metal project to draw us together. We met, connected and engaged in a gregarious relationship for the few years I delivered newspapers to his house.

His expertise once again came in handy when I took on the challenge of casting my own bullets. Not learning my lesson the first time I attempted factory work in the house, I tried it again. The one time I melted lead on the stove inside the house was the only time. Mom, unsuccessfully trying to nap downstairs, was startled awake by my banging around as I dropped a block of lead into an old aluminum pan. She emerged from the den to see what I was up to. Lead has a melting point of about 600 degrees Fahrenheit and the only thing we had in our house that could reach that temperature was an electric stove top burner. Weary and irritated, Mom reminded me that the stove was for cooking and the kitchen was not a foundry. Melting lead for bullets was something to be done somewhere else.

So, off I went to Mr. Parson and asked him his advice. He laughed at my story and then explained all the bad things that can happen to a person if he inhales too much lead vapor. Highly recommending that the process be worked outside, he set up a small torch on a gravely spot off the driveway. Sparking it to a bluish flame, he pointed it to the side of a small iron cauldron in which we had dropped the block of lead. After a few moments, the already misshapen metal had turned to a silvery pool. We ladled the liquid into two hand held molds.   One was designed for round musket balls and the other formed conical, hollow-based minie balls.   The final products popped out scalding and shiny.

WHY the fascination with weapons? My father had no interest in them and neither did his pop before him. I grew up using them for all sorts of recreational uses. By the time I was in my early teens I owned a twelve gauge shotgun and a .22 caliber rifle and by my mid-teens I had expanded my interest to include black powder firearms. The latter supplemented my burgeoning ardor for American history.   Year round, it was a rare afternoon or weekend that we were not in the woods and swampy creek estuary that surrounded our neighborhood, some type of gun in hand, pursuing our legal limit in ducks, blasting clay pigeons or testing our mettle at marksmanship on a distant tree-mounted target.
    We also developed skills as amateur armorers. It was relatively easy to alter toy guns and cannons into working models. A cap pistol that was designed to propel a cork ball down its barrel could also be filled with a very small charge of black powder with some popping corn on top. Thus altered, it made a working scatter gun. That is until the barrel blew off one chilly afternoon sending unburned powder grains into my exposed right hand.   That mishap didn't stop our cabal from pursuing equally stupid experiments. A touchhole, absent on a small brass cannon purchased as a souvenir on a trip to an historical site, was easily created by drilling the soft metal at the breech.   Black powder was rammed in the barrel. On top of that we inserted BB ammunition

as the projectile. Aimed and in battery for firing, the mini-cannon was touched off with a long fireplace or candle match. Plastic miniatures of U.S.S. Monitor and C.S.S. Virginia stood in front of our tiny artillery array and were reduced to shards from direct fire.

THE decade of the 1970s was unique in its social, political and economic make up. Domestic and international terrorism, although not unheard of, was relegated to the back of newspapers leaving inflation, racial tensions and the legacy of the American presence in Vietnam on the front page. In today's world of strip searches at airports, it is unthinkable for a group of teenagers to do now what we did then. But, in the year of the American Bicentennial, obtaining guns and ammunition was easy. Our working, distracted parents would have been shocked at what was going on.

George Hinkel showed up one day in our neighborhood sporting a replica .44 caliber Colt Army revolver. The model was carried by mounted cavalry and known as a Colt Dragoon. He had just purchased it at a weekend gun show and wanted to show it off.

Alongside Abraham Lincoln, George held John Wayne in high regard. He loved the Duke and took great pains to mimic both his walk and his best movie lines. He loved the scene in *True Grit* in which Wayne's character Marshal Rooster Cogburn is surprised at the size of the pistol his soon to be trail partner Mattie Ross pulls out of her possibles sack. "Why, by God, girl, that's a Colt's Dragoon! You're no bigger than a corn nubbin', what're you doing with all this pistol?"

George could recite the scene by heart and his new handgun helped carry it off. The Colt Dragoon joined an already splendid array of weapons owned by me and the other Second Amendment faithful with whom I chose to keep company. The inventory included a replica .75 caliber Brown Bess musket, a .58 caliber Zouve rifled-musket, a .58 caliber 1864 Springfield rifled-musket and a .36 caliber Colt Navy revolver along with cartridge boxes, ammunition and bayonets. A number of Remington, Mossberg and Beretta products, mostly shotguns, and a varied assortment of .22 caliber rifles rounded out the arsenal.

OUR recreational shooting in the woods made a racket and prompted the occasional complaint from a neighbor. But, our minor, extracurricular disturbances paled in comparison to the noise that must have emanated from a volley of musketry coming from a Civil War infantry regiment. One gets some sense of how it must have been to have 1,000 rifled muskets shot in your direction at a Civil War reenactment.

Each July, Union and Confederate reenactors stage a series of mock battles at the Genesee Country Village and Museum. That unique, historical gem is located a few miles outside Rochester in the one traffic light town of Mumford, New York. The hobbyists, some with families in tow, set up camps interspersed throughout the living history village which, over the course of years, was built up to replicate a nineteenth century Genesee Valley settlement.

Some reenactors stick to the rigors of authenticity and stay far from any contemporary comfort while in costume. They engage the curious in nineteenth century language and feign ignorance and surprise when a visitor attempts to converse using present-day idioms. They choose to bed down on a mat of straw with only a blanket and a thin canvas tent protecting them from the elements. In front of their fabric hovel, they cook meals in ironware hanging over smoky fires and take seriously the other aspects of wartime camp life.

Others aren't so diligent and can be found quaffing a beer or soda at the concession stands or munching on a hot dog as they flip through a tattered paperback or magazine, killing time before the next demonstration. Regardless of their level of dedication in recreating the lifestyle of a Civil War soldier, all promptly respond to the long roll of the drum or the requests of their pseudo-officers and non-commissioned officers to take to the line and prepare for the day's battle.

They are a dirty sort. Stained with black powder residue and the dust of camp, soiled by the many death rolls and miraculous resurrections, they tramp into line and march behind fluttering regimental colors and their side's national ensign. A fife's trill and the beat of the drum help them synchronize steps on parade. Lugging the cumbersome infantry weapons of the era and the associated and heavy accoutrements, it is no wonder they sweat profusely in the summer heat. Despite cotton garments underneath, their coarse wool uniforms allow very little ventilation or comfort. The belts, knapsacks and military kit they carry are made of stiff leather and appear to drag them down like sea anchors.

THE rifled-musket they carry in replica form was a cleverly innovative leap in weapons technology. It was also an effective killer. Its predecessor, the smoothbore musket, fired a lead ball that almost never hit what it was aimed at. Despite smoothbore armed masses, arrayed mere yards from one another and loosing volleys of fire and smoke, casualties remained light. The introduction of rifling put a bloody end to that. The lands and grooves of barrel rifling imparted a spin on a projectile, increasing both its range and accuracy. Whether fitted with a patched round ball or the deviously simpler conical round known by its inventor's name – the Minie ball – the rifled-musket could now kill or maim out to hundreds of yards. Civil War battle casualty figures proved its deadliness time and again.

Modern high velocity rifle rounds, some only half the diameter of their Civil War counterparts and moving at muzzle velocities in the thousands of feet per second, do strange things when coming in contact with the human body. The military's standard M-16 5.56mm round, not much larger in diameter than a .22 caliber bullet, will leave the weapon at a staggering 3,000 feet per second. Entering a limb of its intended target, it may ricochet off a bone and weirdly exit somewhere in the body in a totally unrelated place. Not so the larger diameter rifled-musket round. Sized at .58 caliber or even larger, the slow moving, soft lead projectile hit like a powerfully swung sledgehammer, tearing at skin and smashing bones and vital organs.

REENACTORS' choreographed firing, while impressive, displays at best only restricted flashes and muted bangs. Their musketry cannot compare to what were surely far more awe-inspiring sights and sounds at Marye's Heights at Fredericksburg or near the Angle at Gettysburg. This dichotomy exists because, first, there were far more people shooting rifles in actual Civil War battles than are cobbled together for most reenactments today. Secondly, the sound of a rifle or cannon is amplified greatly when it is fired with a Minie ball or round shot rather than with a "blank" charge of black powder alone. The muffled whoosh of a reenactor's bullet-free discharge is no match for the sharp report and mule kick of a fully loaded rifled-musket. Compare cannon fire and the distinction grows logarithmic in scale. The blast from a reenactor's artillery piece firing a blank charge is dramatic. The report is loud and rolling clouds of powder smoke billow into the air. But ram an iron ball or a conical shell down the barrel on top of that charge, jerk the lanyard and the cannon becomes a living beast. It is a barely controlled explosion accompanied by an earsplitting roar. The gun jumps back on its wheels and carriage in obedience to Newton's law that for every action an equal and opposite reaction will follow. The detonation of the shell down range adds to the din.

Aside from unfriendly sharpshooters and pesky counter-battery fire, Civil War cannoneers, while serving their own pieces, faced an array of occupational hazards that constantly conspired to kill or maim them. Ignoring the enemy for a moment, an artilleryman had to constantly handle explosives and with extreme care. He also had to be quick on his feet just to stay out of the way of his own gun's discharge. A misfire certainly caused crews' hearts to jump and the unlucky man tasked with inserting a new primer risked life and limb. Improper swabbing left smoldering embers in the tube waiting to prematurely ignite the next powder charge. For those wearing the red piped uniform of artillerymen, danger presented itself in many despicable forms.

IT'S that way in today's field artillery. I learned that as I became an expert in the specialty during my Marine Corps service. Modern cannons are no less dangerous to their crews today as they were to their Civil War forebears. Both towed and self-propelled guns* are equipped with recoil suppression systems. However, that advance in technology still can't prevent the Marine or soldier from being in the way when the cannon is fired. Arms can be broken and fingers bloodily pinched as the gun jerks to the rear and then floats back into battery. An injury is guaranteed if poorly supervised, lazier individualists, lovingly called "gun rocks" or "gun bunnies" by battery mates, decide to "slap fire" the weapon. The frowned upon practice has the man opt to use an extended arm and finger to activate the constant pull firing mechanism rather than the far safer, regulation lanyard. That length of rope, hooked to the firing

---

* The word "gun" is used interchangeably with "howitzer" in today's modern artillery. Gun is an artilleryman's term of art. In point of fact, a gun and a howitzer are quite different. A gun fires a shell at a higher velocity and at a much lower trajectory and is more appropriate for penetrating armor or reinforced concrete defenses. Naval guns are prime examples. A howitzer fires a shell at a lower velocity and a higher trajectory. Howitzers are better employed to strike targets in defilade. Most cannon field artillery pieces in use today are howitzers.

mechanism and held by cannoneers adjacent to and away from the breech, ensures flailing human limbs stay out of the way of the gun's recoil. The slap fire technique puts the body right in the path of a ton of moving steel. One time out of a hundred, human reaction time is too slow and the gun is unforgiving and cruel. The snap of an arm bone or rib that results is distinct.

An artillery unit carries around with it thousands of pounds of explosives. The physical act of transporting shells, fuzes, primers and powder, keeping the guns supplied and sending the rounds down range requires constant attention to ensure safety to the handlers. Despite intense training and supervision, premature activation of fuzes and the resultant early explosions of shells over friendly heads have prompted many an internal investigation. Faulty ammunition has been known to detonate inside tubes, wrecking the guns and injuring the crews. Short rounds are more common than anyone would care to admit and the jagged steel of shrapnel doesn't care whether it kills a friend or an enemy.

The principles of propelling a modern artillery shell downrange haven't changed much in 150 years. Rather than black powder, smokeless powder is used as the primary propellant. Smokeless powder doesn't explode; it burns and burns very quickly. The grains are small and milled to cylindrical form with tiny holes drilled throughout to increase surface area. That and the addition of an oxidizer during manufacturing ensure faster, better combustion.

When the lanyard is pulled by the cannoneer the firing mechanism triggers the shotgun shell-like primer, igniting the selected powder charge. The energy of the expanding gases is released in the confined space of a howitzer chamber and the pressure created is sufficient to send the projectile down range. The projectile offers less resistance than the steel walls of the chamber and tube. Energy remaining is dissipated as heat, flash and sound.

THE differences between artillery used in the Civil War and today are stark. Modern smokeless propellants burn much cleaner than Civil War black powder and are treated chemically to reduce noise and flash. Thus, on the modern battlefield, there is far less cannon smoke. The faster ignition speed of the powder, improved barrel rifling and longer tubes allow today's cannon artillery far longer ranges. With modern target acquisition devices and firing solution computers, the ability of artillery to mass fire, hit the target and maximize the effects of cleverly designed ammunition is vastly improved.

While Civil War artillerymen had an array of shot and shell from which to choose, they would be amazed with the artillery shells in use today. The menu is varied and lengthy. It includes shells that can be directed to the target by guiding on a laser beam. Others achieve excessive ranges by the assistance of rocket motors. Some kick out landmines from their tail end, forcing an enemy to change his maneuver plans. White phosphorus, known in military jargon as "Willy Pete," is used to mark targets, set fuel or ammunition on fire or signal across a distance. The world's artillery arsenals also include unconventional shells which deploy deadly chemical agents when activated. Believe it or not, some arsenals include tactical battlefield nuclear weapons containing miniaturized fissionable material, shielding, triggering devices and safeties. All of that is crammed into a 155 millimeter shell. The tools available to modern cannoneers are far beyond the Gettysburg artilleryman's iron round shot, conical shells, fuzed round case shot and shotgun-like canister.

FOR our later benefit, many Civil War veterans left a written legacy of their experiences. In contemporary writing or memoirs penned after the fact, veterans tell of the incessant roar of the guns, ringing and sometimes bloodied ears from the concussion and, for some, even deafness. How then did they hear the commands of the non-commissioned and commissioned officers, bugle calls or a beating drum when all around was noisy chaos? The unceasing, cacophonous blasts of rifles and bigger caliber guns, the grunts and groans of their comrades, the banging of ramrods jamming lead into the barrels at a furious pace and the whizzing and whining of bullets and shells passing nearby must have been painfully loud. Frequently, the soldier simply could not and did not hear.

A whack of a sword, a tap on a shoulder or a kick of a boot probably was the best mode of communication. Even those overt signals failed to get the message across to a line of men that sometimes stretched out for well over a mile. Orders at the division or corps level had to trickle down to thousands of people that needed to be told what to do. To defend a hill, take a ridge or shift alignment to address a flanking threat. It is more likely than not that commands went unheard. The destiny of armies was ultimately determined by guesswork or luck.

The object of endless drill was to teach soldiers to be able to react instinctively, en masse, to curt voice commands, a bugle call, a drum beat or visual signals under fire. Drill occupied a soldier's existence when he wasn't otherwise engaged entrenching, on camp detail, sleeping or on picket duty. The units that drilled best stood firm as their world shattered around them. The fresh, green militia units, those with no cohesiveness or lacking in respect for their officers and non-commissioned officers, were the first to break ranks and flee to safety and panic was infectious.

AS a former military man and a Civil War buff, I am frequently asked by friends if I participate in reenactments. The answer is no. I feel that once one has done the real thing, faking it is less than satisfying.

My first year as a Marine lieutenant assigned to an artillery battery at Twentynine Palms, California set the table for that decision. The Marine Corps base there, the largest Marine installation in the world, is without a doubt one of the most realistic training areas offered to any military force. Almost 1,000 square miles of heat blasted sand, mountains and rapidly changing alluvial fans, washes, trails and a host of venomous creatures slithering and crawling about, test those that dare challenge the desert. The nightly yip-yap barking of coyotes is omnipresent. Half of my first year stationed there was spent eating, sleeping and living in the field, preparing for war.

As the end of that year approached, we had morphed into a salty and experienced bunch.

Aside from actual combat, training together in the field bonds warriors as no other experience can. It creates a resilience borne from living under the sun and stars. The Mojave climate is by no means salubrious and its harsh and unforgiving nature breeds a superior fighter. Enveloped by the elements, one is baked, frozen, bitten, drenched, hungry, thirsty, deprived of sleep, dirtied and irritated.

Later in my military life, I lived in the Saudi Arabian and Kuwaiti deserts for almost a year as well. Acclimation to the Mojave helped with the transition to the equally harsh climate of the Middle East. All that mandatory outdoorsy stuff took the novelty right out of camping for fun.

Roughing it under Civil War canvas, cooking over a fire and eating period food without showers or a roof over my head is not something I choose to do in my spare time. That's me, though. I know a bunch of military guys who both served in reenactment units during their service as well as afterwards and enjoyed it immensely. Good for them. They keep alive their own infatuation and provide entertainment for thousands of others each year. And as Cervantes once said, it takes all sorts to make a world.

✳ ✳ ✳ ✳

'ickett's 'harge

MR. Handelsman was a shaggy haired but engaging beatnik. He also happened to be the carefree instructor of our senior high school Film Studies class. In the spring of 1980, he presented us with alternatives for the final exam. The student could either write a paper or, with a group, produce and present a film. Nobody wrote a paper. Although it was unlikely that, armed only with a Super 8 camera, we would produce a cinematographic master work along the lines of *Citizen Kane*, the experience was sure to be fun. In fact, we could guarantee it would be fun. We had, on our own initiative, done it before.

The previous summer, a group of school and neighborhood chums had borrowed Ronnie Galman's father's Super 8 camera in order to make our breakout production. There wasn't much of a script or story line. We just wanted to film some Civil War battle scenes. Being loyal Unionists, we suited up in uniforms as close to those worn by Federal troops 120 years earlier. We armed ourselves with a cobbled together mixture of replica swords and muskets and a few toy guns for effect. Out of convenience, we bore with us a fifty star American flag in lieu of the thirty-four star banner that fluttered over the 1863 Union (thirty-five when West Virginia was pried from its rebellious parent). We borrowed Mom's station wagon, loaded up our gear and drove over to the farm field owned by a cast member's relative.

It was our naïve belief that all Civil War battles were fought in farm fields. The newly plowed rows and recent dry weather provided excellent conditions for explosive special effects. Creating dramatic blasts was no big deal for kids with our pyrotechnic experience.

Gingerly removing an ample supply of tins of black powder from the car, we poured a handful or so of the grainy black material into several plastic baggies. Affixing metal ends from ordinary camera flash bulbs to the ends of twelve gauge wires, the flash bulbs were inserted into each baggie. The package was spun shut and held in place with a twist-tie. Each bag was then placed in a hole in the ground where we wanted an explosion to take place. After a cursory check for rocks that could become dangerous projectiles, we buried the charges and snaked the attached wires to locations about twelve feet away. Before filming any one scene, a brave soul carrying a 4.5 volt battery lay in the prone position holding the bared ends of the wire. His job, when cued by a shout, was to touch the wire to the battery leads. Viola, Hollywood special effects - high school style!

As I wrote this book, an old acquaintance emailed a still frame taken from a negative of the reel. In it, a few of us, wearing jeans and blue buttoned shirts, whatever we dug out of bedroom dressers to simulate Union uniforms, charge up a rise in the field. Behind us, barely concealed in a furrow cut in the tilled soil, the special effects guy lay with his white shirt showing over the top edge of his hiding spot. Next to him, a huge column of smoke and dirt was erupting out of the ground and easily reaching twenty-five or thirty feet in the air. Half the guys in the charging line of troops can be seen looking back, mouths open and blurting something akin to, "Holy shit! What the heck was that?" Unfortunately, the film itself is lost to history.

That cinematic practice run was superb preparation for our Film Studies final project. Each of us had become skilled enough to make a go at it with the camera. Everyone who touched it could load it without exposing the film, could keep it somewhat steady and could pan gracefully so as to prevent motion sickness in a viewing audience.

For the final project, most of us chose to produce non-Civil War related works. I attempted a documentary about our town's Triple-A ballclub, the Rochester Red Wings. It was set at rickety old Silver Stadium in north Rochester on Norton Street, a residential neighborhood much like the one in which Wrigley Field in Chicago sits. For a seventeen-year old, I was given surprisingly open access to the team and the stadium. Management even permitted me to film from the roof of the 1929 structure. I caught a few unique angles of the team on a sunny spring Saturday afternoon. I later played the silent production to the class with an accompanying tape recorded soundtrack. On it, a person searches the radio dial looking for a catchy tune. The radio voyager settles on a station playing Chicago's *Saturday in the Park* which then played throughout the rest of the four minute film.

GEORGE Hinkel, my Lincoln loving elementary and high school pal, had opted to do a much more costly and ambitious production for his final project. He enlisted the same eager crew that had produced, filmed and acted in the Civil War silent short done a year earlier. He invited us to his house, sat us down and walked us through his planned production. We were an unruly and ill mannered cast. Impatient with our tomfoolery, he glared at us in silence until we quieted down. Even though he walked us through the script, it never really became clear what he was trying to tell his film's audience. Whatever the message was, though, it was going to be relayed with plenty of explosions and lots of dramatic and gory deaths.

One complicated scene was set up in a wood lined field and was intended to recreate, with a dozen actors, the wave of 13,000 or more Confederate soldiers attacking the Union center on July 3, 1863. Historians really can't nail down how many Confederate soldiers actually participated in the assault. General Longstreet claimed there were 15,000 in the three divisions and later students who are sticklers for historical accuracy pronounce there were only 12,000. Regardless, as the three divisions left the trees and approached the Union front on Cemetery Ridge, the sublime sight left many Federal observers struggling for words to describe it.

On location with Hinkel, the real number that set across the field on a distant and far more violent afternoon was irrelevant. Some pretty creative camera work was going to be needed to make seven guys look like multiple thousands. Since the equipment produced film without sound, George Hinkel rightly suspected that most in the class would have no idea what the scene represented without dialogue and accompanying narration. To correct that potential problem, he dug up some stencils and poster board. Filming a handmade and explanatory sign before fading to the real action would do the trick. Camera work with Super 8 technology is tougher than it would appear to be. The class was prepped for the battle action to follow by a jumpy five second shot of the introduction informing them that they were about to be treated to a dramatic rendition of the acclaimed:

ICKETT'S

HARGE

Film by
ge Hinkel

The class' titters and guffaws were short lived. They were soon replaced by cheers and loud applause as the film reached its denouement. A John Wayne-like character, played by Hinkel, dressed in authentic Davy Crockett frontier leather and topped with a coonskin cap, is bayoneted by an anonymous soldier. Staggering, summoning his last bit of energy from his dying body, our hero throws a burning brand onto a pile of explosives set in the middle of a sunlit meadow. The resulting blast hurled dirt, stones and junk skyward in an eruption rivaling that of Krakatoa. What a cheesy rendition of the Duke's death scene in his film *The Alamo* and an epic explosion had to do with 'ickett's assault at Gettysburg remains a mystery. But, with this audience, it didn't matter one bit. The home-made production faded to dark accompanied by the roar of the crowd.

George Hinkel, artiste extraordinaire, passed the course with flying colors.

＊ ＊ ＊ ＊

School is Adjourned, Life is Now in Session

MOM and dad beamed when my Naval Reserve Officer Training Corps scholarship was announced to an envious and audibly gasping group of students and their parents at my 1980 high school graduation ceremony. A free four-year ride to college was the fervent hope of any parent of a middle class high school student. In return for the money, I promised the United States Navy my devotion, fidelity and hard work for four long years on active duty and two more in the reserves. During that time, there was the slim but very real chance that someone might actually shoot at me and, although less likely, the possibility I might get killed. But, in the naïve way in which the young take on challenges and opportunities at the start of life, the threat of a violent death on a battlefield rarely crossed my mind. It certainly didn't influence my decision to accept the government's cash.

At freshman orientation, I was sworn in to both the navy and the NROTC unit at the University of Rochester. One of the largest in the country, our NROTC battalion boasted a roster of over 300 midshipmen. The post-Vietnam military was energized by free flowing defense dollars liberally spent by the Reagan administration and his Secretary of the Navy, John Lehman. Their vision was to kick some life into a moribund fleet and face the Soviets head on. The goal was a 600 ship force. The navy, seeing the need to expand the pipeline of officers necessary to man those ships, poured copious amounts of cash into reserve officer training. Graduates coming out of the Naval Academy at Annapolis were insufficiently numbered to fill the demand.

In the break before my sophomore year, I was indoctrinated to navy life aboard ship. In dungarees and set before the mast, I became part of the crew and ordered to learn the ropes of being a sailor. This was to be my longest period to date away from comforting domestic surroundings and a test of my ability to handle shipboard life. My maiden voyage was an uninspiring summer "cruise" aboard U.S.S. Nicholson, a Spruance class destroyer which, for the six weeks I was aboard, mostly sat pier-side in Charleston, South Carolina.

Nicholson's ship's motto was "Fortes Fortuna Adiuvat," the Latin phrase translated as "Fortune Favors the Bold." In my limited time aboard her, I would have suggested something more tailored to my experience such as "Rust is Our Enemy" but I wasn't asked.

After chipping paint, cleaning heads[†] and performing other menial tasks assigned to third class midshipmen, I became convinced that any career would be more attractive than that of a surface warfare officer. The cramped shipboard spaces, tedious daily routine and the real meat of navy life became less and less appealing by the day. The smoky, blue-lighted, frigid Combat

---

[†] A head is a navy and Marine Corps term for a bathroom. It's a legacy of the age of fighting sail when crews of ships relieved themselves through holes cut on either side of the bowsprit at the "head" of the ship.

Information Center, the nerve center and weapons control of the ship, was somewhat interesting. But, even the computers, radars and weapons control systems couldn't keep my attention for long.

Most of the time, I spent endless days on deck dripping in Charleston's humidity, chipping rust, painting bulkheads and applying non-skid to Nicholson's weather decks. Adding to the misery was the unavoidably constant inhalation of the peculiar, sulfurous odors wafting from a nearby industrial site.

Away from the naval base and the stench of the paper mill, Nicholson's home port was a nice diversion. The off duty sections of the crew were released every day at four in the afternoon for liberty. Then, and on the longer, watch free weekends, I was able to enjoy the quaint, historic town of Charleston. When not enjoying South Carolina's beaches, I spent a lot of time leaning on the rail edging the pedestrian walkway along Battery Street. The palm tree lined promenade faces the vast harbor with the famous Fort Sumter lying in the mist shrouded distance. From this vantage point, soldiers and civilians witnessed Confederate batteries around the harbor open the American Civil War. Cannons and mortars roared as they pounded the Federal citadel, three or so miles from Charleston's antebellum splendor. The endless bursting of shells and vagaries of time and tide wore down the once tall and formidable great walls of the fort's outer bastion. The former pride of the Union guarding the entrance to this strategic harbor was reduced to a low silhouetted, rubble strewn hulk. So it remains today.

It was a much anticipated moment when I saluted the officer of the deck and requested permission to go ashore. I then turned, saluted the national flag at the stern of U.S.S. Nicholson and strode down the gangway bidding farewell to my first formal military duty. That was the last I remember seeing that destroyer. She continued on to serve America in an unspectacular career. Used as an offensive weapon once, her crew fired a few Tomahawk missiles in anger during Operation Southern Watch in 1998, a short but heavy blow to Saddam Hussein's efforts to reconstitute his offensive military capabilities after the First Gulf War. Nicholson's hum drum life ended shortly thereafter and in a far more dramatic fashion than she had lived it. She was towed to a target range and sunk by our own navy, sacrificed so that others might get better at what they do. Her corroding hulk now sits at the bottom of the briny deep. Thoughts of her rusting away down there with fish darting in and out of where I once slept give me pause. I think of the debt I owe that ship for driving me to a turn in my life I don't regret. It was aboard that vessel, hating the life of a sailor, tied to a pier in beautiful Charleston, South Carolina that I gave first and serious thought to joining the Marines.

A percentage of NROTC midshipmen are allowed the option of serving in the Marine Corps. Donning jarhead camouflage instead of squid khaki was a big decision but I was eager to see what adventure I could find with America's fighting elite. In the limited time I had spent with real Marines while in college, they certainly presented themselves as a pretty dapper and solid group. Along with very handsome uniforms, they were prouder of their organization and certainly did far less painting and rust chipping than the navy guys. I hemmed and hawed but by the midpoint of my sophomore year, I pinned the eagle, globe and anchor insignia of a U.S. Marine option on my midshipman blues, whites and working khakis. Marine uniforms wouldn't be issued to us until the following summer.

The Marine staff officer and non-commissioned officer assigned to the NROTC unit at Rochester were very helpful in orienting those of us who had chosen the Marine officer option. It didn't hurt that our commanding officer happened to be Marine bird colonel and he was indispensable in providing sound advice and guidance. Boy, did I need all of it.

THE summer of my junior year, the rubber met the road. That's the time I plunged into my first real Marine Corps experience at Quantico and the squat, ugly Quonset huts and low brick barracks of Brown Field, the home to the Marines' Officer Candidates School or OCS.

Flying from Rochester to National Airport in D.C., I came off the jet slightly disoriented and unsure of where to go. Spying a ramrod straight, unsmiling gunnery sergeant, I approached him and inquired if he knew what I should do next. He did not greet me or look at me, he just told me to shut up and sit in a nearby lounge section of the airport and wait for further instructions. Welcome to the Marines!

I sat in the uncomfortable airport lounge section along with a gathering group of equally short-haired and nervous studs, glancing around trying to spot a familiar face. My Rochester

Marine option classmates trickled in from different originating airports. When the drill instructor's attention was diverted elsewhere, we slid next to each other to speculate in whispers what punishment was next to come. It wasn't very long before we found out.

NROTC had taught us how to stand at attention and some basic close order drill so we were able to follow the gunny's commands, keeping pace without him berating us too much. He marched us out of the airport in front of a number of amused civilian passengers. At passenger pick-up, we were packed aboard a Marine Corps green school bus. With no air conditioning and windows wide open, we chugged out of National Airport and on to I-95 for the quick trip to Quantico.

Upon our arrival at Brown Field, the drill instructors lined us up on an asphalt drill field known as a grinder; throwing our civilian gear all over the place and generally treating us as our college military instructors had hinted was our miserable fate. Egged on by lots of screaming and yelling, we were hustled from one building to another and issued our gear and uniforms, taught how to make a rack, organize a locker and sea chest, label all our equipment and obtain a service rifle. That latter, precious piece of equipment, we were continuously reminded, was to be at our side literally twenty-four hours a day. When not in a candidate's hands, the rifle was chained to the end of his or her rack. Lose a rifle and all the angels in heaven could not save that unlucky candidate.

The Marine Corps has developed a straightforward way to teach esoteric military gobbledygook to a bunch of neophytes. The favored method of instruction, outside in a "school circle" or in the sultry and ripe humidity of a tightly packed classroom, is the lecture. Loud, authoritative sounding memorizations permeated our brains. They were shouted over the hum of four large floor fans doing nothing to cool at all. Fetid air swirled from one side of the room to the other. Because lessons were tailored to the lowest common denominator, most figured out that classroom time could be best spent improving techniques to sleep with one's eyes open. Assiduously paying attention when one was dog tired, full of high calorie Marine Corps chow and not interested in the subject being taught was a challenge to say the least. Watching fellow officer candidates trying valiantly to stay awake; heads bobbing and mouths lolling open provided a perverse opportunity for a laugh or two.

Conveniently, at the introduction to every class, students are presented with a list of topical learning objectives. Those, and only those, learning objectives are tested. Simple. As one memorable instructor put it, anything that was not testable was detestable. So, for those that figured that out at OCS on day one, the rest of the academic course of study was no challenge at all. The spare minutes gained by ignoring everything but the learning objectives during study time could be spent refilling drained reservoirs of sleep.

The six weeks of intense OCS training, beginning with a cue ball shaved head at the base barber shop, endeavored to strip us of our individuality and indoctrinate us into the traditions of the Corps. Our OCS company consisted of four platoons. On any day, we were in class, on the drill field, doing physical training or stuffed in cattle cars and trucked out periodically to swelter in the green canopied expanse of the base training area. There we low crawled through swampy, odorous lowlands. Experienced and none too patient drill instructors put us through our paces, taking our measure as potential officers. Land navigation, forced marches, physical training, rudimentary fire team and squad tactics, small unit leadership instruction, military history, drill, uniform regulations and personal hygiene rounded out the curriculum. All along the way, the campaign cover wearing, growling drill instructors poured on the obligatory harassment package. The Marines don't want leaders who can't function under stress. So, they deviously cram eight weeks of training into six and spare no anxiety filled moments doing so.

Despite the strain, I was able to find some humor in the whole business. In addition to the crude and hilarious gems than emanated from the mouths of the drill instructors, we were fortunate to have an entertaining figure in charge of our early morning physical fitness regime. After morning chow, we were chased out of the mess hall, into the barracks to don physical training gear. Seconds later, we were hustled outside and into formation for exercise. A solid, hulking British army Colour Sergeant towered over the morning event, hands on hips and staring from a high wooden platform. Radiating outward from him stood our neatly aligned and similarly clothed company of officer candidate clones. Strutting around the platform, the Colour Sergeant would greet us with a loud hello. "Good morning, Golf Company," he would shout. We responded in unison, "Good morning, Colour Sergeant Russell!" He went on, "I remind you again, Golf Company, to stay away from milk at breakfast. It will turn into cottage cheese in your stomach and end up on the back of the neck of the bloke in front of you!"

Our two platoon drill instructors at OCS were Vietnam veterans. In fact, most of the senior Marines in the Corps at the time had either served or fought in Southeast Asia. They were pretty hard on guys that didn't take well to infantry tactics. They also lambasted the clumsy who fumbled around with the gear. I don't blame the guys who just couldn't get comfortable with some of the equipment. Despite our reputation as one of the world's best funded military forces, we seemed no more technologically advanced than our Civil War ancestors.

The Marines were still issuing C-Rations for field chow rather than the now ubiquitous Meal-Ready-to-Eat or MRE. The field equipment was bulky and barely functional and grew heavier when made wet. Canvas shelter halves and tent poles were of World War II vintage and failed miserably in keeping the weather off a sleeping Marine. They were excellent at filling and weighing down packs on marches. Speaking of packs, aside from the service rifle, the pack was our second best friend. Each of us unselfishly shared a carbon copy girlfriend called ALICE. In military-speak, it was the All-purpose Lightweight Individual Carrying Equipment pack and served as a hard framed sea anchor with limited moisture resistance and not nearly enough carrying capacity.

We also strapped on "782" or "deuce" gear named after a form Marines signed when they took possession of combat equipment. Functional but heavy deuce gear included a web belt and suspenders.   On the belt, the Marine carried magazine pouches, a leather sheath and the Marine "Ka-Bar" fighting knife, a first aid kit, a canteen cup and hard plastic canteens. The more practical and lighter hydration backpacks with a siphon tube, out on the civilian market, took a few years until they were finally integrated into the Marine Corps kit.

All of this stuff, along with a flak jacket, helmet, rifle, chow, a rain poncho and spare clothing, was hauled out to the field for our training exercises. There, in perfectly aligned tent cities, we lived in very close quarters, just like our nineteenth century brethren.

VISUALIZING thousands of Civil War soldiers living on top of one another for literally months or years at a time, one comes to understand that solitude was likely a rare privilege. The military is an open society and personal secrets are simply not kept. Any Marine, at least in the confines of enlisted boot camp or at OCS, soon finds out that an individual's privacy is fleeting. Abruptly taken away, its absence better prepares a person to be integrated into a team.

Today, as I approach my fiftieth birthday, my wife does not understand how I can unabashedly parade around the house in my birthday suit. It would be clear to her if she had gone to OCS. There, the rows of black seated "shitters," as Marines lovingly call them, lined on each side of an open and fluorescent lighted head, left absolutely nothing to the imagination. We learned early on to sit alongside one another and perform our once or twice daily ablution, perfectly comfortable and engaged in conversation as if reclining on a public bench. Some of my fellow candidates, the ones genetically equipped with slower catastalsis, had time to clean weapons or bone up on study material while waiting for nature to take its course. Others strode in and did their business post haste, washed and returned to whatever had previously occupied them. The average man could easily shit, shower and shave in the ten minutes allowed in the morning rush. Stories of characters doing all three at the same time occasionally entered into a discussion. When tasked with scrubbing and buffing the head and shower areas, I used copious amounts of chlorine bleach as insurance. If OCS taught me any life lesson it's that military men don't much care who's watching when they poop.

After receiving graduation certificates and proudly marching by friends and family, we happily took our leave of Quantico and returned to the staid, bricked and manicured grounds at Rochester. Those of us who had chosen the Marine option put on ridiculous airs of being far more experienced than we were. In actuality, we looked downright silly; the southern summer sun having left us with an odd, red-necked sunburn beginning halfway down our shaved heads on the portion of the scalp unprotected by USMC headgear. The farmer's tans extended down to the neckline where the uniform began. Time passed and our bizarre sunburns faded. Our hair grew back and, soon, we were deep into our final year.

SENIOR year flew by with a light class load. I was selected for a six month stint as NROTC battalion commander and that occupied a fair amount of my time. Disproportionately concentrating on preparation to be an officer, I still managed better than passing grades and minor scholastic honors in history, a subject I had attended both in school and as a hobby. Aside from preparation for the military, my primary focus in my last year at college was not on academic accomplishments but on social events: developing life-long friendships, chasing women and consuming alcohol.

Graduation day arrived and, proudly wearing the handsome dress white uniform of a Marine officer, my family in attendance, I pinned on the bars of a second lieutenant. Not long after that, I set out on Route 15. My destination, once again, was Quantico.

AS anyone who has ever served in the armed forces knows, changing duty stations is like changing a worn, sweat soaked and sometimes bloody pair of field socks. It is necessary, sometimes painful and, when completed, it often brings relief. But the process always stinks to high heaven. For officers, a move can be expected about every two years in peacetime. Just as soon as one gets settled and comfortable at a long sought after job or, conversely, itching to get out of a purgatorial punishment, the needs of the service rear their ugly heads. In a frantic change of duty station, the government demands that the individual pack his bags, his household goods, his family, if he or she has one, and get on to the next base. That place might be in the next state, across the nation or anywhere in this world. Because of this, veterans are seasoned travelers. They know the most scenic routes and the best and cheapest motels. They plan the sojourn to the next adventure with the skill of a rugged explorer. With unit farewells and changes of command completed, the migrating veterans, some with families in tow, spread out across the highways and byways of America to get where they need to go.

I joined the ranks of those mobile servicemen and women in the spring of 1984. Quantico and TBS was my destination. That's the school where wet-behind-the-ears second lieutenants begin their real Marine Corps orientation. TBS stands for The–Basic–School. The "KISS" principle applies. Keep–It–Simple–Stupid. Like the soldiers who wore the blue and the gray long before I had the privilege to don a uniform, I soon was made very aware that keeping it simple when all else devolves into bloody chaos is a very wise policy. At TBS, even as older, wiser graduates and officers, we still had only a rudimentary idea of what it meant to lead Marines in peacetime and combat. It was the Marine Corps' job to start filling in the blanks.

AFTER graduation, a buddy and I visited a suburban auto dealer to purchase our first brand new vehicles. I borrowed $9,000 from a credit union used by a lot of sailors and Marines. They were only too eager to lend me the money. Creditors there knew from experience that officers with a steady paycheck coming in were good for the money. Wandering around the lot, we caught the attention of a bored salesman. He was shortly made very happy after he took a chance and got off his duff to talk to us. With limited negotiation, we told him we would sign papers to buy two of the same model of the F-150 Ford pick-up.

Having already filled the tank with gas, I threw a sea bag stuffed with a few uniforms, civilian clothes and some toiletries into the open bed. I hugged and kissed the tearful face of my mother, backed out of the driveway and set out on my military adventure pointed south through New York's Finger Lakes on Route 15.

QUANTICO, Virginia is a tiny riverside dot on the map, wedged into one of the numerous bays and inlets common where the waters of the Potomac River widen perceptibly and then carry downstream to Chesapeake Bay. It is just off the vehicular mania of I-95, within spitting distance south of Washington and almost equidistant north of Richmond. Its low red brick administrative buildings and forested, brambly training areas might just as well be millions of miles from both. On neatly mowed and campus-like main grounds sits the Combat Development Command. That bureaucracy oversees the continual evolution of the Marines' doctrinal war fighting capabilities. Twenty or so miles west, deep in the Virginia wilds, sits the subordinate Training and Education Command's TBS. As each of us fledgling lieutenants arrived, we checked in and were put up in alphabetical order in four-man rooms at isolated Camp Barrett. Over a busy six months, 200 of us would be rudely weaned from civilian normality and learn what it takes to be leaders of Marines. A half a day's drive and a few hundred miles down Route 15, the school of real life had begun.

Chapter 2

THE ROAD

"This new highway program will affect our entire economic and social structure. The appearance of the new arteries and their adjacent areas will leave a permanent imprint on our communities and people. They will constitute the framework within which we must live."

– Robert Moses –

❋   ❋   ❋   ❋

Rust Belt Byway

WHEN first visiting America, Europeans are most impressed by the sheer size of the country. Unlike the Continent, stitched by railroads and crossed by more robust bus lines, Americans get around our vast expanses primarily by car. To do so, we use far reaching and well maintained roads. That was far from the case a century ago.

In the early twentieth century, Henry Ford's genius put an automobile in the hands of average Americans. But, this newly mobile class was forced to drive on surfaces not much better than dirt tracks and horse paths. The flood of automobiles and the lack of infrastructure to support them kicked the Federal government into action. The new demand for cars spurred investment in improving road surfaces for automobiles at the expense of the previous century's rail, canal and steamship infrastructure.

The nascent legislation, in what was to become an expensive history of Federal highway subsidies, was adopted in 1921 with the passage of the Federal Highway Act. The tap was opened and money began to flow to build and maintain an amalgam of interstate roads. Quick on its heels, the United States Numbered Highway System was adopted by joint federal and state agreement in 1926. This rather foresighted report ensured that the growing interstate road network was numbered consistently rather than being subject to a confusing mix of state preferences. Although coming into existence by federal fiat and paid for by taxes filling Washington's coffers, the responsibility for building and maintaining roads was borne by the states. From this era of evolving transportation tastes, the burgeoning involvement of the national government and a plentiful flow of dollars in the roaring 1920s, U.S. Route 15 was born.

U.S. Route 15 was conceived, planned, paved and interconnected in the days when driving was a novelty. In its infancy, it traversed a 794 mile stretch extending from Rochester to an unremarkable intersection in Walterboro, South Carolina. Travelers who first set off on its freshly laid surface would barely recognize it today. It has been altered substantially over the past eighty years. Time and goodly amounts of capital have improved this work horse byway. Much of it has been torn up, rerouted, widened, graded and laid down again with modern materials to accommodate demographic shifts, higher vehicle gross weights and heavier traffic flow. A good chunk of it has been relegated to state control. In New York, for example, U.S. Route 15 in New York, from the Southern Tier town of Painted Post north to Rochester, has been converted to a state route for its entire length.

Like many timeworn and iconic American roads that pre-date the Second World War, U.S. Route 15 was relegated to second-tier status by the 1956 Federal law creating the interstate highway system. Interstate highways were designed and built to move many more cars, trucks and freight across the wide expanses of America. They were poured or asphalted with a secondary military purpose as well. These four-lane highways were built to serve as transcontinental supply routes in the event a war broke out on American soil.

The Eisenhower Interstate System is so well known and used today that other legacies of Dwight Eisenhower's post-war presidential administration are less well remembered. The heady days of the space race and fearful escalation of Cold War tensions with the Soviet Union become more muted as time passes. But the interstates remain vital to most of us in our daily lives.

In Pennsylvania, some sections of the old Route 15 have been replaced by a concrete interstate highway. The quainter two-lane road has been transformed into I-99, a divided, four-lane anaconda with a wide grassy or tree lined center median, the graveled shoulders marked with the red, white and blue numbered shields familiar to interstate travelers.

In areas in southern Pennsylvania and farther south, Route 15 takes on a fresh national historic designation as it passes through areas of Revolutionary War, Abolition Era and Civil War note. It's the same old road but, because it winds past sites of historical interest, local governments and tourist bureaus encourage people to see the countless hills, crossroads, gaps and river fords up, on, through and over which great events in eastern America transpired. The Journey Through Hallowed Ground Byway tracks Route 15's path from Thomas Jefferson's Charlottesville, Virginia to the fields at Gettysburg.

Parts of Route 15 make up what used to be the even older Susquehanna Trail which once led honeymooners from the nation's capital to Niagara Falls, New York. A fair piece of the road in Pennsylvania still retains that designation although only that fact is known only by locals, romantic auto hobbyists and transportation historians.

SOME American highways are known for their spectacular views. Some are known for their traverse through long stretches of colorful desert or along coastal bluffs. Some, like the East Coast's I-95 and the West Coast's I-5, are famous for congestion. What characterizes Route 15 as it winds through Pennsylvania and New York is that this section of the road is a living and breathing microcosm of Rust Belt America. These states suffered while their financially burdened and winter weary populations have migrated to sunnier and lower taxed climes. It is not one of America's prettiest roads. Route 15 is easy to find on AAA maps of course, but, as hard as one looks, it will not be found in the top ten jet-setters' destinations in Condé Nast.

Aside from a few, quite stunning miles on the northeastern fringe of the great Allegheny Plateau and those paralleling the wide Susquehanna River, this working man's by-way is visually dull. In some spots, the eroding, windowless sites of closed factories tell of a more prosperous time. In other places, the lines of worn and dilapidated row houses, set like dirty sentinels barely feet away from rushing traffic, are shells of memories of a once civilized pace. To wonder what they were evokes a menial state of depression which can be exacerbated by the somberness of a bitter winter's day. Layers of dirty snow are tossed aside by wing plows hanging to the sides of salt stained, rusting Department of Transportation trucks. Tons of dirt, ash and road salt are dumped on the potholed asphalt to make travel safer for transients. The plows, roaring by, scrape the road and leave in their wake nothing but garbage strewn piles of slop and grime.

In too many small towns dotting the route, people with the financial flexibility to head to greener pastures have done so. The rest, tied to the place they were born and raised, scratch out an existence. Punching the clock, these hearty souls return from day or night work shifts to their colorless homes.

On the parts of Route 15 where the road is a four-lane, concrete raceway, the whizzing traffic sucks the remaining life out of the surrounding area. This agonizing phenomenon is particularly acute in locales like Mansfield, Williamsport or Duncannon where transportation planners have unwittingly aided the decline of communities by encouraging cars and people to avoid fading downtowns. In a society wedded to the culture of the automobile, stopping or even slowing down to enjoy what the local hosts might have to offer is now troublesome if not impossible.

ON Market Street in South Williamsport, just across a shiny new Susquehanna bridge, rows of ordinary houses sit precariously close to the road. Lined up like pins, they stand ready to be bowled down by an errant vehicle. Drivers are commanded to slow by flashing, cautionary traffic lights and, one hopes, common sense. Half of the strangers passing through ignore both and continue at excessive speed. At night, street lamps and blindingly bright halogen headlights glare on this narrow chokepoint. They easily outshine the twinkle of stars overhead. An omnipresent diesel stench emanating from chromed cab side truck exhausts perpetually hangs in the air. It permeates even the most sophisticated weather stripping. Cars and trucks must negotiate a treacherous left turn as the street begins its ascent back up to the Allegheny Plateau. In the depths of icy winter, this dangerous stretch of road is kept covered in a blanket of dirt and salt to prevent unprepared adults and white fingered teenaged probationary drivers from failing to negotiate the turn and sliding disastrously into a front porch or, worse, a kitchen or living room.

A "For Sale" sign crops up in a random yard now and then. One wonders who would invest here when so many quieter and less trafficked neighborhoods abound. There is a resiliency here, though, a kind of frontier toughness. It can be found in the pride of homeowners who make it a quest to keep some semblance of domesticity with only a thin veneer separating them the apathetic drone of thousands of daily transients. Faded American and decorative holiday flags hanging from porches whip in synchronized motion, dragged in the air streams churned up by passing eighteen wheelers. Quite a few houses sport yellow ribbons or yard signs that boast to all passersby that the occupant supports the troops. It is good to know that these put-on folks still care enough to think of others.

CONTINUING southbound towards Gettysburg and ascending the upslope out of this residential area, drivers pass the headquarters of Little League International and the Little League Museum and Hall of Excellence. Want to get a glimpse into grassy, pastoral Americana? On display are memorials to the men and women who whacked around a baseball or softball as kids and later went on to become famous athletes, politicians, writers and notables in varied pursuits.

The perfectly groomed Howard J. Lamade Stadium, the central and largest venue at the baseball complex, proudly hosts the nationally televised Little League World Series every summer. At times, more people than reside in the entire Williamsport area pack this miniature ball park. Most recline on the grassy berm stretching behind the outfield fence, watching the world's diminutive baseball best run, hit and catch in pursuit of the championship prize. Little League is a major economic generator for this tiny borough of just over 6,000 and its larger sister across the river. Celebratory families of the youthful stars spend freely and these towns could use every dollar. It wasn't always that way. In the late nineteenth century, money was in plentiful supply in Williamsport. The stands of hardwood on the nearby hillsides and the town's proximity to the Susquehanna River drove a vibrant timber industry. At one point, Williamsport was home to the most millionaires, per capita, in the United States. Stately mansions line West Fourth Street in the city on the north side of the river along "Millionaires Row." Time, the decline of the timber industry and the vagaries of the flood cycle of the nearby Susquehanna wore away at the desire of the wealthy to live here. In less complimentary circles, it has come to be known as "Little Philly" and not because of its proximity to the city of Brotherly Love or its trademark cheesesteak hoagies.

Williamsport is better off now than most of its Pennsylvania neighbors. Its hope for revival now rests underground rather than on top of it. The river town is serendipitously perched over a prehistoric geologic oddity known as the Marcellus Shale. This natural gas-rich patch of rock is now being exploited by oil and gas companies using controversial engineering known formally as hydraulic fracturing. Informally, it's "hydro-fracking" or just "fracking." After drilling down to a permeable, gas filled layer of rock, a high pressure water and chemical slurry is blasted into the bore hole. The force cracks the weaker rock around it, releases the gas which is then captured, piped away and put to use. There is a dark side to the process, though. The chemicals that are used in the fracturing can end up in ground water, drinking wells and rivers and streams. It remains to be seen if nature's bounty will be a boon for Williamsport or an environmental disaster.

LEAVING "Billtown"‡ behind, Route 15 continues south past the incomparable Clyde Peeling's Reptiland. From there, it swoops down into a shallow valley becoming the West Branch Highway. Still northwest of the Susquehanna's Sunbury and Northumberland confluence and ever faithfully following the western fork, the road glides into Lewisburg.

This quaint place is the home of Bucknell University, an institution with a stellar academic reputation. Prettily nestled on the river's western shore, the university's power brokers sometimes lament their campus's idyllic riparian setting. When the fickle waterway catastrophically leaves its banks, Bucknell's low areas and basements can turn rather soggy.

Arguably, a bigger point of interest in Lewisburg may just be an ominous looking Federal prison. Officially titled the United States Penitentiary, Lewisburg, it is known by employees and visitors as "Pennsylvania's Big House." While not directly on Route 15, its proximity to the

---

‡ Ask a bar crowd about the genesis of the name Williamsport and you might just kick off a lively debate. Some say the town was named after the son of a large landowner, others say it was labeled after his close friend. Then there are those that swear it took the first name of a state senator. Whatever the true origin, all can probably agree that Bill is a nickname for William.

university has probably spurred many an undergraduate joke. Surrounded by high fences and razor wire, the maximum security prison specializes in keeping the most violent felons behind bars. The nefarious Al Capone, Alger Hiss, Jimmy Hoffa and John Gotti all enjoyed, at one time or another, the pleasure of staying here. Oh, if its walls could talk!

After meandering away from the river for a while, Route 15 inches back towards it and transitions in name to the iconic Susquehanna Trail. The boroughs of Shamokin Dam and Selinsgrove come into view.

In the nineteenth century, Shamokin Dam's city fathers made their splash in the world by constructing a ten foot high, solid barrier across the Susquehanna. That was an impressive feat for the time. If it weren't patently obvious by looking at it, this point in the course the river is not easily tamed. After the winter of 1904, a ponderous mass of moving ice pressing against the dam crushed the structure. The one thing that had given this town its raison d'être, was no more. No worries. Stubbornly inventive Shamokiners[§] weren't about to let Mother Nature determine their destinies. Today, after the ice clears from the river in spring, the world's longest inflatable dam rises. The slowed river water backs upstream, deepens and widens, creating a 3,000 acre state operated recreational lake. If brick and mortar

---

[§] It's my impression that a Shamokiner is actually someone who hails from the larger town of Shamokin a short distance away. Somebody who lives in tiny Shamokin Dam must be called something different: Shamokin Damite? Shamokin Dammer? I claim in this book to know a lot about Route 15 and the places and people on it. This trivial matter, however, stumps me. Email me if you can set me straight.

won't hold back the Susquehanna, a "fabridam" will have to do.

Not too much farther south, a traveler enters Selinsgrove. Since I mispronounced it the first time I visited, I'll save the reader the same embarrassment. Its first syllable is regionally pronounced with a "long e" as in the word seal. The rest is enunciated as expected. Selinsgrove is the home to a homogenous collection of 5,000 people. Quite a few find employment at Susquehanna University, a liberal arts college founded there in 1858.

Like many of its sister cities around these parts, Selinsgrove seems to regret the state's decision to pick up and move noisy, traffic-packed Route 15 away from its main drag. Cars, the protestors alleged, were ruining the ambience of Market Street. The tastes of college students and general population, naturally, moved too. Both groups tend to do their shopping or seek entertainment at the Susquehanna Valley Mall or the box retailers and restaurants that sprung up on Route 15 away from town. The rest of us, jump on the bypass and blow right by the little place heading to points farther south. As probably foretold by some who opined on the matter, progress for Selinsgrove is not what it was cracked up to be.

ASIDE from the regulars, only the adventurous or lost stop at the Horseshoe Bar in New Buffalo about twenty-eight miles from Selinsgrove and fifteen miles north of Harrisburg. On a typical weekend visit to Gettysburg, the drive puts us in the Horseshoe parking lot around four in the afternoon on a Friday. Although a comfort break and quick refreshment are on our minds, avoiding the end of week rush hour is an ulterior motive. Harrisburg's notorious traffic chokepoints are quickly jammed as government workers flee the capital thanking God it's Friday. The resultant traffic mess is a good reason to hold off travel through the capital for an hour or so.

The Horseshoe shares a purely functional looking building with a family restaurant. Together, they are mere feet from the high volume, high traffic highway. On the south side of the restaurant, sits a fifteen foot high, one-of-a-kind, blue-purple painted sea serpent. It might be a dragon. Even after close inspection I can't quite tell which. We simply refer to it as "The Dragon." Its appearance in the front windshield after a four hour drive is a good excuse to stop, take a pee and have a cold beer at the bar next door.

The Dragon is decked in festive string lights for the benefit of those passing at night. Over the years, it has been painted and repainted in various garish color schemes. An advertising gimmick for the restaurant, it has achieved landmark status for us and is a beloved symbol of our Route 15 journeys to the hallowed ground at Gettysburg. Just as we are out of our element here, so too is the fairy tale Dragon. It truly belongs at the gates of a medieval castle. Alas, its sinuous reptilian shape rears up here on Route 15, next to a dive bar north of Pennsylvania's grimy capital. It is as far from Camelot as one could possibly get.

THE Horseshoe is a simple lounge designed solely for drinking. Its existence must be partially responsible for the occasional signs pleading for driver sobriety which plaster the shoulders of the road. The name "Horseshoe" hanging on a lighted shingle outside the place implies luck. The grizzled and downcast souls inside, humped over their ashtrays, rum and cokes and draft light beers, only suggest hard luck. This is a working class joint. I have never seen a white shirt and a tie on any patron at the Horseshoe. The combination would be seriously out of place there anyway. Unlike some of the fancier entertainment establishments in larger cities where after work happy hours are frequented by well coiffed and sharply dressed executives, the Horseshoe embraces the ordinary and the ugly. The inhabitants sport ball caps, flannel shirts and stained, torn Levi jeans. With the day shift just ended, people saunter in to hold a smoke and sip a drink. To them, both are eucharistically sacred. The butts and the cocktails take these people away, albeit briefly, from a hardscrabble life. Everyone I have ever seen at the bar smokes. Cigarettes hang from lips or curl smoke from plastic ashtrays. The hair and fingertips of some are stained from the habit. Acrid tobacco smoke billows, creeping up the tainted walls and ceiling tiles, rusting them to a yellowish brown.

PENNSYLVANIA, unlike about half of the states that have totally banned smoking in enclosed public places, continues to allow the habit in bars. Let them do it I say. Smoke 'em if you got 'em. If the addiction brings pleasure in an otherwise sad or downtrodden life, who am I to say otherwise?

Pennsylvania is one of those states whose manufacturing base has taken a beating for most of the last century. It continues to get thumped in this century's Great Recession. The more economically resilient cities of Philadelphia, Pittsburgh and State College benefit from finance, high technology, biosciences, education or health care. But the majority of Pennsylvanians, according to the U.S. Department of Commerce, still rely on manufacturing to make their mortgage payments. Perhaps it's to get through arduous lives that one in five Pennsylvanians includes tobacco use as a daily ritual. According to the Centers for Disease Control, that puts the Keystone State in the top half of all states in terms of the number of people who light up.

CIVIL War soldiers were smokers. Then, instead of the ubiquitous cigarette of today, cigars, pipes and chewing tobacco were the conduit to the body. Tobacco and coffee were staples to men in camps, on picket duty or during a break on a forced march. Like today, both were used as stimulants to energize worn bodies or when a bored soldier had nothing better to do to occupy his time. And also like today, both coffee and tobacco, when available, were consumed in excessive quantities. When supply lines failed, the soldiers spent an inordinate effort to find reasonable substitutes. Temporary soldiers' truces, declared unofficially by privates on picket duty and frowned on by frumpy officers, were done so to facilitate trades of tobacco or coffee or for other sought after goods. Homemade rafts of wood carrying newspapers, chewing tobacco and coffee beans set sail on many a river in trade between Johnny Reb and Billy Yank.

ULYSSES Grant, the North's most famous smoker, was rarely seen without the stub of a cigar in his mouth. That, however, is not the vice for which he is known. Grant has always been tagged as one with a preference for the bottle. William Tecumseh Sherman, Grant's reliable army commander and friend and somebody who should know, writes that Grant was indeed a drunk for a time. But, he wasn't the whiskey guzzler he has been made out to be. Most of his reputed blackouts were in his days as a company grade officer marking time in tiresome outposts. A far more abstemious Grant rose to command all Union armies.

But, those who were close to him confirm that Grant liked cigars immensely. A famous photo of Grant was taken as he wrote his well received and financially successful memoirs at Mount McGregor, New York. The revealing snapshot shows a weakened and pale man. He is wrapped tightly in a blanket and wearing a watch cap, dying of throat cancer. The malady was certainly due to the consumption of an unlimited supply of cigars always on hand. I doubt if Grant had known his eventual lot, he would have restrained his desire for a smoke or a chew on nub of a cigar as he sent his legions into the fight.

THE military is a stressful occupation. It is equally, at times, mind-numbingly boring. So, as throughout history, soldiers need assistance in enduring both states of mind. With free hands and a ready supply available, a lot of them take up smoking. The military hierarchy is not proud of the behavior. A whopping one third of service members smoke. Depending on which branch of the military to which one refers, that percentage is a bit higher or lower. Lumped together though, the numbers who puff daily average out to a little more than thirty percent of the larger group of men and women who wear the uniform.

There are no statistics on the number of smokers who served in Civil War armies but, in the long and illustrious traditions of military service, a pipe or a wad of chew surely had a special, dry place set aside in a majority of haversacks.

THE Horseshoe boasts a filthy, well worn pool table equipped with a few bent but usable cue sticks. The pool table costs $.50 a play which is indicative of the purchasing power of the locals. Adjacent to the table, the newfangled electronic Internet jukebox hangs on the wall and sits silent. At the back of the bar, a mounted flat screen flashes scenes of the day's news; the four or five customers only partially curious about what the broadcast anchors have to say. During our visits, we'll feed in a couple of bucks to the jukebox to liven up the place. Its jarring beat drowns out the television voices. Our selections of music are usual met with irritated stares but a round of drinks takes care of that.

The draft and bottled beer is cold, cheap and of surprising variety. To get one, the bartender, an ancient, ragged, skeletal blonde with a raspy voice is happy to oblige. She has been behind the bar as long as I can remember. She is welcoming even if the rest of the crew isn't. Around that U-shaped bar is a complement of comfortable stools. A wide, brightly lighted reefer displaying the beer selections caps the far end. Its glass doors reflect the sad eyes and worried frowns of those sitting around it.

The crusty gents park their tired butts on the stools. They are not the chatty sort. When they do talk it is only reluctantly and without eye contact. Responses are mumbles couched in the lingo of central Pennsylvania. They badmouth the politicians in nearby Harrisburg and Washington, no matter which flavor of politics they espouse. Aside from bad government, the sparse conversation sticks to hunting whitetail deer and fishing in the Susquehanna which flows only a few yards from the front door.

THE bartender lights a fresh cigarette and, as she blows out a cloud of smoke, mentions she's had a problem with an electric circuit feeding a coffee maker on the reefer end of the bar. A chivalric gentleman in an oily trucker cap and a snow white beard, who apparently knows quite a bit about alternating current, jumps up. He strolls into the back room where the breaker box hangs. He fiddles with that for a while and then comes back into the bar with a frown on his face. "Not that," he grunts and checks the ground fault on the outlet in which the brewer is plugged. It's tripped. He resets it with a distinct click and the coffee starts brewing again. It'll kick off again and again as long as the brewer makes coffee. The bearded, graying man with the dirty hat and nothing to do, or five or six like him later on, will help out as best they can to keep it doing just that. These folks are eager to come to the aid of a friend or neighbor. They aren't slackers when it comes to national service either.

The images of superficial patriotism around here are apparent. It is the place to see a "These Colors Don't Run" t-shirt, a display of an eagle on a denim jacket or a simple patch of an American flag on a biker's vest or stuck to a car window parked in the lot out front. The simple life of the American worker is on display in this honky tonk as it is in thousands of small towns in America just like it.   And, like the volunteers and draftees before them, the young men and women of the communities that surround the Horseshoe are a tough sort who, if high school proves a challenge or the economy keeps them out of the workforce, will again volunteer to carry a rifle in service as so many did 150 years ago just an hour down the road.

ALMOST in sight of Harrisburg, the harmful legacy of the expansion of a once pedestrian friendly road is poignantly illustrated in Marysville.   Here government traffic planners were presented with limited alternatives to create the promised utopia in which those seeking residential solitude can co-exist with a busy commercial artery. The citizen can have both they confidently promised. Blocked by the daunting flood of the Susquehanna River on one side, the planners had no choice but to rudely exercise the government's power of eminent domain on the other. The victims hardly held enough political capital to stop it.   Their domiciles, naturally, had to remain exactly where they had always been. Once broader, grassy yards were eaten away by pavement; gorging itself via ever encroaching civic rights of way. The steadily creeping road's shoulders were pushed to the very limits of discretion at front stoops, porches and garage entrances.   Windows facing traffic now are perpetually closed and covered with blinds or curtains.   The thinnest of barriers are the only thing standing between these poor people's privacy and the gawking of passing strangers.

Like spectators at a stock car race, the residents stand outside and watch the uncaring traveler race by. A driver's and a local's eyes may meet for a split second. Unimpressed and uncaring, both go about their business. It's hard to believe anybody could grow accustomed to a strip of busy asphalt mere feet from his bedroom. The resilient inhabitants of Marysville and those in South Williamsport too, show us how it's done.

MY darker impressions penned here contradict the travel brochure put out by the Susquehanna River Valley Visitors Bureau. That glossy piece of propaganda claims that if the adventurous decide to travel on Route 15 their time spent on it will be "unexpected, tranquil, engaging and educational."

The hum of countless tires, honking horns, truck brakes and diesel engine noise undercut the Bureau's promise of a soothing, pacifying ride. To be truthful, there are indeed silent and relaxing places just off the road. They may be found adjacent to the highway but only on forbidding, wooded trails mostly inaccessible to the majority not equipped with off road vehicles. Tranquility is illusory on major highways in America and Route 15 is no different. That is no great loss. In the minds of most who travel it, it's not a sought after quality anyway.

If, contrary to government sponsored assurances, achieving serenity is folly then the claim of "engaging and educational" must be scrutinized as well. Surely, though, there must be something along the road to draw the curious? Indeed, every few miles, there appears to be just the right eye-catching venue for some. While assuredly far from the intent of the highway's proselytizers, ramshackle pornography shops crop up periodically along the sides of the highway. The single story, windowless structures are surrounded by broad, crushed gravel parking areas suitably sized for eighteen wheelers. The fronts are splashed with enticing neon signs or brightly printed billboards which tell of "worlds" or "outlets" catering to the sophisticated adult. Like moths to a flame, these showy advertisements draw the attention of lonely long-haul carriers and stimulated voyeurs in automobiles. The screech of air brakes and the rumble of an idling diesel motor give notice to the proprietors that a customer is stopping in to satiate a need. Since Route 15 is busy, proximity to the road provides an excellent medium to push and to sell this lucrative form of entertainment.

PORN shops were rare stops on my off-campus agenda while I attended college. The few times I, along with friends, deigned to enter a selected hovel, it usually met expectations and provided the sought after kicks and giggles. The breadth of artificial merchandise designed by mankind for the sexual pleasure of both men and women astounds. We as college sophomores, living up to every level of childlike behavior that word implies, would drink our cheap beer and then sally forth to the bright lights and big city for some fun. The lure of a porn palace was irresistible. At the time I went to college, the premier and better known of Rochester's purveyors of erotica was in an old theater a few yards from a busy intersection on sordid Monroe Avenue at Goodman Street. The theater marquee's tantalizing Vegas-style lights cast their glow on the four corners and spot lighted the hooded panhandlers bundled against Rochester's chill standing below.

Entering through the heavy, shatter proof glass doors, the aroused visitor cast wide eyes on rows of artificial sex organs, dolls, vibrators, ticklers, how-to manuals and male and female toys in all colors of the rainbow lining the amply stocked shelves. Even better, for a quarter, one could view a poorly filmed and grainy sex act of one's choosing in a dark and stinky room. The feature length version cost considerably more. Whittled through the thin plywood walls, the rough-edged glory holes evinced ribald jokes and memorable pearls of phallic humor. Five drunken college guys crowded into a thirty-six square foot porn theater room, giggling and hooting just like - five drunken college guys - quickly got us asked nicely to leave. We couldn't resist chortling at the oversized dildos and sensually dressed blow-up mannequins as we exited out the door. Fine, we'll take our business elsewhere!

THE Susquehanna River Valley Visitors Bureau, or most regional visitors associations for that matter, prefer those coming in from out of town partake of other, less carnally oriented attractions. Preferred "engaging and educational" distractions include antiquing, taking in a local museum, dining or visits to farm and craft stands. On any late summer or fall weekend, the corn husks, flowers, pumpkins and other festive decorations of the season may be found at several stops along the way. Some travel here for the opportunity to purchase finely crafted Amish furniture at backyard workshops or at more commercially oriented discount outlets.

The Amish are woven into the fabric of this farm country. They are always out and about using Route 15 to conduct their affairs. Slowing to turn into any of these businesses endorsed by the tourist bureaus, one must take care in order to avoid colliding with horse drawn carriages seen frequently riding down the shoulder of the road. These enterprising people, functionally clothed and traveling in nineteenth century conveyances, use the twenty-first century macadam to move between home and shop or deliver goods to produce, craft or furniture stores. The international orange caution triangles mandated for slow moving vehicles like Amish buggies are helpful. Competent horse handling of most of the drivers keeps the rigs sufficiently to the right on the shoulders. But a tiny piece of orange metal isn't going to stop a speeding car skippered by a distracted driver.

If it isn't already obvious that fiddling with a cell phone, texting or doing any number of other things with a handheld smart device while driving a car puts the car's occupants and anyone in the way at risk, then legislating prudent behavior becomes a necessary step. In more and more places, playing with a handheld device while driving is illegal. Pennsylvania was late to jump on that bandwagon, holding out until November of 2011. Wising up, it got in line and became the forty-second state to ban the practice. The drivers of horse drawn conveyances clopping along Pennsylvania's roads breathed a sigh of relief. Smart phones are best tossed in the center console when in Amish Country.

THE people whose mission it is to encourage out of towners to visit southern New York and northern and central Pennsylvania may find it tough to play the hand dealt to them. However, one group they can count on coming, particularly during the fall season, is the folks who like to kill and eat wild animals. Before I-390 was completed, a group of us teenagers, armed with shotguns and warm clothes, would travel part way to our destination down Route 15 to Wayland, New York. From there, we left Route 15 and proceeded over to the speck known as Bolivar where a friend's family owned a few acres and a farm house in a hilly and wooded hunter's paradise. Whitetail deer, turkey and other game animals were, and still are, plentiful. After the leaves fell and the bared trees swayed in the late fall chill winds, blaze international orange vests and jackets of countless big game hunters could be seen dotting the open hillsides and brown fields.

The pop of twelve gauge shotguns rang out and echoed up and down cut valleys. Professionals and novices alike were on the lookout for the perfect rack jutting up behind the ears of a graying, broad chested buck dropping his guard to nibble an ear of dried corn or unwarily standing upwind of a very fortunate hunter's scent. As the day wore on the deer, spooked by all the noise in the woods, went to ground. It was best to drive them out of their hiding and get them on the run again.

As we lined up and pushed through the hardwoods we came across a lone oil pump jack bobbing away. It drew out a few barrels of petroleum a day and siphoned it into a nearby storage tank. The well and pump sucked oil from the then tentatively explored layers of shale which encompass those that sit under Williamsport and also cover a vast area of subterranean New York Pennsylvania and Ohio.

The Marcellus deposits, named after the town near Syracuse where they pierce the surface, are seemingly limitless fossil fuel repositories and a legacy of a massive, prehistoric inland sea. Creatures and plants which thrived in the sea's shallow warmth eventually died; their organic material drifting to the bottom. Layer upon layer of sediment covered the dead material. Over time, the sea evaporated and disappeared as the earth's landforms and atmosphere evolved. Geologic heat and pressure crushed, cooked and transformed the former sea's layered, dead organic compost into an abundant supply of both oil and natural gas. Whether gas or oil depended mostly on the type of ancient flora or fauna and the temperature at which nature cooked the material long after its demise. The current landowners, recognizing the bounty beneath their feet, leased the land to small wildcatters and independent oil companies who are adept at making tiny single well operations profitable. Thus, a pump jack can be found in the most remote and strangest of places.

MY early teen experiences on Route 15 are remembered as a blur of white lines and headlights on a darkening Friday afternoon and the same on the return back home. It was like every other road to me then, just a means to get somewhere. Travel on it was slower than it should have been. Unending and unnerving work was constantly underway and blocked the same stretches of the highway year after year.

One cannot write about a northeastern highway without at least a passing reference to its repair. Road construction and maintenance are seasonal rites of passage for any living in this part of the country. Corrosive chemicals are dropped on the road surfaces to prevent them from becoming vehicular skating rinks in winter. Roads in the northern reaches of the American temperate zone are assaulted by the freeze-thaw cycle. Liquid precipitation seeps into tiny cracks in cement and asphalt and seasonal freezing temperatures turn the water to ice. Unlike most liquids, water expands when it freezes and the solid mass pushes out against the smaller space in which it is trapped. Small cracks are turned into wedges then crevasses. Tiny pinholes in the road surface eventually grow to sinkholes, gobbling tires and keeping front-end alignment shops hopping.

SCURRYING back and forth between Rochester and Quantico, attempting to keep the fire burning in a long distance relationship, I expected to be held up by construction delays all along the length of Route 15. In those tiring but memorable months, bad lighting, faded road markings and the inclement weather common to the area, made travel in my two wheel drive pick-up in the dark just as adventurous as handling explosives earlier in the day out on Quantico's ranges. The narrow, hilly roads and less than gentle turns north of Harrisburg were the absolute worst. Stop and go traffic in all the little towns and villages along the way made an eight hour drive easily stretch to ten or more. My attention was riveted towards keeping on my side of the double-yellow center line. That painted pair of stripes was all that stood between me and the rumbling, high headlight truck traffic screaming by in the other direction.

As I left behind the metropolitan chaos of Washington and picked up Route 15 in Frederick, Maryland, the weather worsened and I steeled myself for the inevitability of road trouble as I crossed the Pennsylvania line. Despite getting little sleep the night before and having a very long day behind me, my twenty-one year old libido kept me alert and ready for anything the road with a nasty reputation was sure to throw at me.

✻ ✻ ✻ ✻

A Mile Wide, A Foot Deep

WHENEVER I look at a photograph of Ambrose Everett Burnside, two images come to mind. One is of a doting grandfather, perhaps bouncing a giggling child on his knee. The other is of a cigar puffing, brandy swilling, portly tycoon with flowing whiskers and a rumbling laugh. He appears a satisfied man with burly arms wrapped around the world. The crow's feet radiating outward from his laughing eyes, carved by endless squinting in the sunlit outdoors, belie the guilt tearing at him as he took in the ghastly carnage of his battlefields. Those unbearable glimpses persecuted his soul. For the body in which it resided was criminally liable for the sanguinary panoramas drawn by his artless hand.

Burnside was anything but an indolent man. In fact, the illusory visage of him as an industrialist is not so far from the one professional niche he carved for himself. But, that occupational diversion was at a pause in a military career. He attended West Point and, after graduation, served inconspicuously in garrison in the Mexican War. After a short hitch and a mediocre tenure in the artillery, he resigned his regular army commission in 1853, eight years before the Civil War began. During the hiatus from the life of a soldier, he kept busy by designing and patenting a carbine. That useful implement was made even more so by a made-to-fit, breech loading brass cartridge. With a workable new rifle and packaged ammunition on the production line, he set out to make his fortune selling them to the army. The carbine was widely used in the upcoming war and came in handy cementing Burnside and his reputation as a vital cog in the army's bureaucracy. Those who trusted his untested martial instincts were soon to learn that a man who makes a good rifle is not necessarily a capable fighter.

Not contented with commercial distractions, he delved into politics and took an unsuccessful run at a seat in Congress. It would have been a blessing to quite a few soldiers if he had been elected and stayed active in civil service. Actually, for their sake, any career which would have made permanent his retirement from the military would have sufficed. But, having kept his militia credentials current during this brief interregnum and riding the wave of his carbine's popularity, he was destined to once again don the uniform. As the guns of war boomed, he reentered active service and was rapidly advanced.

He started the Civil War with a flourish, doing much to ensure the North Carolina coast was blocked to Confederate commerce through a series of effective amphibious landings. Garnering approving back slaps in Washington, he was promoted to command at the corps level in the newly forming Army of the Potomac.

Assigned to handle the right wing of that army at a slow moving creek in Maryland called the Antietam, he proved then and there that large unit combat command was definitely not his forte. In the late morning of September 17, 1862, Burnside was tasked with establishing a bridgehead on the opposite side of the creek and sweeping the Confederates arrayed there from the field. He chose as his primary crossing site Rohrbach's Bridge, a 125 foot long limestone and granite link to the other bank. Puzzlingly, he carelessly sent regiments of his precious charges running across the confining structure. They were easily picked off by Confederates lying covered on an adjacent and commanding wooded ridgeline.

The Antietam battlefield and town of Sharpsburg are only a few miles from Gettysburg. It's easy to pop down and take in the sights if one happens to already be in southern Pennsylvania. With a few friends alongside one mid-September day, near the anniversary of the battle in fact, we stood on the banks of the Antietam next to the infamous stone and mortar bridge that now bears Burnside's hapless eponym. One in our group, lacking in military expertise but intelligent nonetheless, asked, "How come he crossed here? Why didn't he go down a few hundred yards and send his men across the shallower part?" The answer is that a part of his corps did indeed do that. Stubbornly, he opted to channel the rest of his men into a stone killing zone.

At Rohrbach's Bridge, the Antietam is narrow and fordable. A soldier might get wet and would have to take some precautions to keep his musket and ammunition dry, but that shouldn't have been a deciding factor. Some argue that crossing the stream near, but not on, the bridge would have been foolish. Such a crossing would be under fire and slowed by deep water and steep banks on either side. The peculiarities of the creek's bed at that location forced Burnside to his tactical selection. There were other options.

Burnside, prior to launching his ill-conceived battle plan, could have engaged in a thorough reconnaissance up and down the stream's length. If he had done so he would have discovered more than just the one shallow and friendly fording site a short distance away over which he did send a part of his corps. His malignant choice to reinforce failure at the bridge foretold of grislier decisions to come. This man had no business leading soldiers in combat.

What's even more unbelievable is that after his Antietam fiasco he was put in charge of the entire Army of the Potomac. Suffering from what could only be characterized as a congenital bout of amnesia, Burnside sent divisions of men up the impregnable Confederate fortified slopes behind Fredericksburg on a chilly December day a mere three months after his error at Antietam. There he watched, open mouthed like a carp, as roiling smoke blanketed his obedient bluecoats and Confederate lead smashed the life from them. Midway through what was guaranteed to be the most lopsided defeat the Federals had yet to suffer in the war, Burnside, received several reports that his plan had gone disastrously awry. He refused to halt the madness. Waves of his army's finest futilely attempted to seize the heights, failing each time. Daylight, mercifully short this time of year, saved the army from annihilation. The screams and moans of those unlucky enough not to have been killed haunted the untouched survivors throughout the long, brutal night. Under the sharp eyes of Confederate sharpshooters above, they huddled together to stay warm. Surreally, eerie curtains of the northern lights, almost never seen this far south, danced over the now freezing corpses.

Some historians have tried to resurrect the image of Burnside in light of the political difficulties he faced. They avoid harsher criticism of his tactical military skills. Burnside's reputed affability and gentle character appears to have captivated them from the grave. In defense of the man, though, he had refused twice to take command of the Army of the Potomac citing his own mistrust of his martial capabilities. His supple personality, though, allowed him to be shamed into taking the billet by politicians' and fellow officers' appeals to his sense of duty, patriotism and a desire to keep mean spirited Joseph Hooker out of the job. That his Antietam misstep might have been substantive evidence of his lack of military good sense didn't bother his backers one iota.

BURNSIDE, thankfully, had nothing to do with Gettysburg. I bring him up because his troubles fording streams stand in contrast to someone who had managed to repeatedly move his army over riparian obstacles with comparable ease. General Robert E. Lee was immune to the ravages of Burnsideitis. He possessed the uncanny ability to recognize the importance of, or strategic way around, a man-made or natural barrier. Lee was an engineer by training and a crafty tactician in practice. He had blazed a path for Winfield Scott's force through the razor sharp, midnight black lava fields which stood ominously between them and Montezuma's fortress during the march on Mexico City in the Mexican-American War. Later, as he took command of a large part of the military arm of the rebellion, he used valleys to cloak his army, high ground in the defense and rivers to provide security and lines of communication. Nature's gifts complemented his innate capacity to lead men.

In late June of 1863, a portion of Lee's Army of Northern Virginia scampered ahead of the main force pushing into central Pennsylvania. Their mission was to ascertain whether or not crossing the Susquehanna River and moving on Harrisburg, Philadelphia or any number of northern cities was a viable option. Lee felt it imperative that his reconnaissance in force capture one or more of the bridges spanning the great river. While the Susquehanna is comparatively shallow, the river at Harrisburg and farther south is dauntingly broad. It is because of this stretch that the watercourse was aptly nicknamed the "mile wide, foot deep" river. Its expanse stumped even the savviest of Confederate military engineers and logisticians. A soldier simply taking off shoes, rolling up pant legs and holding rifle and cartridge box over his head wasn't going to cut it in getting an army across this imposing spread of water. Without the bridges captured intact, there would be no further advance of the Confederate army into Union territory. There weren't enough pontoons and bridging equipment in the entire South to replace one of the existing spans if it was lost. If any of the bridges had been captured by the Confederates, at Wrightsville or Harrisburg, it is quite likely the battle of Gettysburg would never have taken place.

PAYING homage to the Susquehanna, a couple of less inspiring water sources are companions to those transiting New York's Finger Lakes Region and bound for the Pennsylvania line. On either I-390 or I-86 which, for at least part of their respective lengths anyway, share a highway designation with Route 15, ponds, reservoirs, rivers and streams either lie warming in the sun or flow contentedly alongside the nearby pavement. This is no coincidence. America's highway engineers are not fools. Those experts in survey, materials science and construction wisely take advantage of natural cuts in otherwise unfriendly terrain to place the highways on which we speed to our destinations. As we do so, we give little thought to how the roads get built or why they are where they are.

Rivers do much to change the landscape and they do it in relatively short periods of time. They are nature's cutting tools, scouring their beds, grabbing hold of silt, gravel and rocks. Together, that mixture digs deeper, driven by the power of the flow. Combined with geologic uplift of underlying land, moving water carves out valleys and erodes high mountains. Spring melt water gushes from a river's banks, dropping nutrients and creating fertile plains. Those flooding and ebbing fresh water tides also leave behind ideal footing for manmade ribbons of concrete and asphalt. For much of Route 15's future roadbed, the Susquehanna River was the natural grader that paved the way.

THE Susquehanna is truly a great American river. It well deserves its reputation as a riparian treasure. This important national waterway, at 464 miles in length, is the longest river on the East Coast emptying into the Atlantic Ocean. Where does this wonderful stream come from and where does it go? To answer that, the river is best envisioned geographically as the tongue of a cobra with its two far reaching branches as the split ends of the snake's flicking sensory organ. The main (north) branch, and its partner west branch, twist and turn as they carry water downstream throughout southern New York and western and central Pennsylvania. They each grow in size, taking in tributary waters from any number of other rivers and streams which together drain a remarkable Appalachian watershed. The forks of both branches amble in all cardinal directions but after a while turn south and come together at Northumberland and Sunbury, Pennsylvania.

THE main branch begins its life as an outflow from lovely Otsego Lake in Cooperstown, New York, the storied home of the Baseball Hall of Fame. From there it meanders south, sometimes widening into lakes and then narrowing back into its banks as it flows on. Oxbow lakes, cut off from the main channel, appear now and again along its course. The main channel wanders into Pennsylvania where, not quite sure what it wants to do, it heads back north again and reenters New York. At Binghamton, restrained by engineered cement barriers and fortress-like flood control measures, it gains traction as it is joined by the Chenango River. Emboldened by the increased volume at the confluence, it heads west for a while and then turns to the south and, this time, stays put in Pennsylvania.

THE Susquehanna's aptly named western branch originates as a trickle in the high hills near Carrolltown, Pennsylvania. It is the lesser fork of the snake's tongue and is the half of the Susquehanna relevant to Route 15. For drivers coming off the Allegheny Plateau and down slope following Lycoming Creek into the valley where Williamsport, Pennsylvania is nestled, that ancient western branch, older than the land around it, is just ahead. At the floor of the valley, Route 15 merges into congested U.S. Route 220 and I-180 and parallels the river to the built up area of town. In Williamsport, the Susquehanna is brown, slow and ordinary but the power of its water is evident. The high ridges on each side of the deep depression in which the town sits are the edges of the vast elevated plain that lies to the windward of the Appalachian Mountains. This valley was etched out by the Susquehanna working in concert with the rock strewn slabs of glacial ice that only receded from this area of the country 12,000 years ago. The softer, pliable plateau yielded to the geologic forces working to change it. Slowly, over the millennia, Williamsport's picturesque valley was sculpted.

Along with the much larger Chemung, Lackawanna and Unadilla rivers, countless creeks, streams, manmade diversion of polluted storm water and chemical filth from Pennsylvania's anthracite mines add to the Susquehanna's voluminous drainage. That gigantic watershed, gathering the runoff from a good portion of the northeastern United States, drains almost 30,000 square miles of mountains, ridgelines and farmland in New York, Pennsylvania and Maryland. All that water, sediment and other detritus carried within its banks eventually ends up at its point of termination in Chesapeake Bay.

The bay is the modern vestige of the Susquehanna's prehistoric estuary. The river, at one time long in the past, drained directly into the Atlantic Ocean. As the mile thick glacial blanket, thriving in earth's Pleistocene chill, began to melt, rising water levels inundated the lowland portions of the river and filled the previously narrower and dryer channel. The salty expanse of the Chesapeake that boaters, fisherman, crabbers and vacationers enjoy today was born.

LIKE the main branch, the western branch ends up at Northumberland. There it marries up with its wayward partner. At this dramatic confluence, the newlyweds strut their stuff. The river becomes one as it transitions from two dual personalities to a single, wondrous cascade of water. It spreads from shore to shore in places sometimes to the horizon with islands and shallows throughout. Tree lined, chock full of recreational fishing and pleasure boats, it is a sportsman's ideal playground. Individuals skippering deeper drafted boats should be on their guard. The Susquehanna stays shallow and barely navigable by anything other than small boats, kayaks and canoes. Here its flow quickens. Often it bears white, frothing water rapidly down its course, riding over the bared bedrock, churning and tossing, cascading over stony falls. Many a propeller and deeper drafted bottom have left their marks on a submerged Susquehanna rock.

On a sparkling day, its water reflects an azure blue. Despite the literal tons of polluted runoff from farm fields, towns and mines that populate its banks, it seems crystalline enough to splash in and consume without chemical treatment or filtration. Ancient slides pockmark its banks and, always, Route 15 follows it obediently, taking advantage of its scoured floodplain south. The two do not part company until the capital city of Pennsylvania at

Harrisburg. There, the verdigris covered dome of the state capitol building and the low silhouette of that city reflect impressively in the vast expanse of water. On the south side of the river, the grimy Norfolk Southern run Enola Rail Yard bustles with activity. Engines puff out blue diesel smoke in filthy columns and graffiti marked freight cars line countless sidings. Nearby, infinitely long road and rail bridges cross the river into Harrisburg. Their existence, albeit much improved over their 1863 counterparts, gives us a sense of why General Lee's invasion plans had this city's river crossings in mind.

At Harrisburg, Route 15 veers sharply right through a quiet residential neighborhood putting greater distance between itself and the river. The mighty Susquehanna continues on its own way. Downstream, it races around, and furnishes cooling water for, the notorious nuclear power generation plant at Three Mile Island. It courses under the Columbia-Wrightsville Bridge and speeds on to Havre de Grace, Maryland to the Chesapeake and the broad Atlantic beyond.

IN September 2011, a tropical low pressure system, personalized by meteorologists as Tropical Storm Lee, drifted slowly up the western flank of the Appalachians and parked itself over the state of Ohio. The counter-clockwise flow around the low soaked up warm Gulf of Mexico moisture and carried it north, lifting it, banding it and dropping it in buckets on the Susquehanna Valley. Rain gauges in Wilkes-Barre and Binghamton overflowed. Meters put in place to warn people of the river's rapid rise were uselessly inundated. This majestic river which normally can be waded in places, crested far above flood stage. In places, its forty or so feet of sediment filled water caused heartache and misery for hundreds of thousands. For a time, those turgid waters threatened even Route 15, closing parts to travel. The river that normally partners with the highway to bring commerce north and south was now its worst enemy.

The heavy rain filled the channel and turned the familiar into the treacherous. Boaters, out of their element, now had to contend with powerful currents, poor visibility, trees and other flotsam as well as the damaging effects of floodwaters on docks and landings. They have had little rest from high water. 2011's floods came on the heels of a similar deluge in 2006. Both, notable though they were, are measured against the great flood of 1972. Then, the Susquehanna was at its meanest. A late spring hurricane, daintily named Agnes, wandered up the Middle Atlantic and unleashed its torrents for hours. The continuous and heavy rain drowned the valley setting countless river flood records. To date, Agnes' lofty insurance payouts make it one of the most costly natural disasters in Pennsylvania's recorded history.

But, on most days, particularly when a high sun glances off its clear, rushing waters, the Susquehanna is not only inviting, it is magnificent.

MAGNIFICENT too was the former covered bridge over the broad Susquehanna connecting the Pennsylvania towns of Wrightsville and Columbia. Wrightsville, the unknown borough on the south shore at the foot of the long bridge, is arguably the true place the Confederacy's tide was at its highest.

There the monumental wooden and roofed structure, over one mile in length and set on stone piers in the river bottom, was under the guard of an untrained, hastily assembled and jumpy state militia. Word of Confederate forces running about southern and central Pennsylvania in June of 1863 had gotten the drums of war beating. With the Federal army obviously tied up in Virginia and Maryland, the patriotic Commonwealth responded with the best it had at hand.

Hoping to capture the bridge and thus have a straight run into Union territory north of the river, elements of General Richard Ewell's Second Confederate Corps got as far north as this non-descript place. A few well aimed shots easily scattered the militia which, having no training and a lot to live for, wisely skedaddled.

Ewell's advance scouts must have been mightily impressed by the immense river before them. This was no piddling Rapidan or puny Rappahannock. Even the Potomac, at least the parts north of Washington, bowed in deference to the Susquehanna. These southern boys, unless they had been to the banks of the Mississippi, the Ohio or the Tennessee or, perhaps, to the Atlantic shore at the Neuse estuary in North Carolina, probably hadn't seen anything like it. One thing was for sure, wading across it was not an option. But, if a crossing could indeed be accomplished and a strong bridgehead established on the opposite side, the Army of the Potomac's ability to protect Philadelphia and even New York would have been severely compromised.

Alas, ambitious Rebel plans to cross and march on Harrisburg had to be shelved when Yankee partisans set the covered bridge on fire.

With sparks and dark smoke billowing into the sky before them, and being knee-deep in the enemy's backyard, Ewell's boys turned around and, frustrated at the lost opportunity to take the fight to the heart of enemy territory, headed back to the southwest. Their compasses pointed to the last known positions of their army somewhere near Cashtown and its neighbor, Gettysburg.

✳ ✳ ✳ ✳

Roadside Attractions

PACKED in an Oldsmobile Vista Cruiser, our saintly parents and their five rambunctious kids headed to the North Country on an annual vacation to a lakeside cottage at Brynilsen's Viking Village near Old Forge, New York. The seven of us, after a lunch stop in Utica, exited the crowded car and crammed ourselves into a 500 square foot piney Adirondack box. There we danced on clouds for the next heavenly week. We slept in bunk beds and ate meals on rough hewn furniture. A fire was kindled at first light in a pot bellied stove to ward off the chill of late August's mornings. Popcorn was popped on open fires and the Milky Way blazed overhead. The camp, on the south shore of Fourth Lake, one of eight in the Fulton Chain of Lakes, was a kid's paradise. Fishing, boating, water skiing, campfires, s'mores and scary stories under the crystal clear mountain skies were just a few of the diversions offered by our gracious hosts. Run by a salty Norwegian named Rolph and his wife Jan, the rustic confines were a favorite of Rochesterians who spread the word via the tight knit corporate networks back in the big city. Naturally, the woodsy village took on the secondary title of Camp Monroe or the name of the county in which Rochester sits.

One of the obligatory things to do when we were visiting the area was to stop by the

Enchanted Forest in downtown Old Forge. At the time, in the early 1970s, we were young and easily impressed. The Forest's plywood storybook figures and cheaply constructed, colorfully painted fairy tale scenes were magical to the eyes of elementary school kids. This was the type of roadside entertainment that packed 'em in during the Vietnam era.

Roadside attractions, particularly the chintzy ones, defy explanation. Some pundits claim they are fading fast, just a remnant of the 1950s culture which put stationary Americans in cars to see what the rest of the country had to offer. Others claim that they are even more popular now. Modern marketing makes it so by targeting specific demographic groups. In fact, the battlefield at Gettysburg, in a larger sense, is itself a member of the genre. Thriving roadside attractions do still exist. They are sprinkled like dust all over the United States. South Dakota, of all places, is home to two favorites including the Wall Drug Store and the Corn Palace. Thousands of visitors, usually diverting briefly off I-90 as they head to Mount Rushmore or Yellowstone National Park, can't resist the draw. Both the palace and the drug store have been around for much longer than most of us have been alive. To ensure as many people as possible visit, they are advertised every ten miles or so on billboards set off in the grasslands of the vast and lonely prairie.

There are popular rest and recreational stops in heavily populated areas as well. I doubt any person who has traveled on I-95 in the mid-Atlantic and southeastern United States has not at least had her curiosity piqued by billboard after billboard, mile after mile, imploring us to exit at South of the Border. How can anyone even think of passing by the place that Pedro sez is "Chili today but hot tamale?"

And on the West Coast, travelers on heavily trafficked I-10 near Cabazon, California might exit to dine at the Wheel Inn. That truck stop and its now internationally renowned dinosaurs, Dinny and Mr. Rex, got their fifteen minutes of fame performing a cameo in the 1985 comedy *Pee-wee's Big Adventure*. Stopping for a plate of eggs, sausage and pancakes and mentioning to the waitress at the counter that Large Marge sent you, might prompt a strange look. Most likely, though, she'll comment that she hasn't heard that one in a very long while.

Times change and most wayfarers, on their way to Palm Springs or Los Angeles, are inclined to spend the afternoon at a nearby and newer Native American casino. Those that pause at the anachronistic and homey Wheel Inn are rewarded, not only with good food, but with a breathless view of the stunning, snow capped peaks of San Gorgonio and San Jacinto bookending each side of the I-10. Fantastical wind turbines, set in rows on dusty foothills, sweep up from the gash of the San Andreas fault which cuts though the pass ahead. The turbines inexorably spin at the push of cooler ocean air sweeping east and channeled by the narrow pass into the Coachella Valley beyond.

Dwindling numbers of visitors and the construction of faster, more convenient interstate highways dealt the death hand to a fair number of once very popular roadside stops. Two examples lie also on the West Coast. One of my favorite ghostly roadside attractions bakes on the arid and desolate stretch of Route 66 near Amboy, California. Amboy, once known for its often photographed, perfectly shaped volcanic cinder cone, is also the home to a recognizable film locale known as Roy's Café. Horror movie trivia fans can readily identify this out-of-the-way place. Boarded and shuttered for some time, Roy's has been resuscitated along with the rest of this remote site by a wealthy and nostalgic dreamer. He purchased the entire town and put some real money into it. It's doubtful it will rival Las Vegas anytime soon, but it's nice to see a once often visited stop cheer up with some fresh paint and a revived attitude.

Just east of Amboy, in Chambless, the few loners who survive out there haven't yet discovered their monetary savior. Their luck still waits under some undiscovered four leaf clover. At this insignificant intersection, on a lightly traveled and forbidding ribbon of melting asphalt, is the ramshackle building and its accompanying, towering sand blasted sign welcoming all to the decrepit Roadrunner's Retreat. This forlorn spot was once a café and rest stop for the weary and hot when iconic Route 66 was the only way to navigate this section of the Mojave Desert. The Roadrunner's creosote bush and cholla choked parking lot, from which the long darkened and faded neoclassic sign rises, must have once seen countless cars filled with desert voyagers pulling in to fill up with gas or grab a cold drink and a sandwich. Not so now. The barren and windblown property attracts only shutter bugs and nostalgic wanderers pining for days past.

The aged, deserted section of the famous Mother Road carries only the adventurous crowd now. The common traveler can't be bothered. He or she sticks to the modernity of teeming I-40 beyond the hills to the north. That's too bad. The detour, if just taken once in a life, is worth it. In the setting reds, oranges and purples of a Mojave evening, with a huge moon rising like a plate over the surrounding mountains, an observer can't help but be taken in by the beauty. It is not at all hard to picture a flood of headlights and the glow of neon signs piercing the desert around the Roadrunner. It is a once thriving spot centered now at ground zero in the middle of America's nowhere.

AS I approach my fiftieth anniversary living on this planet, I tend to eat less and be far more discriminatory on what I put in my stomach. I don't reject fast food out of hand but partake of far less than what I once did. Even when I have my son with me, I try to stay away from too much fried and fatty products while he dives headfirst into a Happy Meal. Often, as we cross into Pennsylvania on our annual Gettysburg pilgrimage, we'll avoid the fast food chains and instead make a stop at Fry Brothers Turkey Ranch in Trout Run.

This almost century old favorite used to be right on the edge of old Route 15. I mean, right **on** Route 15. So close, truckers could theoretically grab take-out without stopping. One had to be alert and on one's game to make it safely into the parking lot. It came up on you quick. Flying up a gradient towards the hill top on which the restaurant (and former actual turkey ranch) sits, Fry Brothers popped into sight without much notice. Tires squealing and heart pounding, rapid deceleration was aided by crushed gravel in the outside lot. After the dust cleared and the parking adventure was forgotten, a good hot open-faced turkey sandwich and a cup of Joe calmed the nerves.

Then, progress came along. Bulldozers, graders and dump trucks have picked up and moved Route 15 and doubled it in size, relegating Fry Brothers to a less visible location off the main road. Now, it enviously has its very own exit. Drivers are adequately warned as the turn-off approaches and glide in, far less stressed than those that came before them.

This single story restaurant is a favorite of the big riggers who desire some variety other than a burger and fries. Those are on the menu, though. From Internet reviews and word from the blogosphere, Fry Brothers' reputation isn't as golden as it used to be. The younger set just doesn't stop here anymore. When I walk in and add my fifty years to the combined ages of white-haired, walker-assisted clientele, the resultant math brings the mean down a few points. Some think the turkey is dry and the stuffing and potatoes are mediocre at best. Oh, how wrong they are. I haven't had a bad meal at the place and I should know. As one can probably guess, this isn't a fruit and nut store either. If one yearns for some tofu or granola, keep on going. But, if one wants to stop for a break, get the blood flowing in the legs, use a clean and spacious restroom and end the respite with a big turkey and gravy dinner without the hassle of cooking it, keep alert eyes peeled on approach to Trout Run.

Perhaps I can convince the odd traveler on Route 15 to stop there by laying out the alternatives. There's always the fast food drive-thru. The drill is all too familiar. Peeling off the highway, one queues up into line of cars all having the same idea at approximately the same time. The order is sorted out, the food is handed out in a bag and one immediately gets back on the road. Free now from worry about a left-hand turn, one can now jam the burger or other fried morsel in one's mouth. Ketchup dribbles on a pant leg and, inevitably, a mayonnaise covered onion slice slides on to the floor mat. All of that hassle in the interest of saving time.

At Fry Brothers, an accommodating waitress will bring the food. It'll be hot and served on a plate. It will be placed squarely on a table in front of you adorned with a tablecloth. The patron, if he or she chooses, may use a knife, fork and napkin. A roiled stomach and a harried mind will enjoy the fact that mobile you, for once, chose to eat like a human being.

FAMILIES and other individuals looking for roadside entertainment on Route 15 still have a welcome haven to satisfy their scientific curiosity. In the early 1960s, when theme parks were rare and roadside entertainment had its heyday, a snake lover named Clyde Peeling brought in a Noah's Ark-like retinue of slimy, slithering and scaly reptiles and amphibians to the Susquehanna Valley. Mr. Peeling's Reptiland is on the southern uphill slope leading out of Williamsport in a place called Allenwood. I dropped by with two others once on a tropical, humid day with the rain pouring down in sheets making it feel like we were actually in the native places these animals thrive. Alligators, ancient turtles and forearm thick snakes interest visitors to this relatively small and specialized zoo. Every time we pass by, even in the murkiest of winter weather, at least a few cars are in the parking lot. That tells me that the lure of a unique draw set in some out of the way place still holds a fascination for the bored, harried wayfarers, children screaming the backseat, looking for entertainment on an unfamiliar road.

Sure Beats Walking

AS a student of the Civil War, I am fortunate that its most well known battle was fought a mere five hours by car from my home. That translates into about 300 road miles, most of it, naturally, on Route 15. 300 miles is slightly more than twice the distance most of the combatants had to march to reach Gettysburg from the respective Confederate and Union camps in northern Virginia in June of 1863. Today, in an automobile, we can traverse that distance with relative ease. Our belligerent forebears were not so fortunate.

Roads weren't the only means soldiers could get to where they were going. The Civil War saw the advent of large troop movements via an ever expanding network of railroads; particularly in the industrial North. River boats and ocean going vessels also hauled grateful, foot weary infantrymen to many destinations. In fact, the greatest maritime disaster in United States history occurred as an overworked boiler on the S.S. Sultana, a river steamer on which thousands of Union soldiers were billeted for transport, exploded in late April of 1865. The tightly packed ship erupted and burned on the surface of the Mississippi River near Memphis killing 1,800 blue suited troops frantically trying to escape the inferno.

But rail and ship transport rarely were convenient and available to Union and

Confederate logisticians so marching was the de facto standard to get armies to where they needed to go.

Walking long distances and staying combat ready is easier said than done. Ask any infantryman and he will let the inquisitor in on a little secret that grunts have known for millennia. Forced marching really sucks. Call it what one wants, it certainly isn't anything close to walking. Don't misunderstand me, it's not like the participant is running either. The object is to move quickly, covering the most ground without causing a disproportionate number of casualties among the men.

For hikes longer than five miles, this equates to a pace of about two miles per hour with a ten minute break every hour. Simply math tells us that one is then moving at pace of about one mile every twenty-five minutes. For shorter hikes, a pace of about four miles an hour or about fifteen minutes per mile gets the Marine to where he or she needs to go. That two mile per hour pace sounds pretty slow if one considers that good runners can cover the same distance in roughly one fourth of the time. Marathoners can run even faster. But, runners aren't wearing boots and carrying heavy rifles, ammunition and packs stuffed with clothes, food and water. Believe me when I say it, a two mile per hour pace on a long hike is grueling. A much rarer four mile pace is bone jarring.

Many of the units of both the Confederate and Union armies converging around Gettysburg in late June and early July 1863 marched about thirty miles per day. The sheer physical exertion to do that using the equipment and nutritional supplements available at the time gives one a new found admiration for the Civil War soldier. These guys were tough hombres.

SPEAKING of tough hombres, Kingsley Brownell fits that description to a tee. Although mounted as a horseman in the 21st New York Cavalry and more mobile than his infantry counterparts, Brownell's example gives us some sense of the mettle of the men of the day. Battling Confederate cavalry supporting Jubal Early's summer 1864 Shenandoah Valley Campaign, Brownell caught a round entering near the "short ribs." The ball penetrated his midsection and put a large hole in his back on the way out. He lay on the field for some time until noticed by the enemy. He really must have been feeling poorly as he put up no further fight, was captured and made prisoner and forced to ride nine miles to Martinsburg. There, the logistically challenged Confederates paroled him. Probably tired and fairly woozy, he ended up in a friendly field hospital until he was nurtured back to health. In a brief letter to his mother dated shortly after his terrible wounding he told her in as few words as possible about his adventure. He mentioned that the wound was severe but he was doing well and not to trouble herself. One assumes she ignored his admonition and troubled herself nonetheless. After his convalescence, he returned to his native Rochester and hung around until 1924, probably pulling up his shirt at times and showing one or two grandchildren and the neighborhood curious the big holes in his torso.

ANYWAY, a lot of foot soldiers on a forced march were less rugged than Kingsley. Not having the handicap of a bloody hole in their abdomen to bother them, they, nevertheless, fell out and dropped at the shoulder unable to keep up the pace. Quite a few, in order to keep going, tossed aside heavier stuff they didn't need at the moment; failing to consider that the discards might come in handy later. Roadsides along Civil War route marches were littered with haversacks, blankets, extra rations and whatever else temporarily annoyed its bearer. The weaker and less able stragglers, if they were so inclined, had a bounty of replacement equipment from which to choose.

Stories of men doing these hikes without any footwear at all boggle the mind. Those that did have footwear were equipped with standard issue leather shoes and wool socks which, as anyone who even has a passing interest in hiking knows, aren't the preferred covering for the feet. Even today, with technology giving the soldier the advantage of better foot gear and lighter equipment, a route or road march tests the mettle of even the strongest and most fit members of the armed forces.

As a young officer, I shared many a road march with my comrades as we trained at TBS. Packing about seventy pounds of gear and wearing crappy leather boots, more than a few of us saw our feet turned bloody with blisters and suffered as joints and bones ached with pain. Some of the older and wiser Marines among us, guys who had served in the enlisted ranks before they decided to make the jump to the officer corps, gave bits of advice on how to keep your feet from falling off on a twenty-five mile "hump." The key was to reduce friction and prevent the resultant hot spots that developed after miles of constant pounding. Socks designed to wick away moisture and equipped with cushioned soles were mandatory. The meticulous were rewarded with fewer, tinier and less painful blisters. If one developed, and it was inevitable that one did, the vigilant applied immediate first aid to the area to mitigate further damage.

The item that contributed most to the appearance of blisters was the standard issue military leather boot. Most of the millions who wore them unanimously agree that it was definitely not the ideal piece of gear. It did not breathe and was constructed of materials that couldn't absorb the repetitive impacts of footfalls. They were obviously the product of the lowest bidder chosen to mass produce them. They were designed and constructed cheaply. Their bottoms were unable to properly dissipate the energy created by walking into where it needed to go - the supporting arches of the feet. They instead imparted misery, transferring the force of countless steps not only to the foot, but to the leg and hip bones of the unlucky wearer.

MODERN Marines get to know first-hand how stalwart these Civil War soldiers were. No matter which future occupational specialty an officer seeks, be it tanks, artillery or aviation, TBS makes sure that every student can fall back to their infantry skills if need be. All Marines have drilled in them the skills and knowledge of what the infantryman is going through on the ground. So, when they are called in to support the grunt in battle, they know what he's up against. In essence, all Marines are riflemen. It's a proven formula and builds a lot of esprit de corps but it sure is a pain in the butt for the guy who would rather fly planes or fix trucks.

ONE memorable forced march took us to nearby Chancellorsville, set deep in the thick and dark woods known as the Wilderness. That foreboding place is where the armies on both sides of the Rappahannock tore at each other's existence several times during the war. No piece of ground in America was more fought over than this dense stretch of trees and undergrowth. Armies maneuvered, feinted, attacked and retreated and carried the fight back and forth in the Wilderness over the long stretch from 1862 until 1864. The final abuse to this land and the soldiers who fought on it came at the direction of U.S. Grant. At the head of all Federal armies but packing a ride with the Army of the Potomac, he moved south, slugging it out with Lee's army in a series of horrifically bloody and fierce battles in and around Spotsylvania, Virginia. Despite horrendous human loss, after each fight, Grant, reinforced and resupplied, moved forward again. Bleached skeletons hung with shards of faded uniforms and the wretched human remains from previous battles disgustingly greeted the combatants as the armies clashed once more in the tangled brush.

Staff infantry experts at Quantico determined that young officers would benefit from understanding some of the tactics and maneuvers that a long ago army used to defeat its enemy. Quantico's proximity to the Wilderness battlefields made it convenient to put that lesson in an historical context. Dressed in camouflage utilities, armed with M-16s, carrying food, clothing and supplies necessary to live for a few days in the field, off we went to the woods around Chancellorsville. Being good Marines, we also carried along with us machine guns, mortars and any other heavy weapon an infantryman needs to kill bad guys. Unloading the cattle cars and readying for the forced march, our unexpected and threatening appearance startled quite a few civilians taking in the sights.

The march's objective was to retrace the steps of Stonewall Jackson's corps as he famously put his men on a twelve mile hike and countermarched around the entire Union army. No more deliberate, focused tactician existed in this war than Thomas Jackson. "Stonewall," the complimentary alias he had picked up at the First Battle of Manassas, had perfected the stealthy and quick movement of his units. In his 1862 Shenandoah Valley campaign, his fleet footed men had earned the nickname "foot cavalry" and time and again demonstrated their ability to advance a long way in a day's time. Moving as many as an incredible fifty miles in a twenty-four hour period, Jackson's nimble soldiers confounded Union attempts to simply locate them let alone defeat them. Jackson and his loyal soldiers showed up on several battlefields unexpectedly and at the most inopportune times.

At a few points along his march at Chancellorsville, Jackson's corps was spotted by Federal observers. Considering Jackson's proven skill at maneuver in front of an enemy, Union leadership should have been far more suspicious of his intent. Complacently figuring that Lee's army was retreating or simply failing to comprehend the threat, the Federals stayed put until it was too late. In a typical show of hubris,

Federal commanders were too blinded by confidence in their own plan to bother worrying about the enemy's.

Having completed the march, Jackson arrayed his troops in line of battle. They stormed out of the woods and jumped the Federals in their evening camps, tearing into them on a very exposed flank. The screaming devils soon had the reclining Union boys up and in a panic. The resulting Confederate victory against a seriously shaken and disjointed Army of the Potomac emboldened Lee to travel to Richmond and lobby his government to support his plans to break out of the Rappahannock camps around Fredericksburg and Chancellorsville and head north to Pennsylvania.

ON our welcome but brief breaks on our reenactment march, this information was pounded into our heads by Marine Corps instructors who kept emphasizing that history never fails to repeat itself and that we should keep Jackson's surreptitious tactics in the back of our minds. Most of my fellow Marines, resting weary bodies against bulging packs or rubbing sore and blistered feet, either didn't care about history at this point in the hike or weren't interested in becoming infantrymen. Attentions wandered with some lieutenants taking the opportunity to nod off to sleep. Some, in voices low enough not to be heard by instructors, pondered the odds of us countermarching against an unwary Union army again. That's why we have all those jets and tanks, right?

In any case, we completed the twelve miles in the same time Jackson's men did and I, fully aware of what those men had to do next, was mightily impressed. Considering how fatigued I felt at the time, I was in no mood to fight a battle. Twelve miles, for a Civil War soldier, was a walk in the park.

Later in my Marine Corps life, I was assigned to a Remotely Piloted Vehicle Company. That group of doughy Marines was headquartered in the out-of-the-way place with which I had become familiar, the Marine base at Twentynine Palms. The unit was equipped with boxy, unwieldy equipment containing everything the unit needed to launch small car-sized airplanes with cameras mounted on them. Operators flew them via ground stations linked to the RPV by powerful electro-magnetic signals operating near the bandwidth of broadcast television. The aircraft were undetectable and designed to fly over enemy positions and relay live video back to the ground station. Intelligence experts there could translate and then tell the infantry or artillery what and where to shoot. All this delicate, expensive equipment was dragged around with trucks and humvees. Without motorized assets, we were little use to anyone.

Aside from the Marine Band, in dress uniforms and parading at Eighth and I Streets in Washington, or some of the guys who fly and fix airplanes in air wing, I don't think one can get farther from being in the infantry than serving with an RPV Company. RPV Marines simply do not hike. Or, so we thought.

Unfortunately, at the time, the RPV Companies were attached to Surveillance, Reconnaissance and Intelligence Groups and those guys were led by infantrymen who loved physical training. The First Marine Division, the headquarters organization in which our unit resided, was commanded by a two star general who also enjoyed running, hiking and lifting weights. The guy was approaching fifty years old and could embarrass most of his Marines on a run, on the pull-up bars or on a forced march. A predictably strenuous training regime followed.

One very deflating day word came down that the general had ordered all Marines in the division to complete a fifty mile hike in two consecutive days by the end of that same year. The orders detailed the timing and the amount of gear each Marine was to carry on his or her back. Well now, wasn't that lovely? As one can probably surmise, one does not just suit up and head out on a fifty mile walk. In order to avoid sending half the Marines to the hospital, it is best to train up to that level. Accordingly, being ordered to hike fifty miles meant that we would also do a five, twelve and twenty mile hike to get ready for it. Now we were acting like true Civil War soldiers!

Regardless of how much one prepares, a fifty mile hike completed over a span of forty-eight hours taxes the body. We chose to complete the hike around the low lava and sand hills against which the main buildings of the Marine Corps base sat. As we completed the first twenty-five miles, all of us stripped our packs and took off our dusty boots. We had prepared well but the majority suffered from strains and aches, bloodied feet and skin on the inside of thighs rubbed raw and pink. Liberal doses of Motrin and Advil took the edge off things but, depressingly, there were twenty-five more miles to go! At the merciful end, our bodies were in no condition to do anything other than eat, drink and sleep.

In 1863, after walking up to thirty-five miles in a day to get to the sound of the guns, our long dead comrades not only had little chance to take a break at the end of their travels, but they were thrown into the fray right away. Dog tired and foot sore, certainly without analgesics or anti-inflammatories, these rough and tumble soldiers fixed bayonets and went at each other. Many, like me, pay respect to the men possessing the nerve to charge headlong into a line of opponents firing muskets and loosing cannon shots in their direction on a battlefield. Admiration becomes nothing less than sheer amazement when one understands that these same super humans literally ran without a break to get there!

* * * *

General Lee's Dilemma

IT seems awfully strange that an army would have been interested in Gettysburg. There is no bridge over a major river. No stone and mortar bastion stands defending a strategic waterway or geographic point. No armory or weapons manufacturing plant churns out the tools of war. What distinguishes Gettysburg from the other little towns and villages around it are the roads leading in and out. They are as important to the town today as they were 150 years ago. They spike out from the center of town in all directions and bear the names of the places they go or the places from which people come. The Baltimore Pike. Taneytown Road. Chambersburg Pike.

Gettysburg, for all its rural character, happened to lie at the center of a road network on which armies could quickly march. And if one of those armies has the state capital of Pennsylvania at Harrisburg in its sights and is plodding north through Maryland and southern Pennsylvania in order to get there, then its leaders couldn't help but notice Gettysburg's strategic value in support of that movement. Conversely, it was a very good place for a defender to deploy in their way.

Holding the roads in and around Gettysburg would screen the Confederate army's right flank and provide valuable conduits for the supply train that supported tens of thousands of infantry and artillery troops and their horses. The roads were the bloodstream carrying the baggage and stuff on which armies survive. A Federal army, also marching north to protect the vital seaboard cities loyal to the Union, would also find Gettysburg and its roads very useful for its purposes. So not by chance at all but rather by its location at the center of several routes of commerce; the largest battle in the Western Hemisphere unfolded here.

If Robert E. Lee had had his way, the battle at Gettysburg would never have happened. Lee, normally a man quite adept at controlling events, was not so fortunate this time. His intent was to simply continue the very successful strategy of keeping one step ahead of the badly led but substantially better supplied and superior numbered opponent. The very survival of the Confederate States of America depended on it. A perpetual, credible military threat to the national government would further drain the political and emotional will of the United States. An invading army running rampant on northern soil might accelerate the collapse. And so, after a resounding victory over the Army of the Potomac at Chancellorsville, Virginia in early May of 1863, Lee had convinced his government in Richmond that the stalemate on the Rappahannock was a thing of the past. It was time again for the Army of Northern Virginia to take the initiative, plant himself in northern territory and again chip away at the eroding support for the Union war effort. Further, such a foray deep into Union territory would, it was believed, draw Federal forces away from other key theaters and allow the Confederacy to gain back some of the strategic initiative it had lost elsewhere.

Like his previous invasion of the North, in Maryland in the late summer of 1862, Lee could sense the pressure his victories and freedom to maneuver was placing on Abraham Lincoln, his cabinet and the Republican Party in Washington. In fact, such information was available to him on the front pages of the northern newspapers. Lee had to be careful, though. The foray across the Potomac River and the resulting clash with Union forces at Antietam Creek had cost him almost half his army. Therefore, it was his stated objective to threaten Washington, Harrisburg and the major cities along the eastern seaboard while seeking out a pitched battle only on his stringent terms.

And so north he went, his nimble and tough veterans splashing across that same Potomac River at Williamsport, Maryland and from there onward towards Harrisburg. Screened by the supine bulk of South Mountain, a ridgeline perfectly situated to mask a rumbling army, Lee triggered the very thing he needed in the minds of Union commanders – defensive reaction.

BURNED and bitter over the constant thumping Lee had administered to the Army of Potomac over the previous six months, that battered and weary conglomeration of regular and reserve forces nevertheless could boast of seven infantry corps with attached artillery, one cavalry corps and an artillery reserve. It remained a formidable weapon of war. Despite the defeat at Chancellorsville, the shamed army remained under Joseph Hooker's command. Though humbled himself, Hooker retained the presence of mind to order the army to pull up its tent stakes, saddle its horses and move north on intelligence and rumors that Lee had done the same. All that time he was prodded by Lincoln, army staff and the politicians in Washington to produce evidence that he had a fresh plan. "Fighting Joe," however, was no longer endowed with the personal capacity needed to reenergize his army. Some say his confidence was never the same. It wasn't that way just because of the defeat. That certainly was disastrous enough. His attitude and equilibrium were also knocked silly by a Confederate shell which had struck a pillar on the front portico of the Chancellor mansion on which he happened to be leaning. A man takes it personally when someone tries to kill him and very nearly succeeds.

A capable administrator and organizer, Hooker wasn't always this way. He had faced the guns and the gore at Antietam. After the bloody mess at Fredericksburg, he had picked up the pieces scattered by Burnside's feckless hand and pumped new life and spirit into the shattered army. Personally involved with the smallest of details, he bolstered morale by carting in better food and cleaning up infested, diseased Union camps which stretched for miles near Falmouth on the north bank of the Rappahannock River.

Rested, supplied and ready for a spring offensive, he put his army on the move. His multi-faceted plot involved a bold and original leap across the Rappahannock and Rapidan Rivers and straight into Lee's camps. The trap was set to ensnare the Army of Northern Virginia. The ultimate battle to preserve the Union was nigh.

Despite the upper hand he had gained over Lee, the well fed, well supplied and cocky Union army was again handicapped by indecisiveness and a disturbing lack of urgency. As had been its fate so far in this war, it was out maneuvered, out classed and soundly beaten by Lee at that wooded Virginia crossroads. Hooker's Chancellorsville defeat had punctured and deflated his own self confidence and the confidence of political superiors. Most importantly, the handsome manipulator had lost the confidence of those he was tasked to lead. The luckily aimed Confederate shell was the coup de grâce. Doubters both within and outside of Hooker's ranks had become convinced he was incapable of focusing their efforts on maneuvering to meet the new threat. No one wanted to give him another chance to bring Lee's army to battle again and defeat it.

As a result, Lincoln sacked him and elevated the low key, somber and relatively unknown Fifth Army Corps commander, the "damned old goggle-eyed snapping turtle" George Meade to his place. The Army of the Potomac, a force which had seen leaders move in and out as if through a revolving door, finally had the stable, competent, if not visionary, presence in place. Meade, with Ulysses Grant tagging along, would take the storied army through the end of the war.

Aware that Lee was fully capable of shortening his tenure at army command, Meade drew up a quick battle scheme that, in essence, called for a defensive strategy to not only screen the nervous cities along the eastern side of the Appalachians but compel Lee's stretched force into a fight on Union ground at a place of Meade's choosing. Meade's plan required Lee to do what Meade wanted. The man who had to date run circles around the greatest American army ever put in the field certainly had no intention of doing that.

And so, both leviathans moved north into virgin territory. The newly configured and confident three corps of the Army of Northern Virginia, previously screened by the high green ridgelines of South Mountain, now edged through gaps in the Blue Ridge. They flowed out into the eastern valleys of Pennsylvania, sprinkled with rich farm fields, ripening orchards, tidy barns and prosperous farmhouses. As June 1863 sang its swan song, Lee's army, like ants from a kicked over hill, broke off into parts and scattered. Some tramped northeast towards Harrisburg. Others pushed through the Cashtown Gap and made a bee-line for Gettysburg on the Chambersburg-Cashtown Road.

Lee's cavalry, a force to reckon with, was nowhere near. Galloping behind the solid, unflappable General J.E.B Stuart, the Confederate horsemen left their Rappahannock camps and trooped off on a glorious lark. Their prime duty to support the initial states of the invasion was to keep an eye on the Federals and stay in touch with General Lee and his staff. Frustratingly independent, Stuart opted to move in a far away arc around the Federal legions moving north into Pennsylvania. Accordingly, time and distance kept the talented but rashly disobedient Stuart out of contact with the main body of the army. Stuart was far from idle. Pouncing on and capturing Federal supply trains, the priceless booty did nothing but slow him down. As a result, his tardiness and inattention took him out of the war's biggest fight. In the heart of enemy territory, Lee was without intelligence gleaned from his mobile horsemen and just when he needed them the most.

At the same time at the van of the Federal advance, Union cavalry led by John Buford, who not only knew what he was up against but also knew how to choose terrain to his advantage, clopped into Gettysburg. His troopers tipped their hats and waved to the much relieved civilians who had already shivered at the sight of hungry, shoeless, bedraggled Rebels kicking up dust in Gettysburg streets. Buford moved north and west through town where he deployed his two brigades of the First Cavalry Division on some high ground and oriented in a western and northern direction, along roads, from which he fully expected the enemy to come.

Buford's horse soldiers, albeit some 2,000 strong and armed with carbines, kept hopeful eyes to the south and east as well, waiting for signs of the reinforcing Army of the Potomac's anticipated approach. Even with the advantage of rapid fire breech loading weapons on their side, cavalry cannot stand well for long against dedicated infantry. Buford's staff was not at all convinced that the Confederates would choose this place to fight. If they did, they told Buford, his saddle worn and confident horse soldiers would just brush them aside. A battle tested veteran himself, Buford predicted that well trained Confederate infantry, armed to the teeth and in lines three deep, would attack his tenuous position in the morning. He dismissed his officers' optimistic assessment of the enemy's capabilities and cautioned, "They will come booming," he glowered, discounting their bravado and urging them to attend to the defense. His caution paid off.

The troopers did what they could to catch some needed sleep. The officers and non-commissioned officers inspected the broadly spaced line of dismounted men, deployed to protect the little Pennsylvania town a short distance to their rear. More importantly than that, they would slow the enemy advance until Federal infantry arrived.

THE sun rose, its rays poking through clouds and sprits of rain. The first day of what was to be the continent's greatest battle was at hand. It would be just as the dusty mustached Union general had foretold. Against the wishes of General Lee himself who wanted the army better consolidated, a fractured Confederate division under the command of the tentative Henry Heth of Virginia warily approached Gettysburg. There it collided with a ready, willing and capable General Buford and his deployed blue suited horsemen.

Buford, the man whose division would stand off a much superior and well armed force of infantry for hours, would be dead in six months of typhoid. Those nasty little bacteria thrived in human bodies and were shed in feces. From there they contaminate both food and water and spread like wildfire. They would have found fertile ground in any army camp of that day. It wasn't the feared Confederate bullet but unsanitary conditions and nineteenth century ignorance that were to kill John Buford. But, the man had done what he needed to do.

As dawn melted into morning over the southeast Pennsylvania farmland, the light drizzle cleared. The first skirmishers, probing ahead of waves of Confederate infantry, came into the view of a Union picket. The vigilant blue trooper, chambered a round, cocked the hammer of his Sharps carbine, braced his weapon against his shoulder, aimed and fired. Not long after, the crack of thousands of rifles and the boom of cannon signaled to all within miles that the course of American history was forever changed. It was Wednesday, July 1, 1863.

Chapter 3

A NICE PLACE TO VISIT

"Well I was born in a small town. And I can breathe in a small town. Gonna die in this small town. And that's prob'ly where they'll bury me."

– John Mellencamp –

Samuel Gettys' Burg

PROXIMITY to a natural harbor or a navigable river is the ingredient that has traditionally motivated humans to settle a place and try to make a go of it. The geography on which Gettysburg sits has neither. The location that would one day become the borough is far from any body of water of note. It rests in the shallow and protective depression of an Appalachian valley, nestled at the foot of a nearby extension of the Blue Ridge Mountains. Those low, long humps of the grander range to the south are periodically sliced by naturally weathered gaps allowing cross mountain access to the lower land on which Gettysburg sits. Thus, the geography that was to become Gettysburg was ideally suited for manmade ribbons of commerce since nature saw fit not to provide it with the riparian kind. Indeed, that is what took place. Long before armies were drawn here, early on in its history, a conjunction of roads at this place would tie together the growing cities of the coastal plain with the towns situated on the western side of the Blue Ridge.

In the decade of the 1760s, a wanderer and soon-to-be American rebel named Samuel Gettys stopped in this southern Pennsylvania hinterland and pondered the unnamed crossroads near Marsh Creek. He cast his eye about, took note of the well worn tracks, and determined it was a good place to build a tavern. His commercial instincts proved correct. Those busy commercial arteries then, as they would in 1863, caused many to pass through the area on their journeys elsewhere. Gettys, exhausting his personal wealth in support of his business and the Continental army's struggle for his right to do it without British oversight during the American Revolution, was not to be heard from again.

The vacuum he left behind allowed his equally enterprising son James to parcel and sell to settlers plots of land around his father's roadhouse. These tracts, when cobbled together, were to become a town. A town that would, in the future, adopt the Gettys surname as its own.

Before the year of the battle, Gettysburg's history was inconsequential. Like many small places in America, Gettysburg's early story was a simple one. In consisted of trickling migration, subsistence farming, fruit growing and the odd concern set up here and there devoted to the shelter and comfort of travelers. Mostly a conglomeration of family farms, the town could and did support a few small industries but it was known mostly as a station for wayfarers moving between the larger communities surrounding it. Gettysburg, it seems, has always been a place through which people must pass but have little reason to stay. Nevertheless, it held an attraction for some.

At the time of the Civil War, Gettysburg had become a thriving, self-sufficient town of about 2,500 inhabitants. There they spent their days with dirtied hands, tending neatly fenced apple orchards and fields. Other artisans were hard at work in small shops tinkering away alongside merchants behind counters, servicing tired, hungry and thirsty passersby.

GETTYSBURG today remains the same small and unassuming place it has always been. That fact is surprising since the large metropolitan areas of Washington and Baltimore are both within 100 miles of the place and Philadelphia is only a hair length's distance farther than that.

Ignoring, for a moment, the throngs that mill about the shops and restaurants at the traffic circle in Lincoln Square or along Baltimore Street and Steinwehr Avenue, the rest of Gettysburg is much as it was in the eighteenth and nineteenth centuries. What can best be described as the urban part of town is built up and the family farm plots have been replaced by expanded sections of row houses, small single family dwellings, corner stores, a medical center, small strip plazas and paved parking areas. Downtown's narrow streets are lined with those squat and square looking houses roofed with tin or similar metal. The eave ends are adorned with decorative snow and ice guards to keep melting and sliding sheets of the stuff from plummeting to the ground below.

Off the main thoroughfares the dwellings are rented and mangy. The small yards to the front and sides are weedy and unkempt. Unsightly strings of electric, cable television and telephone wires loop throughout, carried aloft by equally unattractive utility poles. There are quiet cul-de-sacs of better kept houses near the pleasant wooded confines of Gettysburg College and on side streets off Buford Avenue towards Seminary Ridge. But, the majority of the center of the borough, on the streets unsullied by tourists, is made up of structures in which the occupants, and landlords, have more productive distractions to occupy their time than lawn and house maintenance.

The tendency of most in town to gravitate towards the middle-class is borne out by statistics of demographers. The last decennial count put the median family income in Gettysburg at approximately $40,000 per year. That's a sizeable chunk less than the national median level of $50,000 per family per annum. Except for the Eisenhower plot and a few odd large and groomed farmsteads here and there, Gettysburg is bereft of the typical suburban blocks and grassy neighborhoods of over the top mini-mansions one often sees in the outer rings of American cities today. Despite its recession sensitive, service-based economy, the area has shown a small increase in population between the 2000 constitutionally mandated headcount and the one undertaken in 2010. While trailing the nation in annual wage levels, Gettysburg is an attractive enough generator of employment to keep migrants coming in. Its residents also appear both fertile and virile enough to ensure that births outpace deaths by a fraction.

ONE of my pastimes when I visit Gettysburg is to place myself at a location close to where I think a famous period photograph of the borough or a scene on the battlefield was taken. There are, naturally, no contemporary photos of actual combat during the three day battle. Photographic equipment of the time was clumsy and required the subject to remain still during a long exposure. Such a pose would have been impossible if indeed any recording equipment had been present during the fight.

Photographers like Matthew Brady and Alexander Gardner did, however, travel to Gettysburg after the battle and snapped some dramatic and transcendent images. Their work, and the sketches of others who were physically there during the battle, remain prized recollections of what happened during those three days. It is more than meaningful to me to hold a period photo that includes a crack in rock in, let's say, Devil's Den and today place my hand on the very same place. I enjoy stopping at the side of Chambersburg Road, on Cemetery Hill or at the edge of Barlow's Knoll and look down at the town. Photos from similar spots at the time of the battle look uncannily similar. Not much has changed really. Sure, the roads are paved and the farmers' fields nearest the town are now either part of the National Military Park or have been turned into residential neighborhoods. But, steeples still dominate the skyline and the town, from a distance, retains its pastoral appearance. This is particularly so on a fog shrouded morning where tendrils of misty white blanket modernity and allow what only existed in 1863 to catch the first rays of the sun.

Gettysburg, as are many places in the surrounding countryside, is far more wooded than it once was. Those same black and white period photos gracing history books and novelty post cards generally show fewer trees than grow there today. Naturally, the farmers working the land at the time removed most of the trees from the fields. Forested groves near town provided wood for fuel, building material and other nineteenth century domestic uses. Naturally, they would have been consumed in far greater quantities than now. Accordingly, vistas that presented themselves as wide and open to the sharp eyes of Civil War scouts are obscured today by the leaves and branches of resurgent woodlands.

TO really experience the visitors' tumult that can be Gettysburg, do yourself a favor and stop by on a summer's Friday night. Lines of stop-and-go traffic clog Baltimore Street and Steinwehr Avenue. Cars congregate from all cardinal directions at the traffic circle at Lincoln Square in the center of town. License plates from D.C., Maryland, New York and Pennsylvania, with a random sprinkling from throughout the rest of the United States, tell all one needs to know about Gettysburg's proximity to the East Coast's metropolitan aggregation. Eavesdropping on chatter on the sidewalks, in the shops or in queue for a coffee at the convenience stores confirms the obvious. Thick New York and northern New Jersey accents blur together with the similar but milder Philadelphia and southern New Jersey intonation. The oddly endearing Baltimore and Mid-Atlantic "Hon" is heard often as a patron from the Maryland shore clips short a request for more ice water while addressing a hurried waitress at a packed dining spot.

The shop owners, battlefield guides, actors entertaining patrons on ghost tours and hotel proprietors speak in their unique central Pennsylvania accent. That idiomatic articulation is partially adapted from migration of the language of western Pennsylvania to this spot. Once here it mixed with the guttural northern European speak, a legacy of the Scottish, Irish and Germans who immigrated to this rolling and fertile farmland that still bears a cornucopia today.

Like the steady transition to a gentler climate as one approaches the nearby physical and cultural boundary made famous by two surveyors named Charles Mason and Jeremiah Dixon, the language too begins to take on a distinctly southern flair. The balmier air evokes a slower paced pattern of speech, just a tiny bit more pleasing to the ear than its harsher, rapid fire northern counterpart. Not a melodic, slow southern drawl, but something rather closer to it than the coarseness spoken in Philadelphia or Brooklyn.

In Adams County, the political boundary for which Gettysburg is the seat, a dialectical uniqueness is on display as well. One does not snap a *picture* on a smart phone but, rather, one takes a *pitcher*. Another colloquial oddity peculiar to this region may also prompt a second aural take from strangers. Instead of stating that a resident of Gettysburg *knew* a person or a fact; he or she actually *knowed* him or it.

Upstate New Yorkers who possess the unpleasant nasally whine when pronouncing vowels (e.g., Chicaaago or Raaachester), an accent familiar to natives living in a broad Great Lakes arc from the Windy City to Syracuse, are also introduced to a small surprise when first visiting the area. The natives pronounce the name of the place itself differently. To its denizens, Gettysburg is pronounced as "Get-tiss-burg" rather than "Get-tees-burg" as I say it and as the presence of the "Y" would imply.

THE mix of strangers from different cultures and speaking in the varied rhythm of their native English tongue is to be expected in a place that welcomes two million strangers to tramp its streets every year. All points on the map devoted to the drawing of tourists for economic survival should be so lucky. For a borough that just barely squeaks out over 8,000 in total population, or just over three times as many who settled there in 1863, a native keeping a smile on her face when those waves of humanity wash in and out of town is just short of miraculous. If one considers that the Grand Canyon in Arizona sees around five million visitors a year, the number of cars and people that converge on, and move through, this tiny one horse town is astounding. More come in summer, naturally, or when a special event or battle anniversary is circled on the calendar.

The hot season in Gettysburg removes all doubt that a visitor is closer to Dixie than the Yankee North. In the days preceding or following the solstice, the region's uncomfortable heat and clinging moisture are typical of what climatologists categorize as a humid subtropical zone. The guests come by the millions but those that venture there in the high season spend a lot of time in air conditioned buses, museums, shops or relaxing in shaded window and chilled motel rooms.

GETTYSBURG, no matter the time of year, attracts fanatics who come to participate in some sort of reenactment, put on a demonstration for a tourist group or just wear Civil War period costumes for the fun of it. They love to live the experience. The frequency with which some visitors to Gettysburg don Civil War garb may astonish the uninitiated. These vicarious pseudo-soldiers parade up and down the streets of Gettysburg, popping in and out of bookstores and souvenir shops and dining, still fully costumed, at restaurants. Occasionally, they will interact with the contemporarily dressed curious and answer questions. But, mostly, they stay in bunches with their kind and when a group of them gather, it brings to mind a street scene from the Gettysburg of old. In the summer, they exude an essence that's a bit riper than the tourists who, for the most part, bathe once or twice daily. The heavier wool uniforms cause them to sweat easily and those that sleep under canvas in an encampment somewhere nearby usually don't have ready access to showers or laundromats. Their natural bouquet mixes with the rotten egg, sulfurous smell of discharged black powder and the wood smoke from cooking fires. They don't seem to care one whit either way. Get over it, this is Gettysburg.

Some wives, girlfriends or female relatives also accompany these dedicated part-time warriors. Their thick, multiple layered dresses thrown over what looks to be ample undergarments cause these young ladies' faces to quickly turn beat red in Gettysburg's tropical heat. They, however, are evidently also very passionate about the hobby and sacrifice comfort for the thrill of fantasy.

Whether they like the comradeship, the noise and smoke or enjoy being stared at by strangers, these devoted spend a ton of money on period uniforms and equipment. It is quite a lively business for some shops in town. So too is it for the quartermasters and sutlers who religiously tag along with reenactors all around the country. If a Civil War encampment happens to crop up at a place near your home town, the sutler tents will pop up and open their canvas flaps, providing a ready supply of nearly every war tool for the participants along with the knick knacks and souvenirs for the wandering civilian audiences.

The Civil War isn't the only excuse used at Gettysburg to engage in historical imagination. At certain times of year, scores of gentlemen and ladies can be seen parading about town in uniforms and equipment dating back to World War II. Spats, tan field jackets, open topped jeeps and all manner of other gear familiar to that era's American G.I. are worn or on parade. The nearby Eisenhower National Historic Site, the post-military and political career working farm of Dwight Eisenhower, hosts a September World War II weekend annually. The event draws a fair number of devotees who pine after the memory of America's D-Day hero. They gather, camp, listen to the Andrews Sisters and otherwise take themselves back to a time they too probably wish they had lived as it happened.

AS brand new Marine officers, we were required to invest a substantial amount of money in new uniforms. That thought weighed on my cash strapped mind as I continued my brief reunion sojourn at Gettysburg, delaying my trip to TBS at Quantico. Except for a few pairs of camouflage utilities doled out at OCS which, by the way, are soon thrashed by heavy use, the Marine Corps does not furnish a young officer with uniforms. That's on his or her dime.

The choices to shop for those necessities in and around Quantico were limited. In 1984, a Marine second lieutenant had two choices of stores in which to shop. The Marine Shop on the main drag in downtown Quantico had sales and support staff that emphasized customer service. Tailoring was careful, materials were better and, naturally, prices were higher. Alternatively, one could get all one needed at the big box and K-Mart-like Marine Corps Exchange where the blouses, trousers, shirts, covers and the accessories met USMC specifications and that's about it. The key advantage was that the uniforms at the Exchange were cheaper and when a young adult just out of college is laying out a few thousand dollars for clothes, he's going to give the nod to the guy with the lowest price.

I guarantee we as a people love a man, or woman in a uniform and places like Gettysburg prove my case. One of the many reasons the Civil War fascinates Americans today is because of the variety of official and unofficial clothes the conflict produced. At the beginning of the war, it was rare to run across two units wearing the same thing. That non-standardization, from soldier to soldier or from unit to unit, was certainly a nineteenth century convention. More so in the volunteer or militia units rather than those smaller, tighter controlled regular contingents. Uniform regulations were not as stringent as they are now and those rules that were in place, in most cases, were only partially obeyed. The Federal army, naturally, had a very robust industrial base backing it and a lot of government money to ensure that its soldiers were clothed and fed. As a result, variation in Union uniforms was less likely than that in the homespun articles worn by their Confederate counterparts.

The typical contemporary depiction of a Confederate army uniformly clad in gray uniforms with yellow piping, as in the movie *Shenandoah*, is a myth. Except for some privately funded units, the typical Confederate soldier brought along just what he needed to stay comfortable as he fought for his cause. The homestead was his uniform factory and, if that proved insufficient, the decaying bodies of opponents and, perhaps, dead comrades could be stripped of clothing. Supply wagons and commissary store houses were frequently raided and robbed as well. The extensive Federal supply chain involuntarily did much to keep the Confederate soldier warm, dry and walking with, if a soldier was lucky, a good pair of shoes on his feet.

TODAY'S military allows no discretion to the individual and limited freedom to the unit in the wearing of professional clothing. A soldier is told exactly what to wear and how. As strict as the regulations are, they do allow some measure of variation from unit to unit particularly within the U.S. Army. For example, the beret is a U.S. Army or air force convention in head cover. The Marine Corps eschews the style. The Marines, while once having done so, no longer countenance separate unit identification on the uniform as does the army or air force. The Marines seek to attain esprit de corps by consistency across the whole. There are a few very rare and historically significant exceptions. Active members of the Fifth and Sixth Marine Regiments display on dress uniforms a braided rope known as the Fourragere. That honor was awarded to them originally by the French government for bravery in defense of France in the World War I Ardennes Forest campaign. The tradition lives on.

Despite its stinginess with caps and unit badges or sewn patches, the Marine Corps has dozens of combinations of working and dress uniforms styled for multiple occasions. Dress, dinner formal, working, office wear; it is more complicated than one would think. Except for the field camouflage utilities or "cammies," or what the army terms battle dress uniform or BDUs, the uniformed Marine also departs substantially in appearance from his or her comrades in the sister services.

COLORFUL Civil War people wore colorful uniforms. Eccentric personalities and dapper renegades were eager to show themselves off. George Armstrong Custer departed from regulation wear with his gold braided sleeves, a floppy sombrero-like hat and a red kerchief around his sunburned neck. With his long gold locks flowing behind him, he must have been quite a sight.

His southern cavalry counterpart, the equally dashing Confederate General J.E.B. Stuart, was seen often in his gauntlets and feather plumed hat.

A few Union units and even fewer Confederate counterparts dressed in the pantaloons and short jackets made famous by France's North African colonial infantry Zouves. With a fez festooned with a tassel, white spats, baggie trousers and the scarlet piped and navy blue jacket, those units that chose the Zouve style looked like they would be more at home in Morocco than Manassas, Virginia.

Some of the uniform accessories, while distinct, were more trouble than they were worth. Midwestern units, particularly the famous Iron Brigade, were burdened with the army's standard issue dress hat. This was a tall, ponderous, heavy thing named the Hardee Hat after a tactics expert and designer who ignored his oath and eventually joined the Confederate army after Fort Sumter. Practicality took a back seat in nineteenth century uniform design and the Hardee Hat was a typical example. Most soldiers on both sides of the fight, wanted no part of the useless, ornamental Hardee and opted for the more comfortable and practical slouch hat or kepi. Some just wore whatever headgear did the best job keeping out the sun and the rain.

Before the introduction of the various badges, ribbons, shields and medals we see on dress uniforms today, the uniform remained relatively unadorned. There were some exceptions. The famous Irish Brigade, made up of sturdy immigrants barely settled in new homes in New York, Pennsylvania and Massachusetts, would decorate their Union blue with a sprig of boxwood to show their pride in the green of their native land. Stepping off to the tune of *Garryowen* and beneath the emerald banner of the harp and sunburst, they put on quite a profound display. The Confederate Irish units did much the same.

JOSEPH Hooker was the first to initiate a new concept in unit identification. After he slyly conspired to maneuver himself into Burnside's vacated command billet leading the Army of the Potomac, he recognized the value of pride and motivation in enhancing a unit's combat efficiency. Accordingly, he directed that each army corps issue identifying badges that the men wore on their kepis or blouses. A diamond, a three leaved shamrock, a crescent moon or a Maltese cross, colored differently in each of the corps' subordinate divisions, popped up all throughout the ranks. The same symbols fluttered on guidons that accompanied the commanders and their staffs. Corps identification became much easier as generals maneuvered troops in the smoke and confusion of battle. The prominent symbols also made unit identification by enemy scouts and paid spies easier as well. Despite the intelligence faux pas, the little patch of cloth or metal trinket provided the desired motivational effect.

The fact that most units on both sides were volunteers and were formed and funded by a wealthy patron further facilitated the great variation in uniforms. A unit's look was tailored to the taste of the individual footing the bill. But, as the war wore on and more blood was shed, the thrill of volunteering waned. Draftees, bounty men and paid substitutes began to populate the ranks and were provided little choice in dressing themselves. The Federal navy blue blouse and sky blue trouser government standard issue became the predominant Union uniform on the battlefield. The Confederates, with ever shrinking sources of supply as the Union war machine advanced into their territory, retrograded further. The dwindling and evermore chastened southern armies relied ever more on the generosity of citizens to equip their ragged survivors.

* * * *

Monuments and Kitsch

A first time visitor's baptismal impression of the
battlefield at Gettysburg is inevitably one of
surprise at the sheer number and variety of
monuments set on its ridges, rolling hills and
forested paths. The bottomless supply of kitschy
souvenirs runs a close second. One can't move
even a few feet in Gettysburg without bumping
into either. Both make up quite a bit of what most
remember about the place long after they leave.

Most visitors to the Gettysburg National
Military Park, usually diverted as they zip by on
Route 15, are in town for just the day so they stick
to the basics. They head straight towards the
usually overflowing parking lot at the new,
privately run and maintained building operated
by the non-profit Gettysburg Foundation. The
National Park Service Museum and Visitor Center
is located just outside of town on the Baltimore
Pike. Its operation is a partnership between the
National Park Service and the Foundation. Both
paid and volunteer civilians as well as Federal
employees are there to assist a patron if needed.

After paying admission, the majority view
the Morgan Freeman narrated film in the Center's
theater. At the end of that brief presentation, the
audience troops to escalators which whisk them
up to the immaculately renovated Cyclorama. The

canvas has been restored and is illuminated by superior lighting. The painting is displayed as it was originally designed for nineteenth century audiences. The viewers are placed in the middle of the action. A landscaped, debris strewn battlefield foreground, visible in all directions, is seamlessly connected to the painting itself. In such pristine condition, it is easy to see why the artwork once thrilled thousands.

After that rare treat, Cyclorama peepers are ushered out, adjust their eyes to the light and can read about the Cyclorama's bumpy and interesting road to where it currently hangs. Most don't care so they proceed downstairs. Some choose to wander through the sparkling new museum which, at my first visit, fell short of expectations. The exhibits inside focus more on the larger Civil War and Gettysburg's contextual part of it rather than the detail of what happened just down the road. Further, unlike the old museum, there are fewer battlefield artifacts presented and those that are there are scattered and displayed in cavernous and mostly empty space.

As patrons depart the museum, cagey marketers funnel them through the privately run gift shop where an ample supply of souvenirs are stocked. Many of the coffee cups, t-shirts, pennants, posters and art work feature the more popular battlefield monuments. After browsing and spending, the crowds head back out to find a car, truck or recreational vehicle lost in the mass of others in the large and usually humming parking lot.

The next, predictable stage of the garden-variety visit is the fairly straightforward Auto Tour of the battlefield. It is self-guided and allows guests their preference in measuring how much they'd like to take in. Rare is the day-tripper who stops and takes the time to read each and every descriptive plaque on the field. The tour is informative, nonetheless.

Many, after a couple of hours and having seen enough, decide to dine at any one of the fast food joints on Steinwehr Avenue. Distinguished among them is General Pickett's Buffetts. Yep, that's the plural. Why have just one buffet when one can have four? The ample, greasy trays of comfort food dished out at this fine eating establishment satisfy thousands of hungry battlefield wanderers and bused in tour groups annually. I am speculating but it seems to me there is far less foot traffic around the place these days. Like some of the now empty shops nearby, I wonder if General Pickett's has experienced a drop in traffic and loss of business since the original visitors center and museum moved down to its present location on the Baltimore Pike? The new visitor center has a spacious cafeteria with plenty of seats and a fairly diverse menu which must irk competing restaurant owners.

I doubt General Pickett, if he could opine on the subject, would express gratitude at being memorialized in this manner. But, since his division was slaughtered just a few hundred yards away from the restaurant, the reference is understandable. The last time I ate there, more out of curiosity than anything else, it was crowded and the fried chicken wasn't at all bad. There are more genteel places to eat in town but getting a table on a summer weekend is a challenge so I, and a few graduate school buddies, stood in the mess hall-like line with the rest of the stomach rumbling humanity. Trays heaping, we did as much damage to the supply of food as we could.

Stuffed and satisfied, we wandered down Steinwehr Avenue to Baltimore Street, popping in and out of the knick-knack stores, book shops and musty collaborative enterprises that deal in all manner of novelties. Toy soldiers, plastic and wooden muskets, hats, uniforms, magnets, coffee cups, trinkets, bracelets, license plates, t-shirts and every imaginable piece of junk that can display a picture of a bearded Union general, a young, fat cheeked Confederate private or, naturally, a battlefield monument is available for the taking.

In any other American place outside of Gettysburg it would be considered rather odd for a kid to be seen in a t-shirt with the silk screened face of George Meade on the front. After all, his joyless, brooding countenance is nowhere near as attractive as Justin Bieber's or one of the other of today's faddish teen stars.

The Civil War's tug-of-war between a powerful central government and the rights of the individual states seems not to have dimmed in the ensuing 150 years. At least not in the trinket shops in Gettysburg. It is not at all difficult to purchase in-your-face states' rights bumper stickers, window decals or t-shirts. The vendors could care less about any one customer's political leanings as long as he or she pays in cash. The purchasers of controversial items, confident in their decision to show them in public back home, are presumed to be on their own in dealing with the self-inflicted polemics.

Confederate battle flags are in plentiful supply and are sold ready to unfurl on flag poles or front porches. At many shops, the stars and bars of the union of secessionist states, hang side-by-side with the Stars and Stripes and are barely commented on. Try to fly the Confederate national flag or its armies' crossed battle flag next to Old Glory anywhere outside Gettysburg and see what happens.

Want to buy a period, authentic rifled-musket? No problem. A shop near the town square has got them. In the market for a full on authentic cavalry uniform, perfect in every detail from the spurs on up to the badge on top of the kepi? Gettysburg is the place one must go. The bookstores and art shops are chock full of material covering not only every minute aspect of the battle that took place here but pretty much any other Civil War episode that piques your interest. Prints, paintings and photographs line countless store walls. The interpretive war work of artists such as Don Troiani, John Paul Strain, Mort Kunstler and Dale Gallon is all over the place. Some of the prints or original paintings are darn expensive. Some people will pay a pretty penny to hang an oil painting or print of the defense of Little Round Top over their dinner table.

On Chambersburg Street, just west of Lincoln Square and its ever busy traffic circle, is the James Gettys Hotel named after Samuel Gettys' son who had sold the same plot of land on which the hotel now sits to an entrepreneur in the late eighteenth century. Over the years the inn and roadhouse was expanded and improved and, like many period buildings in Gettysburg, served as a hospital for the wounded during the battle. Renovated later in the twentieth century it has adopted the name of the borough's first family and sits above and next to a joint commercial establishment known as Lord Nelson's Gallery.

After a morning of hiking the battlefield and then lunch at the Blue Parrot Bistro, a patron of the hotel might decide to kick back in his Sign of the Buck Suite or the Zeigler-Holtzworth Livery Suite or one of the other choice rooms at the hotel. All are dolled up with lace and colorful bed covers designed to give the visitor a sense of an older, less frantic time. Floors are creaky and doors and walls do not muffle sounds very well so, in some respects, this place does seem just like the crowded, noisy inns of an earlier age. After freshening up in the late afternoon, a guest is sure to wander over to the attached gallery to peruse some of the items for sale. In terms of kitsch, this is some of the most expensive in town. The last time I popped in, the man working the counter stared politely over the top rim of his half glasses at me. I appeared to him not to be the kind of person in the market for $2,000 historical paintings and so he went about his business. The man, apparently, was a fair judge of his clientele.

All manner of humans parade in and out of the gallery and keep the entry door's bell tinkling most of the day. Carved wild animals, pottery and jewelry are generously mixed in with some of the more pricey things in the store. Those include historical paintings which depict events from the French and Indian War to the American Revolution to the Civil War and World War II. If one has to have to have an oil painting depicting the death of British General Braddock on the Monongahela River at Fort Duquesne (modern day Pittsburgh) in 1755 and has a few thousand dollars to spare then he has come to the right place.

ANOTHER way to kill a few hours when not tramping around the battlefield can be found in any one of the many private museums sprinkled around town. They, like the Electric Map, bring a visitor back to a simpler time where cotton ball explosions and parsley sprinkled grass dioramas were at the cutting edge. Jerky animatronic soldiers, acting out dusty versions of the battle, were the innovative technology of the day.

In one Steinwehr Avenue theater, in a comparable version of the Electric Map's basic gymnasium-like setting, the vast battle of Gettysburg takes place on a 400 square foot, poorly lighted floor. Spotlights draw your attention to the scene of interest with flashing colored lights, scratchy sound recordings and unconvincing robots in blue and gray dramatizing the horror of war. Suddenly, mercifully, the war ends. All is hushed and darkened. The saintly figure of Abraham Lincoln rises solemnly from a hole in the floor, the patently fake carnage still surrounding him. A spotlight pierces the smoky gloom, shining on the Great Emancipator. He speaks. His jaw opens and shuts, hinges audibly clicking as the metal parts grind together. He jerks to the right and then left, mechanically making a point with his stiffened arm. If not for the beard and frock coat, believers would think Frankenstein's monster was reciting the Gettysburg Address to a sparse and thoroughly amused audience.

In other museums, wax presidential and other historical figures stare the viewer down. These less carefully made reproductions are not quite up to the quality of Madame Tussauds' detailed work but good enough to keep 'em coming in. In the back corridors and dark recesses of these places, a visitor can stroll through a Civil War camp. Stiff and badly dressed mannequins decorated with ill fitting clothes, glued beards and bushy eyebrows rest against rocks and warm themselves before the pale orange electric flame of a campfire. In the background, a single speaker perpetually plays the chirping of a lone cricket or, if prompted by the push of a red button, explains the scene in a lengthy and overdramatic soliloquy. Despite the overzealous advertisements at the entrances, these figures have absolutely zero chance of "coming to life before your eyes."

THE national historic site that encompasses the battlefield occupies a sizeable 11,000 acres. The smaller, but most visited, part of the battlefield covers a still impressive 4,000 acres. That's too much ground for a corpulent, exercise challenged adults, small children or hurried travelers to see without the benefit of modern transportation. So, most simply opt for the easy way to study what happened. Lines of cars and trucks motor around to the various points of interest highlighted by the ubiquitous National Park Service map which helps them navigate along. The first thing these wanderers notice about the battlefield is just how many obelisks, castles, stones, crosses, scrolls, statues, cannons and various and sundry rock and metal information signs and remembrances mark key points of interest.

Set deep in woods or alongside a trail or road, the sheer number of memorials to individual soldiers, officers, units, states, civilians and even dogs that experienced the battle or fought here is a testament to the reverential treatment the governments of the states from which those units came placed on that sacrifice. If one is looking for a battlefield unsullied by monuments, I suggest a park devoted to a less well known clash than that which occurred at Gettysburg.

The monument phenomenon is so pervasive it has developed its own following. In fact, there are a few websites dedicated to cataloguing them. Stonesentinels.com appears pretty comprehensive if such things suit your fancy. Steve Hawks, the man behind the website, tells his readers that there are over 800 spread across the battlefield. The National Park Service, in a piece of printed literature, tallies not only monuments but markers as well and counts over 1,400 of those in and around Gettysburg.

Rather than pointlessly debating the true number, their mere existence became a point of contention as a friend and I once argued the point at length. He was not so enamored with Gettysburg, dismissing it as too touristy and complaining the many monuments ruined the experience. When he was younger, his father would drag his family around the Washington, D.C. area battlefields and would make sure they walked the same ground as did their forebears. He preferred Antietam which, although it has its fair share of bronze plaques and stone edifices dedicated to the memory of the fallen, is indeed much less congested than the ridgelines, hills and roads of Gettysburg. Antietam is off the beaten path so fewer sightseers visit. The battlefield stays more faithful to its original, once bloodied landscape. In fact, there are places at Antietam where one literally be transported back to September 1862 when the battle took place. Such realness is a credit to the caretakers diligently maintaining the field as it was.   One might catch an odd car whizzing by or a jet contrail overhead. But, kneeling in the famous Cornfield as it browns in the chill of September evenings, one, for a fleeting moment, can share the trepidation of pale young men as minie balls sang around them, slicing withering stalks and smashing into flesh.

In defense of Gettysburg's crop of monuments, I find them helpful in tracing the location of units and the lines of battle.   It's hard for a novice, particularly with a society overly dependent on satellite aided navigation, to orient themselves on a map to physical features on the ground.   The ordinary white knee-sock wearing, pale legged excursionist finds it much easier and informative to know where something happened on the battlefield because big stone obelisks and plaques point that out to him.   To bombard the uninitiated with topographic maps overlain with red and blue rectangles representing units of opposing armies is too much for the modern generation.   Plus, it's kind of cool seeing some of the architecture employed by the states and their hired surrogates in the design and construction of these works of art.

Who knew that Gutzon Borglum, the guy who dynamited Mount Rushmore's presidential faces, is the very same artist that sculpted the State of North Carolina monument which sits right off the park road on Seminary Ridge? Just across from that acorn strewn ground, the 110 foot pillared dome of the State of Pennsylvania Monument pays homage to that state's leaders and its fallen sons. It, fittingly, is the largest monument on the battlefield and recognizes the Keystone State's contribution to the Union victory.   It's large enough to identify flying overhead on a jetliner.

On top of the monument stands a statue of Winged Victory, her sword pointed menacingly towards far off Seminary Ridge and the Virginia, Tennessee and other southern state memorials to the Confederate dead. Fitting for the men whose valor remains in the memories of the people of the states that sent them here.

TO see Gettysburg now is refreshingly different from just a few short years ago. Park attendants, rangers and preservationists, alongside hard working volunteer groups, have made a superb effort to restore the field to its 1863 appearance. It would take some doing to remove the ugly commercial eyesores that line Steinwehr Avenue and encroach on Cemetery Hill. Nevertheless, the removal of hideously incongruous observation towers, permanent and unsightly box restrooms and convenient but poorly situated parking areas has done wonders to bring the field to its original splendor.

For a time, a group of investors and business people, not failing to notice the flood of people visiting the battlefield annually, broached the idea of building a casino near Gettysburg. The announcement and submission of an application to build before the state and local authorities in charge of such things caused sharp dividing lines to form within the community. Finally, after years of partisan wrangling, the casino advocates' plans were rejected by those in the position to make the final call. Anybody hoping to toss some dice or pull handles on slots before or after they visit the military park are out of luck. The monuments, though, are on the battlefield to stay.

The Gettysburg Times occasionally reports a story of vandals defacing or stealing parts off the monuments. Bayonets or swords cast in bronze or carved from stone are sawed off or broken. Sometimes the damage is significant enough to make it on to the wire services and the news gets out to wider distribution nationally. It's a shame but noting the sizeable acreage of the National Military Park and the limited resources at the hands of the park police, it's pretty tough for them to keep an eye on everything twenty-four hours a day. More than a few miscreants probably lurk within the park boundaries after dark for whatever reason. Sneaky and profit driven relic hunters, strictly forbidden entry by park rules, almost certainly wave metal detectors around and dig down to uncover lost and buried mementos long after the sun has set and darkness covers up their illicit quests. On top of handling routine traffic matters, rendering first aid, answering questions and dealing with the normal problems that inevitably arise when two million people show up on one's front lawn, the park police try to keep one eye on the lookout for the nefarious.

Gettysburg National Military Park is just one property in the vast holdings under the protection of the Department of the Interior's National Park Service. Together, with the rangers, the park police are out and about, available to the multitudes seeking information and asking questions. Both organizations employ energetic and talented people with a fondness for their duty stations and, for the most part, they keep a low profile in order to enhance the visitor experience. They try to stay out of sight and maintain the peace and tranquility of that serene place without the need to flash a badge or draw a gun. Except, of course, when trouble brews.

The Evils of Drink

AND brew it did one gorgeous September Saturday afternoon when I and a group of the same graduate school friends, loyalists who frequently joined me in a long weekend at Gettysburg, ran afoul of the law. What happened wasn't exactly a bank robbery followed by a high speed chase. It was, however, the only time I interacted directly with a park policeman. The experience was, for him, professional handled and, for me, instructive.

SOMEWHERE my brother had read that a particularly rare witness tree, a tree that not only had been alive and standing at the battle of Gettysburg but still bore scars from the battle, was just off the road at the top of Culp's Hill. Well, sir, that was something we had to see. Culp's Hill is thick with trees and, after an hour or so of wandering through the woods on the slopes of that famous peak, we came up with nothing. Breaking out of the brush, sweaty and annoyed, we stopped a park ranger and inquired as to a more exact location of this alleged miracle. The ranger was helpful but noted that there are several "witness" trees on the battlefield. With convincing logic, he instructed us that after more than a century of weather and growth any tree that happened to be alive in 1863, survived battle damage and was still in the ground today was unlikely to show the pockmarks of projectile strikes no matter how deeply carved into the wood. As he departed, he appeared to chuckle at our gullibility. It was a good lesson in not taking on faith the rhetoric of some unknown author.

IN any case, we chalked up the wasted hour to experience. It was time to grab a beer. On the way, we took notice of the fine weather and decided it would be a top notch idea to stay outside. It was time to break out the beach chairs, drag out our cooler filled with beer and take advantage of nature's bounty. It was one of those late summer days with a desert-like dew point and the sun hanging like a sparkling diamond in a cloudless sky. With the temperature nearing eighty degrees, we were hot, tired and thirsty. Being both graduate students and guys, we knew just what to do. So, with folding chairs set out and a cooler of beer at the ready, a half a dozen of us settled comfortably down just east of the North Carolina Monument on Seminary Ridge.

We weren't being rowdy or rude. We did nothing more than lazily chat and laugh and take in the sights around us. We even tagged one of our group as a designated driver. It did not occur to us at the time that consumption of alcohol on this particular Federal property, if proven in court in front of a judge or jury of one's peers, is a violation of Title 36, Section 2.35 of the Federal Code of Regulations. It also would be perceived by many to be disrespectful to this the Hallowed Ground.

I happened to be sharp eyed enough to notice a licensed battlefield tour guide helping a group of elderly visitors get back aboard their bus on the road paralleling Seminary Ridge near the memorial to the valiant North Carolina Tarheels. He was extraordinarily interested in what we were doing and couldn't stop staring in our direction. As adults, I suppose we should have tumbled to the conclusion that having even a couple of beers on the battlefield was a Federal government no no. We should have done what every other lemming does when visiting. There were myriad bars and restaurants around and all served alcohol. However, where and how we were doing it on this perfect afternoon just seemed so right. We were in good company, peaceably assembling, enjoying the unbeatable weather and had a cooler with us stocked full of icy cold beer purchased in Rochester.

I'VE got nothing against Pennsylvania beer. In fact, I have it on good authority that the Keystone State's malt masters know how to brew rather excellent beer. Keeping up with the Dutch and German traditions in the state, Pennsylvania is the home to over seventy hops and barley makers including some of the oldest in America. D.G. Yuengling and Son, Inc.'s large brewery pops to mind. That esteemed enterprise puts out a very popular lager among other frosty delights.

Despite a history of pretty darn good beer making, Pennsylvania, frustratingly, is not the easiest of places in which to buy and carry away a cold one. The laws governing the sale of alcohol are drawn up in favor of the distributors. Therefore, dropping in to a convenience store or a supermarket to pick up a case or two is a waste of time. Sure, one can buy a six pack at a delicatessen or a pizza parlor for home consumption but any more than that and the thirsty must head to the central source of supply. I don't make the rules in Pennsylvania but that state's movers and shakers want one to drink at their convenience, not the customers'.   So, we brought our own from across state lines.

In a post-event rationalization, I think that drinking something as innocuous as beer, and to do so where many soldiers before us did the same when given half a chance, was a comradely gesture. A toast from one generation of young men to another, perhaps.   After all, we weren't sloshed and certainly not drinking on or near the plots and gravestones in the National Military Cemetery. That would have been disrespectful and reprehensible. We were enjoying a few cold pops sitting around on a sunny, warm field.

IF one reads any Civil War history one can't but take note how much drinking alcohol played a part in a soldier's life. In a lot of cases, drinking altered the outcome of a battle. Rudyard Kipling knew a bit about the habits of soldiers and warned about the perils of drinking bad booze in his instructive and wholly accurate verse about the young British soldier:

First mind you steer clear o' the grog-sellers' huts,
For they sell you Fixed Bay'nets that rots out your guts
Ay, drink that 'ud eat the live steel from your butts --
An' it's bad for the young British soldier.
Bad, bad, bad for the soldier . . .

Bad for the soldier indeed.   There are literally a basketful of examples of decisions to be made at critical points in any number of battles waylaid by a staggeringly drunk officer.   No wonder. Facing the chaos and slaughter of a Civil War battlefield surely was enough to drive a man to drink. But, to do so when weighted with a command decision is at very least extraordinarily bad judgment and, at most, criminal. But it happened and quite a lot. The callous disregard of a commander that dips liberally into the bottle and then throws his charges into a gruesome cauldron of fire is sickening.

The troops were sure to partake of the grain and the grape where and when available. But all they had to do was what they were told. Except for camp rumor and soldiers' speculation, they had no clue as to the overall strategy or purpose of why they were assigned to take a hill or a fortified position. They just did it. If a jolt of liquor warmed up their bones and steeled hearts prior to the slaughter then whatever made their miserable mission easier was welcome. I can almost guarantee that the canteens, flasks and other containers found in the camps of the Confederate soldiers, those who occupied the same ground on which we were now tap dancing on the limits of Federal law, were filled to the brim with good Pennsylvania hooch.

FOR the first eighteen years of my life I had not fallen too deeply into the trap of intoxicating drink. I don't know how I managed to resist; booze was all around me. The adults who raised us had wild summer pool parties, raucously stirred by all sorts of liquid concoctions and carrying on until the wee hours of the morning. There was the constant peer pressure of casual high school alcohol consumption. A kid growing up in 1970s New York was almost assured to have an encyclopedic knowledge and experience with alcohol. The state drinking age, at the time, was eighteen. That lowered bar further encouraged fresh faced youths to participate.

Nevertheless, I was quite comfortable in my abstinence. That is until I entered the halls of higher learning and, concurrently, joined the military. That combination was a double whammy. There is something about the military that encourages a person to drink. Traditions die hard and one of the military traditions that remains alive and well is the daily gill of grog. In my experience, I noticed a surprising number of service people who habitually drank, daily and in quantity. With the irresistible sirens singing their song, I too crashed on the rocks. College certainly didn't help, with stacked kegs of beer lying around and myriad, specious excuses to drain them dry. Shamefully, but willingly, I became just one of the crowd. Just another in a long line of the post-mortem storytellers with nights barely remembered, wobbly strolls back to the dorms as the sun broke over the horizon and mornings wasted in a snoring, smelly stupor. To binge is the purview of the young and the stupid and I, and many around me, was both.

THE binge drinker, particularly the one who attends university, is part of a troubling phenomenon. Places of higher education, and the responsible adults who send their children to them, struggle to understand it. There are reams of studies analyzing its causes and the impacts on the health of those who participate. I doubt, however, that the heightened awareness has done anything to stunt the practice. It seems to me that a young man or woman, no longer under the close supervision of a parent, is bound to engage a lot of his or her free time doing whatever is made to appear off limits. There is little college administrators can do to prevent it.

On one particularly bad evening, after downing too many cheap pitchers of Genesee beer and baskets of Buffalo wings at a dim riverside honky-tonk, I was mercifully pulled out of the joint before its two A.M. closing time. Dragged into a car, off we went in search of an illegal after hours joint. Erie County, an hour or so to the west, didn't shut down its bars until four A.M. Traveling down the New York Thruway crossed our minds but we prudently decided against it. Instead, we pointed the car towards the city of Rochester. Speeding down I-490 towards downtown, one of the guys in the car decided it would be a good idea to climb out of the passenger window and stand on the hood of the car. So, he did.

The driver, fortunately, was the least drunk of the lot of us and we survived the night. Miraculously, I made it home and was dropped off safely near my dormitory by an unremembered guardian angel. I lurched through the front entrance and stumbled up the steps to the second floor suite I shared with five other buddies. The open lounge in the suite was adorned with tall windows and a sliding door to a small patio outside. That faced the expansive, hilly grounds of Mount Hope Cemetery.

Near our suite, the cemetery grounds hosted a memorial and neatly aligned grave plots dedicated to soldiers who had fought in the Civil War. On the memorial, the frequently quoted funereal words of the poet Theodore O'Hara were carved. A stanza of the *Bivouac of the Dead* reminded the walkers, joggers and cyclists taking advantage of the cemetery's rolling and picturesque trails, that Rochesterians who had proudly donned Union blue were now here and at rest for eternity:

On Fame's eternal camping ground
Their silent tents are spread
And Glory guards with solemn round
The Bivouac of the Dead

On the opposite side of this solemn section stood a memorial to deceased firefighters. On top of a tall, polished cylinder was perched a granite statue of a fireman at the ready, poised to jump into danger, steady and silent, paying tribute to his fallen brethren.

I plopped my soused and wretched self on to the suite's large and filthy couch. There I sat and stared outside trying to focus on that firefighter. He glowed in the fluorescent bath cast by the dormitory complex's security lights hanging off the sides of our unit. Suddenly, there were two firefighters on top of two cylinders. Both, responding to the silent music demon rum conducted in my mind, began to dance in a circular motion, up and down, round and round in front of me. I closed my eyes in hopes that stability would return to my spinning world but that only served to make matters worse. What little function left in my brain lifted itself out of its stupor and, summoning the last, dwindling reserve of its cognitive ability, directed my legs to propel me outside through the sliding patio door and ordered my stomach to empty itself - immediately.

Those that desire to drink alcohol to excess are fated to learn such lessons. The syllabus is painful and intense. It exacts its toll for an endless and miserable stretch of hours thereafter. The only consolation to the tortured is that the experience is less harsh on the young.

AFTER college, at TBS, our ears resonated with countless warnings kept fresh in our minds that any lieutenant snagged by law enforcement with a hint of alcohol on his breath, and found behind the wheel of an automobile, would be subject to the full weight of the Uniform Code of Military Justice. Paying rapt attention to that advice, we drew straws and the unlucky loser became the designated driver. The rest of us tore up the town. If not out in the field training, engaged in a course of instruction that carried over to Saturday or traveling back to Rochester to reacquaint myself with my long distance girlfriend, weekend liberty was our chance to let loose. At TBS, liberty call was sounded at five P.M. on Friday evening. At quarter past the hour a line of vehicles filled with lieutenants in civilian attire raced north on I-95 to the bars and entertainment spots in and around Washington.

Some preferred the Georgetown or Capitol Hill watering holes but I usually veered off at Alexandria, Virginia and hit the bars along King Street. Murphy's, an Irish pub, was a well known Marine hang out. As far as I know, it still is. Wedged into its crowded and welcoming confines, with a couple of ales poured down a parched windpipe, one soon forgot the hard training of the week past. Arms over shoulders with buddies, the band encouraged us to ball out bawdy Irish ballads to the scratch of the violin and the strum of the guitar. During music breaks, we chatted up women with our weekly feats of derring-do. The ladies that frequented the place were used to Marines. The company of the gentler sex was welcomed after being cooped up with a bunch of testosterone laden jarheads. The women that were in the bar were not put off by skin tight haircuts, muscles, uneven tans and bad singing. They knew what to expect when crossing the portals of that place.

Sometimes amorous doors opened in mysterious ways. One morning, my TBS squad and I were involved in one of those physical fitness events that only the Marines can dream up. A dozen of us lay on the ground side-by-side with a heavy section of a telephone pole pressing down on our chests. The challenge was to pump out sit-ups with the pole tucked under the arms. The officer next to me was a much larger guy and as we entered the downswing of the sit-up motion, the size difference caused most of the pole's weight to slam down painfully on my chest. On the upswing, I kept my right arm looped over the log and held it tight to my armpit while slipping my other arm under it. Pressing my left hand against the log's surface, I attempted to secure enough leverage to shift my body into a more comfortable position. On the next downswing, I wasn't quick enough in getting my now vertical left arm out of danger. The entire weight of the 300 pound log came down on that limb. The crisp snap of my wrist bones broke the stillness of the morning air.

I weakly shouted for the team to stop the exercise and they mercifully responded. I stood up. Blood rushed to the injury. Grabbing my useless left arm with its healthy partner, I stumbled light-headedly over to a row of nearby bleachers and collapsed. The group of Marines was now deathly quiet and all that could be heard was my labored breathing and the singing of a few birds hopping from branch to branch in the sun dappled trees above. Our platoon commander, a Marine captain, tentatively approached me. His face looked as ashen as mine must have been. I felt nauseous and faint but cracked a joke about the accident getting me out of physical training. He didn't laugh, instead reaching for his webbed belt and pulling it from his camouflage trousers. He dug up a thick training manual from somewhere and wrapped it around my lower arm and wrist and cinched the web belt around it to immobilize my injury. Good Marine first-aid training came in handy that day.

That evening, after a quick trip to Fort Belvoir's hospital up the road where my arm was set and the injury wrapped in plaster, I returned to my TBS comrades. I watched forlornly on the sidelines as a hand-to-hand combat session wrapped up the afternoon's training.

The injury stopped hurting after a few days and became more of a nuisance than anything else. The cast and story how it came to be was transformed into legend and served as a great excuse to pick up girls. The injury grew more gruesome and I far braver with each retelling. It wasn't long before a few sentimental and unmanly good wishes were scribed on the cast in girlish loops with tiny hearts dotting the Is. For that, I got no end of grief from my buddies. I was able to continue much of the scheduled training despite my injury and, soon, the cast was covered in dried Quantico mud. It was impossible to clean. The grime hid the romantic script and made periodic inspections easier to bear.

WHETHER at the officers' club or out in town, youthful exuberance and liquid rewards for a week's hard work usually resulted in far too much hooch sent down the hatch. It was a couple of beers at times and an all night bacchanalia at others. The binging was an insufficient substitute for more productive pursuits. But, it facilitated the release of pent up emotions gathering as the long days of training dragged on.

Just after I completed TBS, I took some time to visit the base dentist to have some impacted wisdom teeth removed. The navy sawbones put me at ease with several thick needles of anesthesia thrust into my gums. Dr. "This won't hurt a bit" then commenced to cutting and hammering on my skull for what seemed like an interminably long and agonizing hour. After that time, worn and sweaty, he declared himself finished. Still woozy, my tongue rubbed on the sutures and tender caverns in the back of my mouth. I have a high tolerance for pain but, nevertheless, popped a prescription narcotic in a vain attempt to take the edge off my throbbing head. There had to be alternatives.

I ignored the label on the bottle clearly instructing the user not to consume alcohol while taking the medicine. Foolishly, my next stop was the officers' club and a few rounds of the palliative medicine dosed out by the pharmacist behind the bar.

Sitting on a stool, elbows propped on the shiny wood surface and slugging down drinks quickly put me in a worse way. Hopped up on a painkiller, its noxious marriage with the alcohol I had consumed drew out my false bravado. Common sense was shown the door. Liquid courage led me to challenge a barrel chested senior officer sitting next to me, a bird colonel I think, to a wrestling match out on the front lawn of the club. He, despite being equally cocked, destroyed me.

That soured the evening. I was conscious enough to call a taxi which deposited me like a five pound sack of flour at my apartment door in Woodbridge. I awoke the next morning, my head and pillow drenched in blood from my leaking sutures. My head felt as if it had been squeezed in a vice. As I tried to return to the land of the living, I posed to myself the oft repeated question inevitably asked by those who drink too much: "What the heck was I thinking?"

THE same question could have been asked a decade or so later at our Gettysburg Saturday afternoon impromptu outdoor cocktail hour in the shadow of the North Carolina Monument. The alert, licensed battlefield guide at Seminary Ridge, staring at us all the while, finished ushering his doddering group on to the soon departing tour bus and then responsibly phoned the park police on his cell phone.

With chairs angled towards a brilliant sun slowly dropping in the southwestern late afternoon sky and our attentions diverted elsewhere, we were surprised by an officer of the National Park Service who had stealthily approached us from the rear. He was a large guy and his bullet proof vest made him appear even larger. Stopping and placing a foot on the cooler of beer we had with us he asked us if we knew that alcohol consumption here was prohibited by both Federal law and National Military Park ordinances. Of course not, we untruthfully responded, if we had known we certainly wouldn't be doing it.

After a half hour of discussion, we had won enough brownie points from the officer to get off with just a stern warning and an agreement to load up the beer in our nearby car and move on. We profusely thanked him for not ticketing us or otherwise placing us in the midst of messy legal issues. He continued to be helpful and recommended that if we had drinking to do we do it where it's legal. Intimate with a specific watering hole, he pointed us towards Mama Ventura's restaurant and the lounge immediately underneath. It's best entered through the steel door fronting a back alley off Chambersburg Street he noted. "When you go," he said, "tell them the 'Dawg' sent ya."

Being veteran visitors to Gettysburg and its environs, we were aware of the location of all the gin joints in town and we had visited that place many a time. Mama Ventura's is an Italian restaurant just west of the traffic circle in Lincoln Square. Below it, in a subterranean and dank room, is a locally known Gettysburg dive bar. Mama V's, as it is affectionately called by regulars, is much like the Horseshoe bar in New Buffalo. The downstairs lounge has been constructed and decorated solely to support the consumption of alcohol. Often we would stop in here at dusk, snaking our way through the constricted, fire escape strewn alleyway off Chambersburg Street. Once through, we popped out on to the slender one-way access road known as Racehorse Alley. It was hidden far out of sight behind the quaint and welcoming storefronts.

The restaurant's cramped back lot was bare except for a few closely parked cars. The crooked silhouettes of electric poles stuck out from cemented bases; weird sentinels set against a mellowing afternoon sky. Traffic noise was muted and the chirps of sparrows echoed in the emptiness. White clad restaurant workers with dirty aprons tossed bags of garbage in green sanitary dumpsters strategically set and hidden from prying eyes.

Strolling through the steel door and from the glare outside into the dark enclave, our eyes adjusted to the gloom. As usual, late afternoon on a Saturday, a college football game was on a fuzzy and yellowish screened projection television set flush against a side wall. The owner, a hard working man, filled the bar troughs with crushed ice and bottled beers in preparation for the late night Gettysburg College crowd. An amply endowed redhead leaned against the bar, idly chatting with two regulars. The owner's work was interrupted by his Italian speaking, black dressed mother who wandered over to him and engaged him in the melodious conversation of her birthplace. He disappeared upstairs with her to attend to a restaurant matter.

We approached the nearly empty bar and, almost in unison, notified the attractive barkeep that the Dawg had sent us. She shook her head knowingly and asked us what he was up to. We jokingly replied that it wasn't much but whatever it was it was no good. Her unequivocal body language signaled that she might not be interested in a deep romantic relationship with the Dawg. We surmised, later out of her earshot, that she was simply a flirtatious professional. She kept close to him for selfish reasons; prime among them keeping her own bar tab reasonably low. That appeared not at all a hard thing for a good looking woman to accomplish especially in this small town.

Ordering a few pitchers of Yuengling lager, we retired to the pool table and dart board set in the back of this featureless box. Occasionally strolling back up to the bar for refills and a few shots of whiskey, we cheered heartily as Notre Dame was pounded by some Big Ten powerhouse. Our returns to the bar were good enough reason to kid the redhead that the Dawg was sweet on her. She knew that only too well but coyly kept to her game. She assured us that, in an hour or so, after he had finished his shift with the park police, he'd be down there, sitting right where we were, tipping a few back. Great! That would be our opportunity to buy him a round and show him how much we appreciated his earlier forbearance.

By now, after an hour or so more of imbibing, alcohol and testosterone had mixed liberally and made us all very loud and very annoying. The Dawg had indeed shown up, bathed, buffed and dressed in his civilian finest. He sat upon his well worn bar stool and immediately found out that his money, this afternoon anyway, was of no value. After we had slapped him on the back a few times and entertained each other with what we thought was witty conversation, we got the distinct impression that the Dawg was on the prowl and wanted no more of our acquaintance.

We conferred and unanimously agreed that it was time to eat. So, we bid farewell and stomped up the back stairs to get a seat at the restaurant. Being a nice late summer weekend, the restaurant was packed and no tables were available. Our soused little pack of ingrates stumbled over to the tiny restaurant bar, sat down and noisily began to demand food, drink and service. This pedestrian behavior brought only shock and chagrin to the wait staff and the justifiably annoyed patrons. Alcohol can, and did that afternoon, turn normally decent folk into total jerks. Repeated and gracious attempts of the hard working owner and his patient staff minimally pleased us. With gritted teeth and curt responses, they took our orders, served us, watched us eat like animals, cleaned up the spaces in front of us and quickly produced the check. Dessert was not an option. Despite our advanced state of drunken disrepair, we got the message and vacated the premises to the glee of those unlucky enough to have remained. The Dawg was not around this time to scare some sense into us.

A year later almost to the day, on another in a long line of stellar September Saturday afternoons, a similarly composed group of us popped into Mama V's for a bite to eat. The owner, with sharp intuitive sense and an astute memory, recognized us and, with every justification in the world, set us at a table in the very back of the restaurant near the door to the restrooms. Choking on the odor of toilet cakes, we excused ourselves to seek another place. In light of our shameful decorum of the past, we should have accepted the owner's olive branch. Not doing so, we ambled over to the nearby corner Pub and Restaurant. There we placed our names in the long queue of the impatient waiting for a weekend table to open.

Two years to the day later, my brother and I, older, wiser and stone cold sober, walked into Mama V's and sat at the familiar restaurant bar. We ordered a beer from the bartender and then chatted about dinner plans. While talking, we noticed a photo of the guy who ran the place hanging behind the bar. In front of it, on a small wooden shelf, the flickering flame of a votive candle burned. That's not good, we worriedly agreed. Getting the attention of the bartender, we asked about the photo and learned that the man had died a month earlier in a traffic accident outside Gettysburg. We ordered a shot of whiskey and raised our glass to a man we did not know. Despite our rudeness to him, he had treated us with respect and as a valued customer. Humility is taught again and again in the strangest of ways.

Despite his death, the family work continues. Mama V's still serves good Italian food and, underneath in the dingy bar, the hard working owners and staff entertain college kids on Friday and Saturday evenings. As I have grown older and grayer and have more disposable income, I have opted to stay at the James Gettys Hotel downtown rather than the cheaper motels on the fringes of town. Because the hotel is right next to Mama V's, noise can be a problem. The kids leaving the bar at closing time are obnoxious and the live bands playing encores create enough of a disturbance to prompt visits from the Gettysburg police. My family and I have been awakened by the silliness and carrying on of these young carousers out on the town in the wee hours. One thing they'll never know is that I wasn't bothered one bit by the commotion. I've been in their shoes. As long as they aren't hurting anyone or recklessly driving a car, let them have fun. Live and let live. The good proprietor of Mama V's, God rest his soul, and a fine public servant going by the nickname Dawg were kind enough once to think that way of me.

$$* \quad * \quad * \quad *$$

Ghosts in the Snow

THE Farnsworth House in Gettysburg is an early nineteenth century farmstead converted to an inn and, as the establishment's brochure informs, named after a Michigan general killed during the late stages of the battle. He was sent to his certain death by an overly aggressive Judson Kilpatrick, a Union cavalry commander who had graduated in the infamous West Point Class of '61 with George Custer and Patrick O'Rorke.

Kilpatrick was one of an all too familiar breed of officer in the Union army. Selfish, bereft of personal discipline and morals, a loose disciplinarian and, worst of all, reckless with the precious lives of his men. This charlatan got it in his mind to clean up the remaining Confederate units wandering around the Confederate right flank after Pickett's division had been decimated on the third day's carnage at Cemetery Ridge. Ordering Farnsworth to attempt to take a very well defended position, Farnsworth wisely pointed out that the chance of success was slim and the spoils to be won in case of victory were not worth the casualties. "Kill Cavalry," a pejorative nickname Kilpatrick seems to have enjoyed, implied that Farnsworth just might be a yellow-bellied coward if he didn't do what he was told. So, as any military man whose honor has been challenged and possessing a conscience and a spine, Farnsworth sped headlong into futility and was gunned down in a murderous way with a reported five bullets found in his lifeless corpse. If any person who existed has a right to haunt the earth, it's this man. He's probably seeking revenge on one Judson Kilpatrick, the young, mutton-chopped butcher whose stupidity sent Farnsworth and a few others to an unnecessarily early grave.

ON most nights during the warmer seasons, a group of eager ghost aficionados collects around the front of the inn in preparation for one of Gettysburg's most frequented spooky tours. If people can't be intrigued in details of the largest battle ever fought on the continent of North America, I suppose the next trick is to scare them to death.

The Farnsworth House is a quarter of the way down Baltimore Street towards Lincoln Square, a hop and a skip from Cemetery Hill. The inn's side facing the slope is pockmarked with bullet holes from Union sharpshooters returning the fire of their Confederate counterparts who were once holed up in the attic of the now bustling bed and breakfast. Through a tiny window, they rammed minie balls down the long barrels of their Enfield rifled-muskets and popped away at blue capped heads bobbing up and down from dug in positions on the hill anywhere from 300 to 400 yards away. If one doubts the distance, pace it off. If one can't make it to Gettysburg, a cursory look at a map will confirm the range.

The irritated Federals, taking casualties while trying to eat, sleep or do other routine business, were only too eager to return the fire. The rifled-muskets available in 1863 were quite accurate, but a 400 yard hit on a head and upper body poking out of a two foot by two foot window is laudable. In fact, it's a really good shot. These guys weren't fooling around. Speaking as a guy who shot expert on both rifle and pistol in the U.S. Marines, I tip my hat to those boys in blue and gray banging away at each other up and down that narrow street.

Today, a bend in the road, trees and a large, multi-story hotel block the view. In 1863, a clear field of fire allowed this sidelight to the great battle going around them to play out. The irregular sniping was just a nuisance, perhaps, a minor distraction in a much larger event. But so much of the drama of Gettysburg was one individual facing another in a life and death struggle. The young men firing at each other in this serious game were an important microcosm of this broader, seminal affair.

In the chivalric fashion of the day, at least at Gettysburg, the combatants worked to keep the fight between soldiers. But, as in all wars, the inevitable impact on civilians could not be avoided. Miraculously, the resident population of Gettysburg came away relatively unscathed despite the events transpiring around them. Some were already far from the risk of injury, leaving their homes and traveling elsewhere for the security offered by relatives once the first Confederate troops marched into town. Those that remained behind, although scared and hungry, could shelter in dank basements away from singing bullets and bursting shells. Private property was indeed destroyed or commandeered for the use of both armies. But, civilian casualties were held to a minimum. In fact, the only civilian death at the battle of Gettysburg is attributed to a Confederate sniper either holed up in the Farnsworth attic or somewhere close.

At the start of the fight, the McClellan family had welcomed their relative, Mary Virginia "Jennie" Wade, to stay in safety with them at their brick house where Baltimore Street turns southeast and heads out of town. The larger group felt secure behind their sturdier walls and in closer proximity to the Federal lines. The fact that Federal officers were seen going in and out of McClellan's house caught the attention of one or more Confederate snipers paid to watch out for such things. The house became a target. Ms. Wade, believing she was safe inside, happened to be in the wrong place at the wrong time. As she baked bread for the hometown troops camped nearby, she caught an errant and unintended round that penetrated a door and then her back, killing her instantly. History records her as the only civilian casualty of the battle. One civilian killed? Considering 165,000 soldiers were banging away at each other for most of three days around the town, that statistic amazes.

THE Farnsworth House Ghost Tours, one of many spooky choices in Gettysburg, collect cash by luring a willing audience inside and frightening them with tales of spirits of the dead Confederate soldiers roaming the attic and house. The tours are led by a period actor dressed in Civil War garb and familiar with enough details to wow the crowd. On a warm September evening a few years back, jammed on stacked bleachers in the claustrophobic peaked garret space with the actor seated and narrating before us, my wife, my young son and I listened to the show. I am not enamored of such things and because of a lack of imagination can't see what other ghost spotters swear on a stack of bibles moan, groan and otherwise haunt all the nooks and crannies of the town. Occasional television documentaries focus on the subject of the ghosts of Gettysburg. Producers follow amateur photographers as they meander around the battlefield and snap pictures with expensive equipment. From all I can tell, what they capture is the same stuff one sees in the day only it's darker. They, however, claim some of the photos show wispy spectral figures abounding in final prints. Perhaps.

But, I am in my jaded forties. My then six year old son was far more impressionable. He sure bought every line of the story told on that September night in that spooky attic. Wriggling and uncomfortable next to us, confined in the midst of sweaty and tightly packed humanity, he jumped up and made his way forward. Free, he plopped himself down right next to the animated and amused narrator. We watched him, as did the others in the crowd, as his eyes grew wider and more petrified at every gruesome new turn to the tale.

The prospects of a pale, gray uniformed apparition clomping by at any moment grew ever more likely to him. He was not in the slightest bit interested in seeing that. At some particularly important part of the story, our son looked at us and, paying the utmost respect towards the rest of the crowd listening to the story, signaled urgently with his hands while silently mouthing the words "I want to go downstairs, NOOOOWW!" The kind people in the few rows in front of us chuckled. With a gentle tap on their shoulders, they parted and allowed us to squeeze past. We picked up our petrified progeny and hurried downstairs NOOOOWW for a breath of fresh air in the alley outside. There we eventually managed to convince him that he was in good hands and safe from a prowling Confederate wraith.

THE Farnsworth House is also where I spent one frigid and snowy weekend in February. My incurious fiancé was at my side. Let me clarify. She's not at all lacking in curiosity, she's just not that enamored with the Civil War. She puts up with my fanaticism and has survived several visits to the battlefield. I keep telling her that at least I am not a reenactor and don't require her to wear a hooped skirt when we travel. However, if she had been given the choice, she would not select Gettysburg, Pennsylvania as a top ten location to spend winter break.

Gettysburg's Convention and Visitors Bureau employees are aware that Civil War buffs sometimes drag along a spouse of relative that simply is not interested in anything related to the battle. Responding to demand, they do a commendable job of coordinating other forms of entertainment. Organizers periodically hold barn dances, antique shows and sales and apple harvest festivals. These events do wonders to palliate the potential marital stress that arises when one spouse or partner, usually the man, drags the other spouse, usually the woman, into town to see the sights. In February, though, the list of alternative things to do in Gettysburg is short.

With the weight of evidence far away in her favor, I still managed to convince her that it would be fun to stop there and dangled a preparatory two day visit to Washington, D.C. as bait. On the way home from D.C., passing through Gettysburg, on Route 15 of course, we opted for a first time visit to the Farnsworth House. It was cold and snowy. In fact, Washington had seen a five or six inch snowfall. We Rochesterians, used to over 100 inches of the white stuff annually, marveled at how poorly a city like Washington is prepared to handle that type of precipitation. Watching a speeding fire truck hit a patch of ice and move sideways down Connecticut Avenue convinced us to stay off Washington's streets until order was restored. Nature and the hard work of civil servants slowly cleared the streets. We were free to head back north to our prearranged rendezvous with our Farnsworth hosts.

LATE in the afternoon, we checked into the mostly empty inn as the cloud blanketed sun was setting and a tundra wind was blowing. We were assigned the Custer Room which was well appointed and comfy and included a gas fireplace. Naturally, being the Custer Room, a few rustic western prints decorated the walls. Over the bed, George Armstrong, along with the remnants of his decimated Seventh Cavalry command, was getting his just desserts from a group of agitated looking Sioux and Cheyenne. On another wall, a frightened family out for a winter's sleigh ride was being chased by a pack of wolves nipping at the horses flanks and eyeing the terrified human morsels above them. Native Americans, dead or dying cavalrymen, wolves and scalping were themes appropriate for the room but my fiancé thought them creepy. Nevertheless, she slept comfortably and reported in the morning that she had only occasionally opened one eye to confirm no scalping or mauling was taking place.

We awoke bright and early to take in the breakfast part of the bed and breakfast. Outside, the storm raged on. After we ate, we suited up in winter garb. The plan was to head out into the weather for an eight mile self-guided and narrated stroll. The only way to see the battlefield, in my astute opinion, is to walk it. So walk it we did.

The saga began with us shuffling up Baltimore Street towards Lincoln Square and then out to the Lutheran Seminary and McPherson's Ridge. There I gave Jill the lowdown on the first day's battle. She nodded patronizingly as she squinted through horizontally blowing ice pellets at the barely visible monuments lining the ridge ahead of us. From there, we turned back, walking past the Lutheran Seminary, its famous cupola covered in a steadily piling layer of white, and out to Seminary Ridge near the North Carolina Monument. The weather was getting worse. The snow piled deeper.

SPANNING the low rise of Seminary Ridge, Confederate troops of Pickett's, Trimble's and Pettigrew's divisions, picked from both A.P. Hill's Third and James Longstreet's First Confederate Corps, sat hiding in the woods preparing for the infamous assault that history chose to place solely on one man's shoulders. Pickett's unsullied division had arrived fresh to Gettysburg the previous evening and its commander was itching to get it into the fight. Lee knew just what to do with it.

In an elongated, shallow depression, lorded over by a thick canopy of oaks and maples, the anxious masses nervously waited for the end of their side's artillery bombardment on the Union line about three quarters of a mile east across the rolling fields. Like soldiers told a tale so many times in the past and those who will be told the same story so many times to come, those frightened men and boys surely tried to reassure one another that the artillery would do its job. It would obliterate the enemy where he lay. The only thing the infantry would have to do is march smartly right up to their lines and mop up the few remaining stragglers. The only other bigger lie told in war is that the whole darn thing would be over by Christmas.

The artillery, as the cannoneers drew down supplies and held remaining ammunition so as to support the assault, became quiet all at once. In the new silence, the waiting troops were hustled to their feet and hurried to formation to step off toward the Union center located on the ridge beyond.

SHIVERING, my fiancé listened to me pontificate on the critical tactical importance of this location. I also touched briefly on the controversy within the Confederate brain trust just prior to the failed assault. The key players in that saga were the commander of the army and his loyal man "Old Pete" Longstreet.

James Longstreet, the bearded and talented strategist, familiar to his loyal lieutenants in a slouch hat with a cigar dangling from his mouth, was lovingly known as Lee's war horse. Longstreet leveraged Lee's familiarity almost to insubordination on that Friday afternoon, warning the commanding general that no 15,000 men ever arrayed for battle could take the Federal position.

He realized that the army was deep in Union territory and, while quite successful so far at giving the Federals a lashing, was adamant against a bold offensive operation with a force badly bruised as well. At most, Longstreet urged, Lee should consider another flanking movement to the Union left. Lee had his mind set. Some say angina and fatigue were too much for the old soldier that day. Whatever the case, he should have listened to his war horse. Something bad was about to happen and everyone at Gettysburg could sense it; all but the man who had worked miracles with this army. His tough-as-nails boys had never let him down before and they would not do so today. Plus, he had a fresh division of Virginians to rely on. Lee, emboldened by the success of the first day's battle and the near success of his forces on the second, could not pull himself away from the opportunity to defeat the Army of the Potomac on its own ground.

Things likely would have turned out differently for the army if Stonewall Jackson was there. Jackson, Lee's right hand man, his useless left arm sawed off at the shoulder by a surgeon after being shattered by friendly fire in the confusion of a moonlit night at Chancellorsville, had faded and died of pneumonia shortly thereafter. In the short period since, the old man was less sure of himself. He was subdued and cautious to the point of error, his confidence eroded by the loss of the steady and reliable Jackson. He leaned heavily on "Old Pete" for military counsel. But here on Seminary Ridge, after two days of brutal fighting, the old man brushed aside Longstreet's prudent advice.

The charge, which the Marines term as "hey, diddle, diddle, right up the middle" was supposed to be a coordinated assault with another Confederate corps assaulting the Union right at Culp's Hill and East Cemetery Hill. Meanwhile, J.E.B. Stuart, who had eventually arrived on the field from his grand escapade, was tasked with the third prong in the plan and asked to harass the Federal rear. But, as in many plans and in many wars in the past, when the guns boomed the whole thing quickly fell apart. The assault on the Union right petered out, Stuart's jab was stunted by Union cavalry and the men of Pickett's and Pettigrew's and Trimble's divisions were on their own. The brilliant Lee, the wizard who had vexed the Army of the Potomac since the Peninsula Campaign, was committed to this lone and futile effort.

Out of the trees, the 13,000 men in the three divisions plodded on. In front of them, prone men in blue, shaken but mostly surviving an intense ninety minute artillery bombardment, waited to deliver revenge for the slaughter they had suffered eight months ago at Fredericksburg.

SCHOOL kids, tourists, buffs and historians have long believed that the famous Copse of Trees was the focus of the Confederate assault that day. A recent body of evidence has come to light that contradicts conventional wisdom. The argument is simply that, in 1863, the famous group of trees was too small to be seen from Seminary Ridge and that Lee actually pointed towards the much more visible and elevated wooded mass at Ziegler's Grove for the focus of the attack. No matter. On our winter's foray, neither Ziegler's Grove, the famous Copse of Trees nor the equally famous

Angle formed by adjoined stone fences nearby were evident to us.

I decided to show my partner exactly what those soldiers experienced. We set off to walk across the field as those soldiers did. "I don't think it was snowing this hard when they attacked," my fiancé snidely remarked. I answered with an equally flippant response. "Marines spell the word "tough" as d-u-m-b," I reminded her. She laughed. "There?" she queried as she pointed to the foggy distance. "Yep," I replied. Off we went across the wintry plain. Nothing was visible ahead.

THE wind whipped the snow around us as we walked in the footsteps of the men of Pickett's Division. Not really. We hadn't gone that far down Seminary Ridge to the place where the Virginians had kicked off their part of the assault. Most strollers, thinking they are recreating Pickett's Charge, are actually taking the well worn footpath along which Isaac Trimble's North Carolinians made their way across to the Union line. Even with a significant layer of snow on the normally flattened, well worn ground, that route was still discernable.

In the distance, the tall and imposing monuments to Union army greatness now guarding Cemetery Ridge were lost in the blowing and drifting whiteness. Reveling in the exhilarating experience, I sprinted ahead while my fiancé trudged in my footprints left behind. The snow was collecting knee deep and walking became an exertion. Alone, I ambled through an opening in the rail fence, crossed the unplowed and empty Emmitsburg Road and mounted the gentle slope to Cemetery Ridge popping out of the soup at the obelisk dedicated to the relatively small number of regular U.S. Army units that fought at Gettysburg.

MOST of the Federal units on the field that day were volunteer infantry, a kind of National Guard or Reserve of the day. It's only a fairly recent thing that America has kept a regular standing army in peacetime. Throughout most of its history, the American regular army, Marines, or navy for that matter, were tiny cohorts of underpaid professionals ignored until a threat to national security raised its head.

In the twentieth century, until the Japanese attack on Pearl Harbor, the numbers of Americans serving in the armed forces sat at a paltry seventeenth on the list of the world's military forces. That changed almost overnight. A pre-World War II force consisting of about 200,000 active duty members and about an equal number of reserve forces was transformed into a force of sixteen million men and women in uniform by war's end. Most of those service people were reservists. To a society that is used to an active and quite competent regular armed force as we are today, it seems odd to not have one well armed, trained and ready to deploy if needed.

With the advent of intercontinental ballistic missiles and the threat of an immediate strike on American interests in foreign lands, the United States no longer had the luxury of long periods of preparation and mobilization to bring the armed services up to required strengths. Technology has shrunk vast oceans and compressed expansive air miles. Today, unlike 1863, American relies on a much larger and permanent active duty military and a reserve force that stands ready to go to war with very short notice.

When the first shots of the Civil War were fired at Fort Sumter, a call for volunteers in the northern states was answered with gusto. Thousands of inexperienced and ignorant boys and men gathered in temporary camps and put on fancy new uniforms and learned how to march. So too was the call answered in southern cities as men crowded at public gathering points to join up with a forming unit and defend the interests of their state.

Serving in the Marines as regular officers or regular enlisted, we tended to look down at the part-timers as inferior. Even though they wore the same uniform and served the same country, they did so only on weekends for a stretch in the summer. When they showed up in the field for active duty training, the stories of their inexperience were legend. Nothing could be further from the truth. In recent American wars in Iraq and Afghanistan, American reservists have, despite an unfair reputation, done a fantastic job fighting for the national interests.

As today, the American volunteer, at Gettysburg and many other battlefields of the Civil War, was the largest contributor to the fight. Those buoyant youths, joined at the hip with a band of hometown buddies, committed to ninety day, nine month or two year enlistments. When their time was up, these part-timers, having seen enough of the horror of war and the incompetence of their leaders, were quick to throw off their uniforms and head home. Volunteers still made up the bulk of the forces but the government had to sweeten the pot to encourage men to join. Cash payments took care of that for a time. Waving a bounty in front of an impoverished lad's face was sometimes too tempting to refuse. When the supply of free or paid volunteers dwindled, the War Department was left with no choice but to institute an involuntary draft to help fill the ranks. High casualty rates and the battlefield disasters befalling Union military efforts stymied interest in serving for purely patriotic reasons. It is one thing to join for a neat uniform, camping and a lark. It is another to be mowed down by cannon fire or walls of lead marching elbow to elbow in a direct frontal assault. The word got around quickly and by the time armies marched to Gettysburg either greed or coercion supplanted altruism as the primary motivation to serve.

I paid homage to my brother regulars at the monument dedicated to them and glanced back to see where my partner had gotten off to. I could see her safely across the Emmitsburg Road, coming along in my rapidly filling tracks. Confident in her safety, I continued on the now deeply covered paved Park Road toward Little Round Top where I would lecture her on the details of the battle's second day. As far as I could tell, we were the only two idiots on the battlefield. The very few others who had chosen to stop at Gettysburg that weekend were wisely holed up in a bookstore or tavern, waiting out the weather.

I maneuvered along Hancock and Sedgwick Avenues, climbing the paved road leading up to Little Round Top from the dip in Cemetery Ridge. It was midday but the heavy cloud cover and swirling precipitation made it seem like evening. The normally expansive view from the rocky peak of Little Round Top was limited to the bared trees nearby and I could only partially make out the ever vigilant statue of Gouverneur K. Warren perched on a flat rock.

That foresighted man, General Meade's Chief of Engineers, scouted out Little Round Top prior to the real fight getting underway on the second day. Seeing it unoccupied by anything other than a lone Union signals unit flapping red and white flags to distant stations, he realized that a Confederate force on top could flank the entire Union army and threaten their tenuous line on Cemetery Ridge. Warren quickly directed nearby Federal units up to the top to remedy the situation and just in the nick of time. A Confederate assault on that part of the Union line was already underway.

I was eager to relay this information to my fiancé but I couldn't quite see where she was. Knowing her as I did and confident in her survival skills, I still deferred to my instincts and trudged back down the hill to see what was keeping her. Along the way, a half mile or so closer to the Round Tops than where I had initially detached from her, I met up with a car moving slowly. The vehicle was disobeying the one-way park road signs and headed in my direction. Seeing me emerge from the gloom, the car stopped. Its rapidly moving windshield wipers were not doing a very good job keeping the gobs of heavy snow clear. The driver rolled down his window. "Looking for someone?" he queried. I nodded and at the same time noticed my future spouse in the front passenger seat. She appeared cold, wet and irritated.

Discretion being the better part of valor, I thanked the kind stranger while assuring my partner that the hike was done. I threw her a bone and offered to buy her lunch. I lied. There was still a hike left back to town but at least she could see the end in sight.

On we trudged, passing again the most well known Cemetery Ridge monuments. In a little over a mile, we stopped at the Dobbin House Tavern. Still in heavy winter boots, we clomped down the entry steps into the warm and inviting underground restaurant and bar. There, with just the two of us and the bartender and waitress in the dark, candle lit and normally overflowing dining area, we stripped off our winter duds and sat down next to a roaring fire for a nice bowl of piping hot French onion soup and a cup of coffee. The winter tour of the battlefield at Gettysburg had officially ended.

There was far more to see on East Cemetery and Culp's Hills but a team of artillery horses could not drag my fiancé out of the tavern. Unlike a typical, jammed, chaotic summer day, the waitress and her co-worker had plenty of time on their hands. We conversed about the unseasonable weather this far south and what a novelty it is for Gettysburg to experience such a heavy snowfall. Their eyes widened a bit when we relayed that Rochester, in the lee of Lake Ontario, is routinely dumped on during the winter by persistent lake effect snow bands. It can be sunny and bare ground in one spot and a raging blizzard half a mile down the road.

They, like the staff at the Farnsworth House and the other places we popped in that wintry weekend, weren't so busy and had time to smile and chat and demonstrate the friendliness that is an admirable but often hidden character of the residents of this service oriented borough.

We stayed longer than we otherwise would have, toasty, snug and full of good food. We enjoyed the company of strangers and let the time pass in front of the fire before we reluctantly bundled up for the walk back to Farnsworth House for a well deserved winter's nap.

(Detroit Publishing Co.)

High Water Mark of the Confederacy

In reality, the Confederate army ranged far to the north of this spot at Gettysburg. This solemn monument marks the symbolic high tide of the rebellion and is the rise on which General Robert E. Lee wrecked the Army of Northern Virginia. With the army went the hopes for an independent Confederate States of America. This sorrowful place is where I reacquainted myself with the battlefield after a long hiatus. Over eight years separated a middle school trip in 1976 and the diversion on my way to my first active duty military station. In one later winter visit, I noted the High Water Mark is hushed and hauntingly beautiful when covered in a layer of snow.

Alexander Gardner

Subsumed in the shadow of his former boss, Matthew Brady, Gardner's genius was ultimately revealed via his portrait work. No one captured the majesty of Abraham Lincoln like this man did. He has been criticized for faking battlefield scenes in order to create more dramatic photographs. Despite that, his work is hailed as a precious, unparalleled film record of the American Civil War.

(Alexander Gardner. Library of Congress)

Gettysburg Lincoln – 1863

Enlarged using computers and photo analysis technology, this portrait of Lincoln fascinates. Note the lazy left eye. Lincoln, emboldened by victories at Gettysburg and Vicksburg, is at his best in this Gardner portrait. George Hinkel copied it exactly. The most brilliant speech in American history would be given by this iconic figure a few weeks later at Gettysburg.

(Alexander Gardner. Library of Congress)

Cracked Glass Plate Lincoln – 1865

What a difference a year and a few months make. This is a man who bears the weight of 600,000 corpses on his shoulders. Some say he would have been dead of natural causes if not shot in the head by John Wilkes Booth in April, a few months after this photo is believed to have been taken. Despite his obvious fatigue, a wisp of a smile on his lips can be detected. The end of the slaughter was in sight.

"The Dragon" – New Buffalo, PA

When the dragon appears in your front windshield, the Horseshoe bar isn't far away. The Horseshoe is a working man's hangout and a good place to have a beer while one waits until Harrisburg Friday evening traffic clears. And, by all means, smoke 'em if you've got 'em.

(Author)

High School Cinematic High Jinks – 1979

A grainy still exposure taken from one frame of a Super 8 negative. This homemade Civil War extravaganza was the prelude to George Hinkel's Film Studies opus. The producers, directors and actors in this film did not give much thought to the danger to which we exposed ourselves. We all survived. The film did not. This and a few other shots are all that remain.

(Heintzelman Sales via CardCow.com)

Fry Bros. Turkey Ranch Restaurant

Now no longer a few dangerous feet off Route 15 as this old photo shows, Fry Bros. is still the place to stop, relax and have a good meal before getting back on the road. As one approaches Trout Run, Pennsylvania, jump off the shiny new and ready-made exit dedicated to those with a hankering for the place. Set your tired body down and enjoy a plate of sliced turkey, gravy, stuffing, mashed potatoes and cranberry sauce served on a table and eaten with utensils. It beats a fast food burger any day.

Ambrose E. Burnside

Those in his charge at Antietam, Fredericksburg and in a crater near Petersburg, Virginia, wish he would have picked another occupation. At Antietam, he was incapable of taking the initiative to get his men across a narrow, shallow creek to establish a bridgehead on the other side. Instead he threw them into a shooting gallery. A few months later at Fredericksburg, he directed bloody and failed assaults on an impregnable position. Many more today indirectly know about his famous sideburns than care about his hapless performances on battlefields.

(Library of Congress)

Winfield Scott Hancock

The true warrior leader of the Army of the Potomac at Gettysburg. He won the moniker "Hancock the Superb" on the Peninsula. At Gettysburg, as George Meade administered to the army, Hancock brilliantly conducted the fight. His equestrian statue rules over the East Cemetery Hill, the place where he brought order to chaos after the first day's battle (see cover). But, it could have rightfully been placed anywhere on Cemetery Ridge. The statue is awe-inspiring in the cloud scattered light of the moon.

(Alexander Gardner. Library of Congress)

Execution of the Lincoln Conspirators

One can almost feel the blast furnace heat and feel the raspy hemp on necks in this Gardner treasure, one of a series he took of the event. The soldier standing below waiting for the order to remove the support is visibly ill. He leans against the post and suffers. Despite a belief that no woman would die at the hands of a hangman, the only woman conspirator - Mary Surratt - hooded and bound like her male counterparts, dropped to her death moments after this photo was taken.

Young Lion of the West

One of four frames of a 1906 panoramic view of a vibrant and growing city. The broad Genesee River flows northward and crosses under the Erie Canal aqueduct and then under the built-up Main Street Bridge. Look closely, this is a city that hums. Rochester is nothing like that today.

Smugtown – 1964

Police and firefighters attempt to gain control of a riot torn neighborhood in Rochester. The chaos erupted as a result of economic and social divisions brought on by a somnambulant and ignorant population. The result: a city is wrecked. White flight to the suburbs and to the Sun Belt, already underway anyway, accelerated after this hot summer of 1964. Rochester never recovered from it. Today blacks and whites in the metro are more segregated than they have been in their history.

Frederick Douglass

His iconic name is now plastered all over Rochester, the city from which his national reputation was made. Douglass capitalized on the region's religious fervor to peacefully advance his political and social goals. His body lies, aptly, in pastoral Mount Hope Cemetery, near the desolate northern terminus of Route 15.

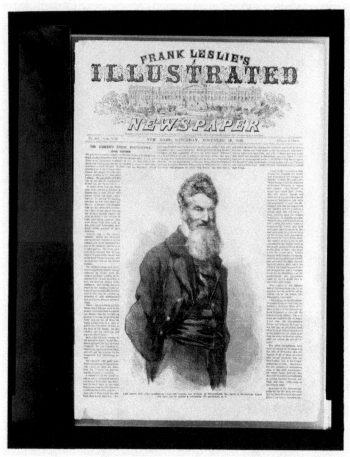

John Brown

If one didn't know him, one would think him mad. In a sense he was. John Brown was Frederick Douglass' alter ego. A man of action, he preferred the sword over the pen and was hanged for it. He produced twenty children; literally his own private army.

Joshua Chamberlain

The modern, popular hero of Gettysburg; made so by Michael Shaara's novel *The Killer Angels* and its 1993 cinematic interpretation *Gettysburg*. Chamberlain survived the battle and the Civil War and, thus, was able to polish his already Teflon coated reputation. His leadership of the 20th Maine at Little Round Top and his unorthodox but hugely successful tactics there are still studied and admired today.

Patrick O'Rorke

The bullet to his neck at Little Round Top ensured that others would have to advocate for him. "Paddy" lies in the ground in Rochester in a cemetery down the road from a brand new bridge with his name on it. His quick thinking and bravery saved the Union army on the second day at Gettysburg. His last sight on earth was of Confederates swarming in the Valley of Death and up the slope of Little Round Top.

Daniel E. Sickles

It's hard to imagine a life more exciting or tumultuous than his. Sickles' actions at Gettysburg are the subject of endless debate. His decision to push out to the Emmitsburg Road contrary to orders bled the Confederates dry as waves assaulted his soon to be wrecked Third Army Corps. Severely injured on the field, Gettysburg was his final military hurrah. Sickles is one of two Union corps commanders not recognized with a statue at that shrine-rich place.

(GettysburgDaily.com)

Paddy's Lucky Nose

The National Park Service asks that visitors not deface battlefield monuments. Thousands ignore the requests and rub Paddy's nose every year giving it a brilliant, golden sheen.

Chapter 4

NORTHERN TERMINUS

"Rochester is for us, who don't know it at all, a city of any time or country, moonlight, filled with lovers hovering over piano-fortes. A city of handsome streets wrapped in beautiful quiet and dreaming of the golden age."

- William Dean Howells -

"I dearly hope I am never fated to live in Rochester."

– Simone Beauvoir -

✹　✹　✹　✹

Young Lion of the West

CIVIC pride burns in the hearts of the boosters of the too many decaying whistle-stops that straddle or sit beside the New York and Pennsylvania stretches of Route 15. Better days for these blighted burgs are long past. Dansville, Painted Post, Mansfield, Williamsport, Duncannon and Marysville devotees, far from alone among a dreary and substantial number of other blighted places, still carry the dimming torch and grasp at tatters of community pride. The fire still crackles intensely in the hearts of some who live in and around my beloved hometown of Rochester. Rochester's blood is in my veins. It is the city in which I was born and the city to which I willingly returned after my hitch in the Marines.

This once rollicking Erie Canal port holds the distinction of being the northern terminus of now fractured U.S. Route 15. Before interstate superhighways crisscrossed America, the northern run of the road took strangers to this "big city" and dumped them off in a bustling downtown. It still performs that function but does so now as a less urbane, uninviting gateway.

Picking up city street names as it crosses the southern metropolitan boundary, Route 15 transitions to West Henrietta Road. Slicing straight through an insipid southern Rochester suburb of the same name, it doffs its rural mantle revealing a congested strip of car dealerships, restaurants, plazas and box retailers. Welcome to Gemerica; that predictable, generic four-lane eyesore that is indistinguishable from countless others found in any city in the United States. Usually near a university, an airport or a business park, the Gemerican thoroughfare is tailored for rapid movement of cars and trucks and treats people as the body's immune system treats viruses. Pedestrians are unwelcome here.

A few miles north, West Henrietta Road's ugliness morphs into Mount Hope Avenue. That street is unable to shake off Route 15's bland character as it slips past more commercial nothingness. Next, it parallels the gargantuan, industrial park-looking complex of the University of Rochester's Medical Center. All is not lost, though. For a brief stretch anyway, Mount Hope, having left the boxy piles of the medical center campus behind, begins to parallel the hilly and leafy setting of a large and quite beautiful cemetery.   In and around the graveyard, sidewalks, trees and attractive residences line both sides of the road and provide the traveler with something other than mini-marts, parking lots and fast food restaurants on which to gaze.

Over 350,000 dead are interred in Mount Hope Cemetery's rolling grounds. It is a telling statistic that the dead inhabiting this necropolis greatly outnumber the living and breathing people residing in the city. Within Mount Hope's spiky wrought iron fences; the Victorian era gothic crematoria, worn and mossy stone monuments and garage sized crypts draw the neighborhood curious. Joggers, bikers and strollers frequent the paved roads and trails and take advantage of its park-like solitude.   Under the stately oaks and pines of Mount Hope's canopy, historians, school kids as well as the thoughtful anonymous place small stones and decorative remembrances on or next to the markers set over the remains of Rochester's renowned freedom fighters; Frederick Douglass and Susan B. Anthony.

This pastoral slice of Route 15 is bluntly cut short as the road descends into the center city of Rochester itself. Planed flat now as it nears the high cement flood control walls holding back the Genesee River, the road passes a new multi-dwelling public housing project, a gaudily painted public housing tower, abandoned and crumbling commercial fronts and weedy open lots sitting on the river's banks.

Just at the fringe of the city's small, compact core, Route 15 meets and joins an unattractive bundle of unsightly overpasses rising from a paved, lightly traveled moonscape. Enmeshed in that loathsome urban can of worms, it works its way out, crossing over I-490 and an ill conceived concrete moat known as the Inner Loop built to move traffic at a time when the city was more heavily populated and bustling. It now lies mostly unused. In its last few hundred yards, posing as South Clinton Avenue, Route 15 cruises underneath a misleadingly artistic welcoming sign and into a once vibrant but now sparsely visited downtown. There it dies at Washington Square Park. This small grassy and shady rectangle has as its centerpiece the Soldiers and Sailors Monument. The statue is an interesting, dramatic slab of rock and metal sporting a cylindrical pedestal on top of which stands, oddly, not our first president but a pensive Abraham Lincoln.

Futile have been the many attempts at rejuvenation of a city one can literally hold in the palm of one's hand. It once boasted street cars, packed sidewalks, shopping, restaurants, nightlife and a lively business and residential mix. Theater marquees lit the night and a taxi could be hailed at the curb.

The white flight of the 1960s and 1970s to Rochester's suburbs along with the inexorable migration of mobile, weather weary northeasterners to the Sunbelt ate away at Rochester's once lofty population of 350,000. Those leaving the city but staying in the area preferred free parking at suburban malls, better schools and the tranquility of new neighborhoods with houses spaced apart. Like Detroit, Buffalo, Pittsburgh and Cleveland, Rochester bled population and now barely contains 200,000 souls living within city limits. Those that remain are predominantly black and poor. Immigration and births in Rochester couldn't then, and can't now, keep pace with the diaspora.

At the terminus of Route 15, where South Clinton Avenue cuts into Woodbury Boulevard, the urban landscape is devoid of the round-the-clock hum of life and commerce. The tick of the clock to closing time sees the city's office towers empty and cars flooding out of ramp garages and parking slots with the sidewalks rolling up conveniently behind them.

One of America's first boomtowns, Rochester is a shadow of that nineteenth century hub of limitless energy and ideas. It baffles visitors when they are told that this place was once so cutting edge it dared call itself the "Young Lion of the West." Here the very word entrepreneur could have been coined as freewheelers, inventors and risk takers milled about Rochester's streets. The westward migrating population of America stopped and settled here on the frontier to take advantage of the river's power, access to the canal and cheap, plentiful farmland which, unlike New England, was free of plow denting rocks. In fact, early Rochester once lorded over a tiny and insignificant midwestern backwater known as Chicago.

Early in the nineteenth century, millers capitalized on the fast moving Genesee River, channeling it over enormous water wheels which transferred river energy to gristmills. Those enterprises lining busy millraces ground wheat into high quality flour providing Rochester with another fitting nickname: the Flour City. Teamsters, stevedores and money men loaded the product on canal boats teeming on the nearby Erie Canal and barely kept up with the demand of millions of eager purchasers waiting on the Atlantic seaboard and beyond.

THE Library of Congress holds in its collection a remarkable panoramic view of the once fair city. It was taken in late spring or early summer of 1906. Then, Rochester was on an upward trajectory. The connected photos are taken later in the morning with the shadows cast westward. Trees are fully leaved and green. The camera looks south down the length of busy South Avenue and to the upriver course of the muddy Genesee. The scene pans northward, looking west down the length of Court Street and, finally, northwest to the heart of the city to the packed and smoky Four Corners. Rows of tenements and businesses hang precariously from the bridge carrying Main Street over the river.

Transportation is highlighted in this rare view of early twentieth century life in Rochester. The Erie and Lehigh Valley railroad stations hum on opposite sides of the river. At the time, they and three other rail lines served the city, whisking passengers and freight to all destinations. Both terminals are bustling with customers waiting to board the trains idly puffing at the stations' platforms.

The Erie Canal passing by the storefronts on South Avenue leaves the photo in the foreground and then reappears bending languidly around to the west and passing over the river within the walls of its amazing aqueduct. No boats are on it the day the photo was taken. That makes sense.   Competing rail transport had already stuck a stake in the economic heart of the American canal.

The engineering marvel of its day, the Erie Canal aqueduct today no longer holds canal water as it crosses over the Genesee River.   The municipal brain trust, doing what other forward thinking civic visionaries have done, put a road on top of it. Currently, this architectural gem is now hidden by the arches and concrete streetscape of Broad Street.   In the years after this photo was taken, the Erie Canal was rerouted to travel well south of the city. The empty aqueduct and canal bed presented a challenge for a growing city's planners.   Thinking Rochester would keep its position as one of America's most populous cities; the old canal route was engineered to carry the single line track of Rochester's short-lived subway.

Parallel to the Erie Canal aqueduct and pointing like an arrow outward in the center of the photo is Court Street carried by its bridge across the flood of the Genesee. Shiny twin street car rails line its surface.   The Kimball Tobacco Factory's brick bulk takes up the space just to the right on the opposite bank.   On top of its ornamental spire sits a riveted bronze statue of winged Mercury, symbolizing commerce and the prosperity of the city far below. After Kimball's products fell out of favor, Cluett Peabody took over the space and set up manufacture of collars and shirts. When that business faltered, the empty hulk was torn down and became the current site of the civic arena.

The Rochester Community War Memorial, until its expansion and renovation in the 1990s, was a diminutive horseshoe shaped structure barely squeezing in 7,000 seats for indoor sports and only a few more folding chairs for concerts. For a brief time, it was the home of the Rochester Royals, Rochester's only major professional sports team. The Royals won the NBA title in 1951 beating the New York Knickerbockers and moved into the War Memorial in 1955. But glancing into the crystal ball and gazing at Rochester a few years down the road, the moneymen behind the venture saw little future. After giving the city its sole major league sports title, the Royals packed their bags and moved to Cincinnati, then Kansas City and finally ended up in California as the Sacramento Kings. Rochester was now permanently minor league.

Across from the thick walled and steel framed arena, which also served as a civil defense shelter during the age when Soviet atomic bombs and missiles were a threat, sits Rochester's gulag-like Civic Center. This utilitarian collection of cement squares houses the county jail, the court system and several public service agencies. It is a glaring example of what planners should avoid when renewing urban centers. Its drab and uninspired style would fit just as well in 1960s East Berlin as in downtown Rochester. Soviet style apartment blocks have equal allure. Rows of quiet streets and pretty houses were torn down and carted to the dump in order to erect this monstrosity.

Demolition also cleared blocks of quirky and seedy stores and apartments on Front Street and the admittedly shabby tenements hanging precariously over the sides of the Main Street Bridge. Such destruction in the name of progress chipped away at the brick architectural originality that gave Rochester its very own unique municipal shape. The panoramic photo captures that fast disappearing, gritty industrial and energetic character sandwiched between the cascading falls at Court Street and the higher, more dramatic ninety foot High Falls just out of sight to the north. The center city of one of America's early twentieth century metropolises pulses. Church steeples and smokestacks jut up here and there. The twelve story Powers Building, topped with an oversized and barely ruffling American flag, towers above the rest. It is the most imposing structure in the growing city.

That growth continued even when the Erie Canal became a stagnant ditch, antiquated by the railroads and slowly filling with the detritus of a people too busy to care. And busy they were. Industry was Rochester's new course; its reason to live.

At the tail end of the nineteenth century, George Eastman's Dry Plate Company had whitewashed the brand Kodak in bold letters across the frontages of its factories and office buildings. Assembly lines churned out cameras and film which were mailed back to Kodak for development and printing. Eastman bestowed the gift of one-click photography on the average citizen who could simply press a button while Kodak did the rest.

Eastman's deep pockets stoked Rochester's early philanthropic fire too. The generous patron handed out millions to local charities, social programs, cultural institutions and colleges and universities. But time and disease took its toll. The aged and infirm Eastman, the man who had revolutionized photography in his adopted city, cloistered in his East Avenue mansion. Fearing his remaining days would be spent in a wheel chair, one day in 1932 he triggered a single gunshot into his own heart. Perhaps also haunted with a vision of what his city was to become, Eastman's suicide note resignedly told all who cared to listen "[m]y work is done. Why wait?"

In the wake of Eastman's blazed photographic trail, Joe Wilson's Xerox came along and brought to market Chester Carlson's electric photography process. Mass produced and simplified, the new office management technology refashioned the way the world did business. While Kodak and Xerox were building empires, Bausch and Lomb introduced cutting edge optical products for the world. The "Big Three" in Rochester created an environment that bred innovation and growth, similar to the impact high tech companies have today on Silicon Valley or the Carolina Triangle. Rochester's industry was world renowned. Its reputation even leaked into fiction as Sam Wainwright, by telephone, almost convinces Jimmy Stewart's character George Bailey to move to Rochester to take a job in his plastics factory there in the 1946 movie classic *It's a Wonderful Life*. "Rochester? Why Rochester?" asks Bailey. Wainwright responds, "Why not?"

But, in a story told in other manufacturing based cities in America, Rochester was victimized by newer technologies and the shift of labor to cheaper, less regulated nations worldwide. Xerox, although still a sizeable employer in town, moved its headquarters to Connecticut in the 1970s. Kodak, which at its peak employed 65,000 people in Rochester, failed to exploit its self-invented digital camera technology. It milked its dwindling prospects from film dry. At last count, Kodak employs fewer than 8,000 in the area and is operating under Chapter 11 Federal bankruptcy protection brought on by a severely degraded revenue stream and poor cash flow. The value of the company to shareholders now comes primarily from the patents Kodak holds and not the company's potential for growth. Kodak Park, once one of the largest manufacturing facilities in the world, has dramatically shrunk in size as Kodak bean counters order buildings imploded or otherwise demolished to take the unused and unnecessary real estate off the tax rolls.

Despite the transition, loyalists with strong family roots stick here. Rochester remains a sizeable metropolitan statistical area with over one million people in the city and surrounding counties. But because that population is static, the Flower City slowly declines in relative influence to other more dynamic areas that steal the spotlight and the political clout. Gutted and bleeding from the trauma of fading industry, enervated by the gloom of endlessly gray winters and kept down by its inability to break the hold of a downward pulling vortex, Rochester barely plods along.

Just north of Route 15's urban end, past the ebony and featureless rectangular mass of Rochester's 440 foot Xerox Tower, the tallest in the city, a pile of debris and bare iron skeletons are all that remains of a once innovative indoor mall, a first in America. Once known as Midtown Plaza, its demolition at the time of this writing is underway. City blocks of a once teeming place are being torn down to make way for redevelopment. Egged on by the grandiose dreams of a businessman and a handshake promise to construct his company's world headquarters on a shovel-ready site, the plans vanished in a flash when he sold his company to a bargain bidder. Midtown is presently nothing more than cleared land, piles of rubble and the skeletal frames of buildings that could, if the spirit and the money will it, be something again someday. But like the other New York and Pennsylvania cities that have seen better days, there is more hope in Rochester than anything else.

On a summer evening, one can wander the streets with friends at one's side, enjoying one of the many festivals whose food and entertainment tents spring up overnight with the advent of pleasant weather. Then it is much easier to bask in the sense that the community is one big project away from restoration to greatness. But summer in these northern climes is short and soon departs in a hurry giving way to the blustery, chill wind and perpetually battleship gray skies of winter.

Reuters, in an October 2011 article on the social impact of Kodak's demise on Rochester, called the residents who have watched the giant tumble "weary and resilient." That characterization seems overly optimistic. Those that depended on Kodak's salaries and its post-retirement largesse are unlikely to strike out in other American cities also suffering from the decline of American industry. They remain anchored to the land of their birth and wait for the next shoe to fall. Some, who have already gotten the employment axe, are forced into a lower paying job most likely in a service to others. They watch helplessly as their prospects sag and stare out the window as wave after wave of frigid frontal Canadian air sweeps over Lake Ontario and dumps loads of lake effect snow on dimming hopes. By March, the drifts are waist deep, piled mountain high on empty lots and decrepit real estate once occupied by a thrifty and industrious class. This enterprising and trailblazing city, lovingly succoring an inventive and diligent population, has fallen into malaise and disrepair. It was victimized, almost brutalized, by social and economic change that even the blindest observer could see coming a mile down the road.

※ ※ ※ ※

Aldine Street

A few short miles west of the empty city center, just off the run down, trash strewn Genesee Street, sits the one time home of my maternal grandparents. Separated from Aldine Street by a weedy grass strip and a broken, uneven sidewalk, the worn and inhospitable pile holds memories of grand houses in a fairer Rochester of the past. Colored glass windows, the sweet, omnipresent smell of rosewood architectural molding, pass-through milk boxes and coal chutes were standard accoutrements to the houses in the working class, tidy neighborhoods that made up this city. It wasn't at all out of the ordinary to see black Ford Deluxe Coupes parallel parked at the curb. Nearly touching, the three story single family or duplex houses on Aldine were once immaculately kept. Their tiny lawns, evenly trimmed with a push mower, were edged by flowery gardens tended with hand tools stored in the buggy garage or stable out back. People strolled the sidewalks, chatted with neighbors and rocked the hours away on wide front porches.

My grandparents had been in the same house on Aldine for many years, giving birth to my mother and her brother in the late 1930s and raising them through the war years before Mom and Uncle Dave left home in the late 1950s to pioneer their own families. After my mom had met my father, married and broke ground on a new house in the suburbs, Gram and Gramps helped tend to the five grandkids that my mother and father were only too eager to share with them. We all looked forward to our visits to Aldine Street. But then, as in countless neighborhoods across urban America, the specter of change hung over the lives of the people living there.

PRIOR to World War II, the northeastern metropolitan centers were populated with an energetic and industrious class of mostly European descent, well established after generations living in their ancestors' adopted land. Mixing in with them were fresh immigrants and their descendents leaving Europe for a better life in America. Jewish, German, Polish and Italian ethnically pure enclaves were common no matter which city one spoke about and Rochester was no different. People gravitated to live where common culture and tastes could be found.

As industrial production skyrocketed to support the material needs of a nation at war, the northern labor force was supplemented by African-American migrants from the South seeking good paying jobs in northern factories. When the war ended, flush with war time salaries and a new outlook, blacks remained to build lives in their new surroundings. As had been the case in the post-Civil War Reconstruction Era in the South, the natives of northern cities, they themselves all too familiar with not so subtle bias against immigrants, were incapable and unwilling to integrate African-Americans into their neighborhoods and lives. African-Americans were subject to segregation and overtly racist treatment by unwelcoming communities. The

1950s saw western societies trending towards conservative public policies and ramping up consumer based economies. The American middle-class, newly empowered with political and economic muscle, sought alternatives to the heterogeneity and constriction of city life. The gulf between peoples constituting the essence of cities, those who had once melded peaceably if not harmonically, widened.

A Rochester newspaperman captured some of this social angst in a scathing review of his restless city. He stomach punched his sycophantic neighbors by labeling them indolent, butt-kissing yes men. In his now out of print *Smugtown*, G. Curtis Gerling called out the feckless socialites and business people in town for their destructive emphasis on the selfish and the mundane at the expense of the infinitely more important social contract. The complacent attitude not only leaked into and began to corrode Rochester's industrial base, it led to the inevitable alteration of its collective structure. The monied class, the civic leaders and the culpable citizens never thought to imagine how bad it could get. Being labeled smug was the least of their worries. Their selfish myopia was soon brought into focus on the mean streets on a steamy July night in 1964. Everything that came before that summer in Rochester was no more. It was the time, if any such time can be identified, where the Young Lion of the West no longer roared. Rochester stepped into the abyss as simmering discord and hidden, seething hatred broke out into open violence.

Just a few days after President Lyndon Johnson signed the Civil Rights Act, black families and neighbors on and around Joseph Avenue in Rochester's north side Seventh Ward were hanging out on porches, front yards and streets trying to catch a cooling breeze. Some in the crowd, mostly teenagers, were entertaining themselves by gathering to drink booze at street parties. Rochester police on the lookout for trouble and cruising Joseph Avenue pitched into one of those impromptu celebrations and arrested a young African-American man for public intoxication. Word spread about the arrest and rumor quickly trumped fact. False stories of teen beatings at the hands of law enforcement and a little girl being attacked by a snarling police dog raced around the city and grew more agonizing and gory at each fantastic retelling. Incensed, angry groups of African-Americans gathered in predominantly black sections of town to protest the unconfirmed police behavior. City police and firefighters raced to the scenes to counter enhanced and unsubstantiated public violence. The inevitable clash of two sides working off false assumptions kicked off a three day savage melee. Overwhelmed, Rochester police sought the assistance of the State Police and the National Guard to restore order. Rock throwing, assaults on bystanders and Molotov cocktail fed blazes were phoned in to city police and fire stations. Though first reported in predominantly African-American enclaves on the city's north side, emergency calls now came in from the south and southwestern wards. The city roiled.

When the fires were suppressed and the smoke cleared, more than a thousand people were arrested, scores wounded, four were dead and the image of Rochester as a tolerant and desirable city in which to live lay in the ruins of rows of stores and houses burned to the ground. Across

America, throughout that decade, that same story of interracial tension exploding into uncapped mob violence was repeated in Philadelphia, Watts, Newark, Detroit and countless other places where people divided themselves by skin color alone.

Eight years after that summer of despair, I unknowingly frolicked in the perfection of suburban childhood, my family and I insulated from the city's problems by a long stretch of interstate highway. By then, the racial tension had quieted down and a restless peace held sway. Visits to the city, however, provided a fresh perspective for me. There were very few black families in Penfield so to run across an African-American in Rochester was a first. Riding my wagon down my grandparents' short driveway one day, an African-American kid about my young age of ten came by on a bike. I was as studiously interested in him as he was in me. We chatted and then he offered to trade his bike for my wagon. The side of the wagon, once owned by my long dead Uncle Dave, bore my name painted by my grandfather on its side. Realizing that the proposed exchange would not go over well with my elders, I politely declined. We talked for a while, sizing up each other as kids tend to do. He was as amazed at my skin color as I was his. I took notice that his palms were nearly the color of mine. As an ignorant ten year old, I naively thought that being black wasn't permanent and the act of washing hands was all that was needed to correct it. I queried him on that. He looked at me in a quizzical manner, laughed and then got on his bike and rode away.

As I mentioned, the demographics of that west side Rochester neighborhood were changing then. What had once been a street of middle-class whites became a street of mixed races. Soon the formerly common sight of couples strolling arm-in-arm in the neighborhoods became rare as distrusting strangers insulated themselves from their irrational, internal fears and ventured only out to porches or locked their doors at the first hint of twilight.

IN a rectangular cinder block building just a few streets north of Aldine on Genesee Street, my now retired grandfather, who loved to take shots at squirrels from his back porch with a .22 rifle as he tried to keep them from gnawing their way into the attic, took on a part time job as a liquor store clerk to bring in a little more cash. On Friday nights, he'd drag me along with him and sit me down in the back storage room until closing time. There, surrounded by cases of mostly cheap booze, I watched television on a junky black and white set. Gramps tended the register and dealt with the spare number of customers. His domestic proficiency with a small caliber rifle got me to wondering whether or not he carried a concealed pistol at the store but that's a question that won't ever be answered. Armed with a firearm or not, it was not a great place to take a kid but I needed watching and so he did what he had to do. In between his curt dealings with customers he editorialized to me, and to anybody else that came in and sported Caucasian ears, on the changing face of the neighborhood. He was none too subtle about his distaste for black people.

To have heard common, racially charged insults when one is young makes an impression. I couldn't understand most of it and through inexperience certainly passed no judgment. All I did was listen and keep my mouth shut not daring to comment or otherwise dispute my grandfather's beliefs. I guess if inaction implies guilt then I was culpable. My ignorance was just a less overt example of the same blatant prejudice that had contributed to white flight and the segregation of American cities. But Gramps was family and family trumps.

When it was time to leave for the night, he hustled me out, turned the keys in numerous deadbolts and slid the bars down over the entire front glass face of the store.

MY grandparents slept in queen sized beds in bedrooms at opposite ends of the house. When I stayed with them, I chose to sleep with my grandmother because she neither rolled about much nor did she snore. After I had bathed, brushed my teeth, put on my pajamas and got myself ready for bed, Grandma tucked me in and stood by as I said my prayers:

Angel of God, my guardian dear,
To whom God's love commits me here,
Ever this night, be at my side,
To watch and guard, to rule and guide.
Amen.

I then begged God's blessing for every known relative I could think of and every pet, living or dead, that we had ever owned. When finished, Grandma kissed me and promised to see me in the funny papers in the morning and off she went to play cards with invited guests.

Through the heavy bedroom door, I could hear the sounds of the foursome playing bridge, laughing and enjoying the evening. The sweet pipe smoke of the male visitor, whom I never remember seeing without that black stem and bowl sticking out of his mouth, wafted under the door to my nose.

On summer nights, as I fell into dreams in my grandmother's queen sized bed, the orange glowing face of a small electric clock set on top of a dresser wandered aimlessly as I drifted in and out of consciousness. Eyes opening and closing, I struggled to remain awake and focus on the conversation outside my door. Above the tall bureau on which that clock sat, a framed print of Jesus Christ holding the Sacred Heart was barely discernible in the diffuse light from a city streetlight cast through the lacy draped open window. To my young eyes, it looked as if the bearded, robed man was holding a flavorful pink frozen treat one got from the neighborhood ice cream man.

GRANDMA took great comfort in her Catholic upbringing. Each day she wrapped a rosary in her hands, reciting prayers in a Latin mumble or reading her frayed prayer book as she reclined in the quiet of the afternoons. On Sundays she would attend Mass a few blocks away at Saint Monica Parish on Genesee Street often with me in tow. Gramps wasn't a big fan of religion and, on good weather mornings, kept company with a favorite foursome at the public golf course in nearby Genesee Valley Park.

Saint Monica, an older parish filled to the brim with false idols, displayed its trove of sacred regalia in a manner incomprehensible to my ten year old mind. The Stations of the Cross, mounted high on the walls adjacent to the pews, told a story of pain and sorrow. The undecipherable Latin script, arced on the sky blue apse, was the language of deities. The very mystery of the spoken mass, whether sitting, standing or kneeling, kept my eyes and ears wandering throughout the liturgy.

Sunlight beaming from the outside illuminated the nave's stained glass windows depicting beneficent scenes of chromatic glory populated by haloed demigods. All were foreign to me. Centered high center at the rear of the church, facing Genesee Street and the sunrise, a brilliant rose window magnetically attracted my stare. I could not resist looking over my shoulder to ponder man's creation rather than attending to the priest's spiritual incantations.

LYING in my grandmother's bed and well on a drowsy path towards sleep, I mutely dissected my underdeveloped faith under the withering stare of the Son of God. The sounds of the elderly card players grew less distinct as other distractions caught my dwindling attention. Through the open window, the nightlife of Aldine Street passed by. The laughs and loud chatter of people having fun could be heard over a car's motor revving. Its radio, too, blared noisily. The sounds of the street floated to my ears. Intermixed were the rhythmic lyrics of a 1972 O'Jays' tune:

They smile in your face
All the time they want to take your place
The back stabbers

The song was about a guy complaining about buddies who paled around with him only to keep wandering eyes and hands on his girl. My grandfather, if he had any desire to listen to the tune, would put a far different meaning to it. The neighborhood around him was evolving in a way not at all to his liking and the ascending generation was taking away, at least in his mind, whatever little he possessed. Gramps did not like soul music. But, to me, the gentle sound, the mix of R&B and gospel music popular in that decade, caught my fancy and lulled me to sleep.

IN the morning, my grandfather lit the gas stove with a match and began preparing breakfast. After a time, I heard his steps on the creaky floor of the kitchen and awoke to the aromas of sizzling bacon and brewing coffee. Grandma sat at the table and enjoyed the time off. As Gramps hustled about, she sipped her coffee and chatted. The rest of the day, she was on the job.

The first chore was setting the dining room table right after the breakfast dishes were washed in preparation for the bigger midday meal. That practice is unheard of now. But, people who made it through the Great Depression and the shortages that came about as a result of the demands of World War II had a different perspective on mealtime. Fast food was anathema to my grandparents. They weren't at all interested in gobbling their meal. They preferred to sit and enjoy it and setting the table long beforehand was a means to that end. Eating was a slow and deliberate practice and preparation for each one was done as if the next repast was their last.

There were no store bought pies or prepackaged dinners. Grandma, her strong wrists and hands soaking and wrinkled as she washed green apples in the farmhouse style kitchen sink, would pare the skin from the fruit as a first step in her recipe for apple pie. She did not waste a morsel of the fruit. The fragrance of cinnamon and perfectly baked crust filled the house, mixing with the other smells that when whiffed today evoke fond memories.

The ancient clock mounted on a decorative mantel above the bathtub-sized sink, ticked away. At the quarter hour, its rapid bong sounded without fail. Gramps stood on a kitchen chair and religiously wound it on Sunday evenings. Its pendulum swung loudly, keeping time for the rest of the week, waiting for its next appointment.

THAT appointment was missed one day a long time ago when Gramps fell to the floor. A stroke paralyzed his left side and left him dependent and angry. He had worked all his life and raised a fine family but diabetes and the constant struggle with high blood pressure finally took him down. He was never the same after that. Quiet, uninterested in other people, he figured his life was over.

Grandma, whose son - my uncle Dave, had died of testicular cancer in his youthful twenties, had then always favored me as the oldest grandson. Strangely, she never took to my younger brother and her ambivalence to him was obvious. During our boyhood tussles, when Grandma was babysitting, even though he was the younger, more vulnerable sibling and I was the instigator, to her my brother was always to blame. I became her son incarnate and she did not spare the embraces and kindness. She doted on me and I was enamored with her. My love for her was so deep that it led to an irrational pattern of psychological speculation about life without her. On occasion, I would experience a bad dream portending her death, where she and my grandfather would fly west on an airplane, waving goodbye to me and my family, never to return. I would be wrapped in internal malaise for days, hiding it from my family and friends and only coming out of it when again I had the chance to come in contact with her.

That long flight out of my life was an eventuality with which I had to come to grips. Like most children, sickness and death are first thrust upon them with the aging and passing of grandparents. Indeed that was the case for me. While in my later life, I would have the misfortune to see the untimely death of soldiers on the battlefield and a Marine under my charge, my first experiences with death were of the painful but quite ordinary kind.

As my crippled grandfather clomped around the house, assisted with a cane, cursing and surly, my grandmother slowly fell victim to the scourge of Alzheimer's disease. She first lost track of simple things and then, later, was involved in minor fender benders or unable to find the car after shopping. She went downhill quickly, wandering about the house at three in the morning dressed and stepping through the front door into the winter dark as if to go to church. She was the sweetest most generous person I think I have ever met and it was excruciatingly painful watching her fall away from reality.

My grandparents became unable to live without assistance and soon had to sell the place on Aldine Street and move to an apartment near my parents' Penfield home. Mom wanted to be close just in case something happened. My last proud moment with my grandparents, the last time they together could as husband and wife enjoy their grandchild's success, was during the period when senior classes had ended and before my college graduation. Preparing for my senior year midshipmen's ball, I put on my dress whites and visited them at their apartment. My grandmother recognized me and was demonstrably pleased as she beamed looking at my white uniform and the gold buttons. My long dead uncle, her precious son, had been in the navy and served aboard the venerable U.S.S. Forrestal. My presence surely enhanced those faded images in her mind. But, I could tell she wasn't quite the person I had always known. Grandpa was proud as well but, as he sat helpless in his favorite chair, I could see him taking his eyes off me and glancing out the window at the busy street outside. His mind was elsewhere and I suspect he was, mostly, pondering his life past and the rapidly approaching end. He may also have been recalling the day when his own son, on active duty in the navy, stood in a white uniform before him. Today, though, he was in a small, unfamiliar place, keeping company with a woman who was daily becoming more of a stranger.

Later, a few months after I had graduated from TBS, I learned Grandpa had tried to kill himself by turning up the temperature and sticking his head in an unlighted gas oven. He survived that but died shortly thereafter a very bitter and sad person. Grandma held on for a while but, now alone, she came to live with my parents.

Anyone who has ever cared for a relative with a degenerative brain disease knows full well that such home care is extremely expensive and emotionally draining to the hosts. My mom gave it a try for a good while but that became too much for her and my dad to handle. When the money ran out they placed Grandma in a nursing home. Her house and husband gone, her savings eaten away by medical bills and possessing only a few old dresses and some bedside knickknacks, my favorite person in the world spent her last few months in and among people she did not know.

On leave from the Marines, the last time I saw her alive, I visited her at the nursing home and, despite the ravages of the disease eating away her very being, she immediately recognized me. Her strong hands grabbed mine as I sat next to her at a round table in the social area of the facility. Alzheimer's had ruined her ability to speak but her smile told me everything I needed to know. Whether she actually saw me or saw her dead son I can't ever know. Not that it mattered. I just knew, for that one bright moment, she was happy. Something inside of her dysfunctional brain was able to connect my features to a long lost and pleasurable memory. We hugged tightly as I departed and I never saw her again.

Her death closed the book on my connection with Aldine Street. It was only later that I looked back and recognized how much that one street in a small American city helped me understand the state of race relations in our country. I loved my grandfather even with all his faults. But, he had neither the time nor the inclination to come to grips with the reasons why he felt uncomfortable when people with colored skin came around.

Sometimes, I will drive by the old house, sadly remembering happy times with my grandparents. It is such a different place than the one I once knew. I guess the change is just one more ingredient in my desire to study our great conflict. A violent chapter in the seemingly eternal and very human story of the subjugation of one man by another. Today's Aldine Street and the ward and the city in which it lies, remind all of us who still live here that much of that endless book is still to be written.

Every Marine is Green

IN my high school class I was surrounded by primarily white friends of equal socio-economic backgrounds. Thinking ourselves the funniest, cleverest observers of the human condition, we ignorantly snickered at our underdeveloped views of race relations. Labeling one of our group, an olive skinned, curly black haired kid of partial Italian descent, as "Bunny" or an abbreviated version of the pejorative "Jungle Bunny," we perpetuated the most despicable traits of our forebears. The only positive aspect of our use of that slander was that we kept it to our group's ears only. At least, we were ashamed enough to realize that its spread would be looked upon with disdain by those more enlightened than we were.

While I attended the University of Rochester, African-Americans remained in the distinct minority among the whole undergraduate class and in my circle of friends. So, it wasn't until I joined my first Fleet Marine Force unit at Twentynine Palms, California that I interacted daily with African-Americans and tardily and embarrassingly recognized how harmful stereotypical views can be.

The Marine Corps is a great teacher of social, cultural and racial equality. Rather than put in place entry quotas or channel funds to one class of disadvantaged people over another, the

Marines abruptly tell recruits to check race, sex, economic background, and all that makes candidates who they are, at the door when one crosses the portal into their domain. All who wear the eagle, globe and anchor bleed Marine Corps green. That straightforward, rather simplistic statement is the view the Corps has about race. Naturally, it's more complicated than that. However, I give the Marines a lot of credit. I think they do a lot better than most organizations in knocking down color barriers and, for as long as I wore the uniform, most of the Marines I served with, of all races, did not complain about discrimination or criticize a promotion or other benefit because they felt it was either unfairly given or stonewalled because of race.

I must admit, I heard my fair share of invectives liberally tossed back and forth between bored Marines. Tongue-in-cheek, racially laced jokes were evenly distributed about those with different racial backgrounds; Hispanic, Black, White and a few Asians and Pacific Islanders here and there. That humor, however, is the language of people who have too much time and energy on their hands. The guys who traded indiscrete barbs were busting each other's rumps and any outside accusation of overt racism would fall apart under the barest scrutiny. Even though they took aim at each other's familial origins, when the crap hit the fan, these Marines loved each other, watched each other's backs and tolerated no one strange to them who attempted the same tricks.

In the First Gulf War, I served as the Fire Direction Officer for the Third Battalion, Eleventh Marines. That unit provided fire support to Task Force Ripper. Ripper was a Marine combined arms organization honing its edge in order to help kick Saddam Hussein and his army out of Kuwait. After Saddam invaded that tiny Arab nation in August of 1990, we were rushed to Saudi Arabia and deployed into the desert to ensure that the Iraqi army strayed no farther than it had already had. Operation Desert Shield, as it came to be known, was an opportunity for the United States and its allies to build up forces in anticipation of the eventual liberation of Kuwait. In the meantime, we were invited by Saudi royalty to array our guns north to protect the kingdom's oil fields from an Iraqi attack. During the tedious, uncomfortable months we lived in the Arabian desert, we stood watch, tried to keep clean, ate bad food, alternately froze or boiled and swatted ever present flies. Training for war wasn't the only thing that occupied our time.

The daily administrative grind that burdens officers and staff non-commissioned officers in the rear cropped up now and again. It didn't go away just because we were in the field. Promotions, disciplinary proceedings, new Marine orientation, evaluations and a litany of paperwork kept us busy when we weren't practicing to kill Iraqis. Being one of the junior battalion staff officers, I had the misfortune one miserably torrid day to be assigned as investigating officer. My task was to look into a complaint lodged by a Marine assigned to one of our subordinate batteries. His beef was that his unit had discriminated against African-Americans and that senior members of that unit condoned the behavior. That was a pretty serious charge and demanded that someone to uncover the facts. I drew the short straw.

I pushed the work off for as long as I could. I dug up excuse after excuse to delay the interviews that needed to be conducted. We were on a war footing and I had duties to attend to. Shortly, the battalion executive officer, exasperated that I hadn't even started the investigation after a week of delay, took me off the battalion watch schedule and told me my sole duty until completed was to look into this allegation. I never thought I would be sent off to a combat zone and be doing legal administrative work. I picked up a pen and a pad from our fire direction center, found a Marine to drive me around and motored over to the unit in question to begin my queries.

Over the course of a few days, I spoke with numerous Marines in the battery trying to ascertain whether or not any of the allegations were true. The discrimination was alleged by an African-American Private First Class who had been in the Marine Corps for four years. That told me a lot. Sharp enlisted Marines are promoted to PFC out of boot camp and to Lance Corporal not too long thereafter. The fact that this young man was still a PFC with that much time in service indicated he was a below average performer. But, I had to find out whether or not there was a systematic and intentional favoritism going on in the unit detrimental to black Marines. I certainly didn't expect to find a burning cross in the middle of the unit's position in the desert. Further, it would have surprised me to find out that the unit had condoned Ku Klux Klan rallies. The racist undertones, if any existed, were going to be hidden and hard to find.

Meeting with the battery first sergeant, I examined the unit promotions over the past eighteen months to see if white Marines were disproportionately promoted over African-

American Marines. I interviewed the plaintiff's section chief, his platoon commander and the battery gunnery sergeant to ascertain whether or not any of them assigned duties based on race rather than capability and rank. I also interviewed the plaintiff and a fair number of randomly selected Marines of all races, to get their impressions of the issue. Finally, I interviewed the battery commander and the executive officer and attempted to gather information regarding the command viewpoint on the issue and what was done to ensure that Marines were treated based on merit rather than the color of their skin.

After a long few days, I wrote up my summary, conclusions and recommendations and presented them to the battalion executive officer. He was a low key, country Texan and took my report in stride. He stayed out of the fray and simply forwarded my report to the authority that requested the investigation at First Marine Division headquarters. I felt my report was a thorough but an empty piece of work. How would I explain what could be considered common in mixed race organizations throughout America? I, in a few short pages, was expected to summarize the continued evolution of race relations in post-Civil War, post-Civil Rights Act, and post-Rodney King America. My task could not have been fulfilled with a 1,000 page, well documented book let alone a Marine Corps investigation no matter how thoroughly I did the job.

The Marine who had alleged discrimination was pretty savvy. But he was also a punk and a trouble maker. He was more interested in investing time figuring out ways to get out of work than in doing the work itself. He was a rabble rouser and a talker and would do all he could to poison the minds of the other junior enlisted African-American Marines. He was a big fan of Malcolm X and twisted that leader's philosophy to fit his distaste for the Marines.

I had no doubt one of the young man's fellow Marines slapped him with a racial slur. Such behavior was not endorsed or encouraged by the command nor was the command culpable for failing to stomp out non-existent discrimination. The problem was that a small group of jerks, both white and black, wrongly felt the other race was conspiring against them and using skin color to game the system. Two groups, from radically different cultures, backgrounds and poisoned by long held stereotypical views, clashed. Unlike most Marines, they weren't harmlessly kidding one another. They truly did not like to interact with people with differently colored skin. Their hatred was not inconsistent with prejudice one would find in a high school class, on a factory floor or, frankly any place in America.

That's what I put in my report. I found out later, much later, that the commanding officer of the unit had gotten the official findings back from the division. The staffers there took my research and report as factual and complete. There was no sanction and no punishment meted out. Instead a suggestion was proffered that the command refocus its efforts to enhance cultural and racial sensitivity. How and what that would be carried out in the middle of an endlessly flat, sandy and baking wasteland was never made clear. The commander of the unit did not like that at all. He assumed that any investigation would find that all his Marines were color blind and that the complaint of the one was simply sour grapes. The problem was he should have recognized that his Marines were people and a few of them were going to retain old, bad habits. He also should have realized that the America of today is in many ways the America of 1863. That's something that a Kumbaya moment of hand holding and spiritual togetherness is not going to change. There were a few bad white apples that didn't like blacks and a few bad black apples that didn't like whites. He didn't want to hear that. Later, when I would run across him in the Saudi desert he would not speak to me. After the war ended and we were all back at Twentynine Palms, the silence continued. To this day, as far as I know, he still thinks my conclusions were wrong. I looked around me then and I look around me now and can still see that my observations were spot-on accurate. They will remain so as long as humans of different nationalities, races or creeds try to co-exist.

✳ ✳ ✳ ✳

Moldering in the Grave

FEW would disagree that John Brown was one mean, crazy looking guy. The photographs that do exist of the man show him to be exactly the personality that history tells us he was. His thick mat of wild hair and the blazing fire in his eyes reveals the excitable and unquenchable energy of a man who would sire twenty children, kill men in cold blood and lead a failed effort to violently overthrow the government of the United States. He took his abolitionist fervor to a level of lunacy when he and his cohorts attempted to seize a Federal armory at Harpers Ferry, Virginia. Their ambitious plan would have them remove the weapons held inside, blaze a path throughout slave territory systematically freeing blacks held against their will, arm them and, alongside them, carry out an armed rebellion against any American governmental authority that sanctioned human bondage.

The sheer scope of the grand plan guaranteed the scheme barely got off the ground. The timely arrival of Federal troops was the nail in the plot's coffin. The conspiracy petered out in a brawl in and near the fire station in this high bluff pinched river town. Brown was manhandled, handcuffed and dragged to court, easily convicted and hanged by the neck until dead for the crime of treason.

This firebrand, this man of action had, in his wide travels, the fortune to meet the milder mannered Frederick Douglass. Douglass carried equally bona fide abolitionist credentials but practiced much more restrained methods to accomplish his goals. His pen and his fiery rhetoric were his unsheathed sword.

Writing to an abolitionist friend in 1847, Douglass revealed that he had ". . . finally decided on publishing the *North Star* in Rochester and to make that city my future home." Noting its distinct geographically racist boundaries of today, it is ironic that he chose to do so. Rochester was a different place altogether in the mid-nineteenth century. Douglass' choice rested on the then forward-looking city's early reputation of attracting political and religious leaders; fervent advocates for the fundamental rights of all humans. Its fortuitous geographic location not only energized its industrial prowess, but it placed it smack in the center of a revivalist band running through central and western New York.

The nineteenth century's Great Awakening had reenergized the spiritually lazy and set new fire under the region's religious torpor. Like hand in glove, reaching out to God also inspired a nascent social radicalism which spanned all manner of social and economic reform. A pillar of this new order was the anti-slavery movement. Such zeal for the rights of African-Americans flourished here in the "burned-over district." This evangelized swath of upstate New York, cutting from Syracuse to Buffalo, was claimed to have been so razed and so cleansed by the conflagration of transcendent reform that it now was bereft of sinners to fuel the fires of evil. Since sins against

God were wrapped up nicely and topped off with a bow, it was time to get down to business working on sins against humanity.

Well, despite those ethereal assertions, I suspect some rather dry tinder of damnation still lay around the taverns and cheap lodging houses of Buffalo and Rochester. Pious passengers, journeying up and down DeWitt Clinton's famous ditch, must have turned beet-red observing the ribald antics of the canal boatmen crewing the packets.

Regardless, there was sufficient support among those with financial and political means for Douglass' message on the injustices inherent in human bondage to take firm root. That message grew and flowered in the same garden as the Women's Rights Movement. Douglass, never hypocritical and certainly aware of the ties between the two causes, was eagerly supportive of both.

During his time in Rochester, he left his imprint on both the city and the rest of America. Before he moved to the nation's capital and the much bigger national stage, Douglass cemented his place in history. His name and god-like image can be found all over Rochester today. Schools, public buildings, statues and streets are titled in memory of this iconic giant. He used his power and influence to attempt to peacefully change America and his work did not go unrewarded. The former slave was a brilliant self analyst, critic, debater and public servant. His work on the abolitionist paper the *North Star* provided him with a forum to express his views and the views of the anti-slavery movement. His autobiographies and his journalistic prowess placed him among some of the most often read and influential writers of the time. While John Brown was leading armed and masked bandits to the houses of slave holders in Kansas, beating them and gunning them down in cold blood, Frederick Douglass wielded the pen in order to force the abolition of an evil he himself only knew too well.

150 years after the Civil War ended, on the decaying streets of Rochester and in too many places elsewhere in America, bigotry and interracial discord remain with us. There have been major strides towards equality to be sure, but distrust and antipathy thrive. Although prohibited by law, segregation is condoned by the ungovernable forces of social and economic preference. It flourishes in the poisoned fallout from misguided public policies intended prevent exactly what has occurred.

Just a stone's throw from the northern terminus of Route 15, the mean streets of Rochester are living examples of the uncaring and unattractive tendency of Americans to congregate around their own kind, to choke off meaningful dialogue, to find compromise to lessen the tensions that historically flare into deadly violence and to eschew the right economic policies that can substantially mitigate that risk. Concentrated poverty, inefficiently run and crumbling schools, lack of opportunity, a dramatically higher unemployment rate than that of white suburban towns surrounding the city and an overall sense of despair hang over the former home of Frederick Douglass, George Eastman and Susan B. Anthony.

Despite what those three did to bind the racial wounds of the nation, lend a hand to lift the underprivileged and advocate for those with a limited voice, places like Rochester continue to suffer. It, and other cities, home to predominately African-American populations continue to lag behind the rest of America. Inner city dwellers are at the bottom of the social and economic totem pole. They show higher percentages of school drop outs, higher mortality rates from disease, higher poverty rates and are surrounded by skewed rates of violent crime. Those with the economic means and a choice flee this dead end hell. The Rochester metropolitan area becomes more segregated with each passing year. It is almost as if America had never even fought a civil war. Like my grandfather two generations before me and a select and hard headedly ignorant group of young men serving in the Marines, we seem to never learn.

Chapter 5

WATCHING A MAN DIE

"Do you remember the stretcher-cases lurching back with dying eyes and lolling heads, those ashen-gray masks of the lads who once were keen and kind and gay?"

– Siegfried Sassoon –

❋ ❋ ❋ ❋

The Smell of Death Surrounds You

GETTYSBURG is awfully quiet at three o'clock in the morning. So it was on September 17, 2011. Earlier the day before, after an enjoyable drive from my suburban Rochester home in Pittsford, accompanied by my brother, we had checked in at the Gettysburg Travelodge. After parking the car, we went to our assigned room facing Steinwehr Avenue and dropped our bags. We then stepped next door to a bustling O'Rorke's Eatery and Spirits. The building replicates a quaint Irish cottage, sports a trellised outdoor patio and takes the name of a son of Erin whose parents had died in transit to America and who had subsequently been sent to an orphanage in Rochester.

PATRICK O'Rorke, known as Paddy to those with whom he was familiar, had been offered a scholarship to the newly organized University of Rochester but had opted for a life of military service instead. So, he packed his bags and stepped aboard a New York Central rail car and was off to the bricked fortress on the Hudson at West Point. At the academy he set the pace, keeping a fine polish on a sterling record. His work paid off and Paddy graduated at the top of his class of 1861. He was in very good company. Civil War trivia buffs can reel off the list of famous names that graduated in both the May and June classes of that momentous year.

The inventory includes arguably the most famous of the lot, George Armstrong Custer. With his attention directed elsewhere other than the army curriculum, Armstrong, as he was known to family and close friends, didn't do nearly as well as Paddy and barely hung on to the last position in the class. Custer, despite his academic struggles and penchant for disciplinary trouble as a cadet, managed to stick it out and got a commission anyway.

The Civil War was already underway and Custer's academic record soon faded into the past. Unfettered by school or other conventional constraints, Custer quickly proved his merit on wild and violent Civil War battlefields. With reckless abandon, he and his troopers helped stop a serious threat imposed by J.E.B Stuart's Confederate cavalry to the Union rear on the third day's fight at Gettysburg.   At the van of his Wolverines of Michigan, Custer pitched into the Confederate horsemen and blunted Rebel plans that may have changed the events transpiring later along Cemetery Ridge.

More than a decade after Gettysburg, Custer's rash and impetuous nature that served him so well in the Civil War was to doom his Seventh Cavalry Regiment on the grassy, dusty slopes along the banks of the Little Bighorn River in Montana.   Headlong rushes into an equally sized and comparably armed force is one thing, attacking an enemy force hundreds of times larger is quite another.

A young Custer, from all we can discover about him, was both a dandy and a rabble rouser. Eschewing authority and finding rules inconvenient to his lifestyle, Custer made trouble. But the 1861 army was far more tolerant of that behavior than it is now at least as far as an officer was concerned.   More importantly, the army needed men.   The saddle worn troopers of his future Seventh Regiment would have been better off had the army been less tolerant and had cracked down on his tomfoolery but the rebellion intervened.   And so history's course, twisted and confusing as it may be, had the rebellious one stand at the tail end of the long, gray line of West Point's graduating Class of 1861.   Patrick O'Rorke took higher honors and stood first.

AT the pub carrying O'Rorke's sainted appellation, my brother and I sashayed up to the bar and ordered drinks.   Time flew as I chatted with a decent fellow from the panhandle of Florida who was up north visiting an army son stationed on recruiting duty in a nearby town. The battlefield at Gettysburg is a natural draw to visitors, of course, and, after a day's sightseeing, they too sought refreshment. I paid little attention to the amount of alcohol I was drinking and shortly had overindulged. The last shot of Jameson Irish Whiskey kicked my irritable bowel syndrome into full motion.

Later, as I lay flat on my back in the darkness of the room at the Travelodge, my stomach was flipping like a trapeze artist over the center ring at a circus. Despite downing copious amounts of bottled water and crunching and swallowing a chalky over-the-counter anti-acid, I knew a rough, sleepless night lay ahead of me. My brother, who shared the room with me, slumbered peacefully. Wisely placing a set of headphones attached to an iPod over his ears, he was insulated from the gurgling of my stomach and the annoying regularity of my trips to the restroom.

After tossing and turning on my bed, I finally gave up. As a faint bell in the distance chimed the early three o'clock hour, I shuffled out into the silence of morning. I paused and quietly clicked the hotel room door shut behind me. Under dressed for the chill, I knew where to go. I had to head up Cemetery Hill to the entrance to the National Military Cemetery. That's where the dead go, right? And boy did I feel like death. Nothing is worse than a hangover induced irritable bowel episode. Those who suffer from the malady know what I mean. Doctors suggest that people with IBS shouldn't drink alcohol but this night I ignored that advice and now paid dearly for it. This was my walk to Golgotha.

My progress took me up the street past the water tower, gift shops, private museums and the other tourist havens that have for some time taken over the Gettysburg facing slope of Cemetery Hill. I paused near the famous Gatehouse marking the entrance to the civilian Evergreen Cemetery whose presence gave the hill its name. The waning gibbous moon, a whittled chunk of this year's Harvest moon, was poking through a surreal looking stratus layer of clouds. Its milky beams bathed the colossal equestrian statue of Winfield Scott Hancock nearby. They reflected dully off the broad chest of his obsidian mount. Hancock lords over East Cemetery Hill. I admired him from across the empty Baltimore Street which sharply bends leaving town and moves uphill to where I now stood, dizzily hoping for some calm to return to my agitated gut.

Lynyrd Skynyrd's song "That Smell" kept going through my head. Ronnie Van Zant's confessional and warning about the pain experienced through heavy drug use blared from speakers in our car as my brother and I made the long trip here. My personal character, thankfully, remains strong enough to resist the temptations of sticking a needle my arm, taking another toke or having a blow for my nose. I wish I were equally resistant to overconsumption of beer, wine and spirits. The piper on this moonlit morning was exacting his toll for my rare indiscretion. One more drink, fool, sure drowned me. One hell of a price to get my kicks! Van Zant brilliantly called drug addiction the smell of death. My discomfort hardly came up to that but it sure felt like the hooded grim reaper had his bony grip on me.

SPEAKING of the smell of death, it must have overwhelmed every nostril and been taken in with every humid human breath on that long ago July battlefield. After the guns stopped firing and the carnage was surveyed, approximately 50,000 of the 165,000 combatants were killed, wounded, missing or captured. Who knows how many horses and pack animals were slaughtered by cannon fire and musketry. 3,000? 5,000? Black and white photos of General Meade's headquarters at the Lydia Leister house and the scene of fighting around Abraham Trostle's barn display torn horses lying in the sun, bloated and festering.

Digging a pit in which to throw a dead horse would take a long time with a bulldozer or a backhoe let along hand digging with a shovel. So, on top of the ground the mangled horses stayed, fly covered and rotting until someone got around to dragging them to temporary piles and burning them. The air was reported to have been polluted with the vile wind from these disgusting pyres.

Oddly, I knew what that must have smelled like. Near my childhood home in Penfield, New York, on one of the meandering bends of the Irondequoit Creek, an animal rendering plant turned carcasses and other animal parts into the grease, tallow and meal. When in operation, the trucks hauling carrion moved in and out regularly and dumped their cargo in heated steel vats. On windless summer nights, when the plant was in full production and cooking, the smell was distinct and unbearable. The same odor wafting to the noses of the citizens of Gettysburg must have been only one disturbing part of their excruciating post-battle hell.

It was early summer in southern Pennsylvania and it was hot. Combined with the reek of decaying horses and thousands of dead men, 165,000 dirty, sweaty soldiers who had little time to dig proper latrines or clean themselves and the stench hanging over the field must have been omnipresent and unavoidable.

NO wonder disease in those days killed more of these people than combat. Sanitary conditions even in the most peaceful of times were shoddy. Cleanliness under the stress of battle was non-existent. Even today, in a field training environment, it requires a diligent effort on the part of small unit leaders and medical experts to ensure soldiers and Marines keep clean and healthy in the absence of running water and porcelain toilets. A short stay in any place and waste disposal is straightforward. Soldiers and Marines dig a hole, squat, wipe and cover with a layer of dirt or sand. That field expediency is insufficient and unsanitary when water supplies are limited and a unit stays in one out-of-the-way location for any length of time.

With open and flowing supply channels, adequate material and attentive supervisors, a permanent field position can take on the comforts of home. Slit trenches or individual cat holes common to temporary encampments are soon replaced by solidly constructed outhouses with multiple, comfortable seats. If all goes as planned, these are cleaned routinely by the unfortunate junior man on the hierarchical totem pole.

In this more civilized arrangement, the daily waste of dozens of soldiers or Marines is not deposited into hole dug out from the dirt below but rather into quarter cut fifty-five gallon empty fuel drums. At a predetermined time, an unlucky sod carries out his assigned task by dragging the containers out from underneath the structure, pouring diesel fuel into the mix, stirring generously and setting the putrid mass on fire. Continuing to beat the mixture with a stick, his job is done when most of the solid, disgusting mass is vaporized.

Woe to the unwary if that young Marine has failed in his task. In the dark of night when nature calls, Marines have been known to stumble hurriedly towards the "shitter" in the pitch dark. They enter the outhouse and disrobe only to plop down dishearteningly and directly on top of, as Marines lovingly term it, the peak of Mount "Shitabachi."** Peril in the field comes in many guises.

POST-BATTLE Gettysburg survivors, civilians, some families of the dead or strangers hired by government did the best they could by digging shallow trenches in which to place the bodies. A thin layer of dirt was then thrown over the deceased. The living figured that would have to do as they had other worries on their minds. Revulsion was the prime motivation behind these temporary burials. Alone or in mass graves, in a furrowed field or a farm house yard, the dead

---

** In February 1945, at the tail end of WWII, the Marines invaded a small Japanese island in the Pacific called Iwo Jima. After a few days of brutal fighting and having suffered several thousand casualties, the Marines and a Navy Corpsman raised the Stars and Stripes above the highest point on Iwo Jima called Mount Suribachi. The battle continued on for another month or so but the volcanic hill shortly became a centerpiece of Marine Corps lore.

were all eventually covered with the fertile soil of Gettysburg's countryside.

The smell of death lingered though. It did not disappear until the summer faded and cooler weather arrived. Then, a more formally organized process ensured all that remained of the once living beings was either interred in more formal settings at the Soldiers' National Cemetery or transported to a plot far away in a hometown. A few, naturally, were forgotten. Nature, before even a wink of time had passed, had disguised their temporary graves. Without markers, they remained covered and hidden. They lay at or near where they fell on the hills and fields outside the little town for months or years to come. Some waited decades until a plow, a heavy rain or a National Park Service reclamation project churned their bones to the surface.

❋ ❋ ❋ ❋

Bound to Act

ON top of Cemetery Hill, I diverted my mind from my personal grief and focused on the scene around me. My eyes settled back on the statue of the Army of the Potomac's magnificent Second Army Corps commander - "Hancock the Superb."

General McClellan, who had stood at the head of the very same unlucky army twice in his brief and tumultuous career, had bestowed that epithet on Hancock for his bravery during the Peninsula campaign. McClellan's futile attempt to march up from tidal Virginia and take Richmond early in the war reaped few benefits for the Union cause. The revelation of Hancock's martial skill was one of them. McClellan's observations were spot on and Hancock's spanking new nom de guerre stuck.

Hancock's striking monument silently commands the rise where on the eve of the first day of the battle of Gettysburg, in the absence of George Meade, the army's commander, the Superb looked about in disgust and dived in to take charge of a very dispirited and scared rabble. He did so with vigor and over the sullen protestations of the more senior, one armed Oliver Otis Howard. Earlier that afternoon, Howard's Eleventh Army Corps had picked up and skedaddled after a sound beating on the other side of Gettysburg. George Meade may have had his faults but, to his eternal credit, he did have an explicit understanding of Hancock's ability. After a messenger brought him word of the death of the stalwart John Reynolds, the First Army Corps' leader and senior man on the field, who got caught in the dead-eye sights of a Confederate sharpshooter at McPherson's Ridge, Meade delegated the authority of command to Hancock. Meade did so until he himself could spur his horse and his headquarters north to the fight.

As a Pennsylvanian and a steady military hand, an abler lieutenant could not have been found. He looked the part. With wavy black hair, a full goatee and moustache, Hancock's handsome head sat on top of a lofty stature, his frame filling out his double-buttoned dark blue uniform. Mounted on a black stallion, Hancock was regal. After his summary dismissal of Howard, he busied himself with the Cemetery Hill defense as darkness fell on that very confusing first day. His firmness and confident direction set the groundwork for the eventual Union victory some forty-eight hours later.

Hancock wasn't far from the fray at the key moment on the second and third days' battles as well. Meade, having now arrived at the scene, directed him to temporarily hand over his beloved Second Corps and head out to the Third Army Corps' salient to restore a semblance of control after its leader, Daniel Sickles, was stretchered off the field with a severe injury.

Hancock's solid and unflappable personal touch brought the situation under control at the threatened Union line both in front of and, later, at middle Cemetery Ridge. There is absolutely no question that this valiant soldier was the de facto leader of the army on the three days at

Gettysburg. Meade readily deferred to this giant of a man. Stolidly cantering about during the Confederate bombardment of the Union lines on the third of July, Hancock dismissed his rash exposure as both routine and necessary. As shells screeched angrily overhead and shrapnel riddled the ground around him, Hancock deflected his staff's cautionary pleading by reputedly saying that "[t]here are times when a corps commander's life does not count."

As reluctant Confederate General Longstreet followed up the brisk ninety minute cannonade with his assault on Cemetery Ridge on that same afternoon, Hancock, whirling about in attendance to his command, urged a subordinate officer to plug a gaping hole in the Federal lines with the memorable "[y]ou better get in there goddamn quick." The officer and his willing charges did so and the threat was ended.

Hancock's aura of good luck was bound not to last forever in the free-for-all enveloping him and his corps. On the late afternoon of the third of July, when the situation looked well in hand for the boys in blue, a minie ball struck the pommel of the saddle on which he was sitting. The missile drove jagged shards of metal and wood debris into his groin. While surviving the bloody and painful wound, he never attained the same level of invincibility he projected at Gettysburg. He was a later and powerful presence on the national stage and even took a run at the U.S. presidency but those challenges were breezy diversions for this man. It was on the battlefield that he was in his element. He was always there to do his duty.

ON July 7, 1865, a day where the temperature ignored the thermometer as it soared past 100 degrees, he presided over the execution of the conspirators convicted of assisting in the plot to assassinate Abraham Lincoln. That day, Hancock would order four of the conspirators, judged guilty by a recently concluded military tribunal, killed. The condemned group included a woman named Mary Surratt. Mrs. Surratt ran a boarding house in Washington. Several of those involved in the attempt to decapitate the U.S. government the night Lincoln was shot either lived with her or used the place to draw up their plans. She was found to have been a willing participant. However, the chivalrous America of that time believed, no matter what her crime, a female would be spared the plunge at the last minute. A frothing horse and dusty courier carrying an expected presidential pardon never arrived at the front gate of Washington's Old Arsenal Yard. The patiently waiting Hancock blanched. He quietly cleared his throat and strode empty handed to the temporary gallows. He entered the prison courtyard and approached the solidly constructed platform. Squinting in the glare, he directed that the orders detailing the conspirators' guilt be read and the sentences of death carried out. Later, he compartmentalized the emotional strain rather calmly noting that "every soldier was bound to act as I did under similar circumstances."

That understatement may have also applied to one very unhappy and very sick man appearing in one of Alexander Gardner's poignant surveys of the gripping scene. Framed moments prior to the tightening of the nooses around necks, a viewer's attention is drawn to the crowd on the platform itself. Less noticeable below, a uniformed corporal stands beneath the tall structure. His job is to remove one of the platform's wooden posts when the order to do so is given. He is quite visibly ill. He leans against the thick post, green at the gills. One wonders if he had overdone it the night before at a tavern with a couple of buddies or, perhaps, maybe the stress and the heat were just too much.

Gardner, in these precious historical frames, brings us to the courtyard and ushers us to front row seats. His work is so detailed, so real that one could almost cock one's ear and the sounds of vertebrae snapping and spinal cords transecting might be heard as the conspirators drop.

Gardner worked hard that day and kept his camera busy. In his post-execution photographs, the holes in which the dead criminals will be temporarily buried are neatly dug, deep, square and in a row next to the gallows. As the victims swing, the coffins in which the bodies will be placed are stacked and ready for their occupants.

The rotting dead at Gettysburg got nowhere near the same respect. There wasn't time. Care and decency afforded traitors would have to wait until a more convenient occasion for heroes.

AT the end of that momentous third day at Gettysburg, the Superb, suffering as did so many others around him, unwillingly joined the ranks of the casualties that had fallen on the field. Hancock's wound, while bloody and painful, was far preferable to trauma inflicted on those far less lucky. Even more horrible disfigurement caused by relatively slow moving lead and steel projectiles either brought immediate death or put the soldier on an excruciating path to a lingering demise.   Despite the copious arterial flow from his wound, Hancock survived.

MANY of those who did not survive, who paid the ultimate price, lie beneath the stones of the graveyard adjacent to the civilian plots at Evergreen Cemetery and the place where I stood early in the wee hours of that September morning. What I saw and heard before me were eerily reminiscent of the same sights and sounds that surrounded the Union occupiers on a moonlit night long ago. Then, as was my experience, the hill fell quiet. The guns were mostly still. Their exhausted crews lay in lumps underneath. Only worried leaders paced about, lost in thoughts of tomorrow.   An edgy picket here and there, roaming in front of campfires flickering through the gloom, cracked off a shot at a shadow or the snap of a dry twig. Most in the army collapsed where they were and slept among the graves and the freshly killed as the stars winked above.

THE log and dirt breastworks, muddy limber and caisson trails are no longer visible. The broken headstones have been repaired and lines of military markers lie row after row surrounded by neatly trimmed grass and manicured paths. All lie covered under the umbrellas of lofty pines. In these places of eternal rest, the filth and waste of war have disappeared.   Torn ground is now graded, planted and landscaped.

Across the road on a rise, the statue of "Hancock the Superb" watches over the untroubled remains. Clouds scurry in front of the bright moon. Their shadows are cast far below. They flit in silent rhythm above his ebony majesty

and carry on over the incandescent white stones
guarding his former charges.

* * * *

Dear Madam, It is with Sincerest Regret . . .

THAT same bright moon lighted the sands of Kuwait and Saudi Arabia in the early days of 1991. The moon is the bane of the modern night fighter. Its full or near full phases reveal even the most cleverly concealed plans of a foe to the laziest eye. A modern force prefers the cover of darkness brought on by a new moon. Stealth is far easier when ambient light is limited to the glow from a distant city or the dim light from pinprick stars. But, even those dull sources of light can illuminate a battlefield when an observer views it through the lens of night vision goggles. A bright star like Sirius or Arcturus can shed just enough light to cast a column of trucks or troops into an observer's field of vision. The planet Venus can, in certain phases, be bright enough to throw shadows. The radiance emitted by the tinier of heavenly bodies orbiting in the night sky is perfect for the silent warrior who prowls the dark.

KNOWING that the Iraqis had suffered much at the hands of Coalition airstrikes and were at the point of breaking, the senior commanders leading the 1991 invasion and eventual liberation of Kuwait chose to kick off the ground war when the moon was past its first quarter phase. Strategic planners figured that the extra illumination would be more of a benefit to Coalition forces than the detriment it could have been with a better prepared enemy before them. So, with the moon shining above, the tanks, artillery and humvees began to roll early on the twenty-third of February.

As part of Task Force Ripper, one of the ground combat elements of the First Marine Division, we lined our trucks, humvees and guns up on the Saudi Arabia-Kuwait border. Like our Civil War brethren so many years before us digging gun pits and throwing up defenses in the moonlight on Cemetery Hill, we gathered and prepared to tangle with a tough enemy under that same colorless light. The vast expanse of the Saudi Arabian desert spread endlessly before us, the sand palely reflecting the moon as it reached higher in the sky. Tired and jittery, we donned our mission oriented protective posture gear – military jargon for a gas mask, boots, gloves and a suit that protects a Marine from a potential biological or chemical attack.

It was brisk that winter's night. Coalition fighters and attack aircraft zoomed low overhead, dropping ordnance just ahead on the Iraqi minefields and defensive lines set up to prevent us from doing what we were about to do. Even with the late night and early morning chill, the charcoal laced suits drew sweat with the mildest of exertion. Gas masks, packed away in their hip canvas pouches, served as field expedient pillows. Leaning against the tires of a humvees or trucks, the calmer few caught a few winks of sleep before the assault began.

Pre-war intelligence estimates had trumped up Saddam's chemical and biological weapons capabilities. Grim faced analysts believed at least a third of us would be killed or wounded in the upcoming fight. We were up against a tough enemy, dug deeply into the ground and, for the most part, capable of putting up a stiff defense even with all the airpower thrown against them.

We took some comfort in knowing that, if wounded, we would enjoy the benefit of trained medical professionals tagging along with each unit. Even better, a well equipped battalion aid station and even more sophisticated triage and operating stations were never too far away.

NOT so for the men who fell wounded on the first day at Gettysburg. It's hard to conceptualize what could be worse. The injured soldier, on either side of the line, suffering a wound so severe that the primitive medicine of the time and the guesswork of the surgeon ensured there was little chance of healing. The overworked doctors and their assistants grew immune to their agonized cries. Nothing, really, could be done.

Most of the wounded ended up in the cemetery and the only solace to a dead soldier's friends and family was if he was buried with something to identify him to comrades and loved ones poking from the surface nearby. Today we pass by a soldier's stone and read "Unknown" and think nothing of it. Surely, though, a name and memory of a face or a touch meant something to those who once cared.

The American Civil War saw the deaths of 620,000 or roughly two percent of the population of the country at the time. In its beginning, energetic volunteers, proudly wearing newly tailored uniforms and gaily following fluttering banners, fell to its wrath. The ignorant were rudely matured by terror none could comprehend.

At its end, the butcher's bill was paid with the lives of conscripts, volunteers, civilians and non-combatants alike. As if to punctuate the lengths to which death would go to meet its grisly quota, the war took the life of the nation's chief executive in a story of assassination that fascinates and compels today.

ON plots marked by white stones at Gettysburg's National Military Cemetery, and thousands of other veteran gravesites in America, flowers placed by families or volunteer groups on the neatly mowed graves of the military's dead wilt after only a few days in unforgiving weather. It is heartening, though, to see that the sacrifice of those known and unknown soldiers is not forgotten. Each time I visit the place where Abraham Lincoln delivered arguably the 268 most important words in American history, I pause to remember another country's soldiers. Six men of the Iraqi military; victims of the First Gulf War. Each was once somebody's father, son, or brother. When I saw them last, on a dismal night in February 1991, two were lying on the hood of an idling humvee. The other bodies rested side-by-side on the oil covered ground.

THE day, if one can call it that, had started early as the Marines' Task Force Ripper and the artillery of Third Battalion pushed through the Iraqi minefields and razor wire defensive positions ringing occupied Kuwait. The sun never rose. The inky-black oil smoke created crypt-like darkness at high noon. It robbed the senses, hiding from sight the war that raged around us. But our ears heard the tom-tom of artillery and the roar of F-18s overhead as they paved the way north towards

Kuwait City. Their devastating power opened gates for the massed armor and infantry coming in waves behind them.

Not long after Task Force Ripper maneuvered through the minefields on the Saudi Arabian border, a strange and totally unexpected sight greeted us. Out of the darkness they walked. Filthy, skeletal figures. Thousands of them. Iraqi soldiers. Hungry, tattered, harassed night and day by Coalition air power, they had no more fight left in them. Their white flags, made from underwear or medical bandages, were prominently displayed. Machine guns, rifles and other weapons of war were tossed away as they emerged from their battered subterranean bunkers.

One hollered in perfect English that he was from America and sought a ride with us. He had chosen a very bad time to visit his relatives in Iraq. It seems the Iraqi press gangs found him and "volunteered" him for national service. He, like the other bunches and clumps of the gaunt and defeated foe, was told to move southward into the hands of rear area administrators and safety. The fast moving force could not be burdened by prisoners of war.

Up ahead, Task Force Ripper's infantry units were tangling with an Iraqi armored brigade in and around Al Burgan oil field. The rabbit quick Marine light armored vehicles moved past our artillery positions and charged headlong into the fray. Awestruck myself at the power surrounding me, I questioned why any foe dare challenge a Marine combined arms force. It is suicide.

We fell in behind the armored infantry and set up in the center of the Al Burgan complex. One of the world's largest oil fields; the entire expanse was on fire. Thick columns of brownish petroleum spewed from wellheads, chased by the immense pressure built up underneath. As the yards high gushing oil mixed with air, the combination turned to flame. These huge candles roared all around us. The unburned petroleum rained down in a slimy, misty shower coating everything. The sound split ears. A shout could barely be heard by a comrade standing a few inches away. Hand signals became the lingua franca.

As we scrambled to set up communications at our new position, a detachment from a reserve regiment was busy nearby. The infantry Marines were occupied herding a surrendered Iraqi militia unit into a tight square. The Iraqis, on their knees with hands clasped behind and tied with plastic restraints, were methodically searched. In the gloom, it was difficult to tell friend from enemy.

I stood between two high backed humvees that served as our operations center. With one hand on a radio to Task Force Ripper's headquarters and the other calling our subordinate firing batteries, I went through the obligatory communications checks. As I did so, I blankly stared at the Iraqi prisoners under guard. They kneeled or sat waiting, illuminated by the fires of hell around them.

Without warning, artillery starbursts popped above their heads. It was American artillery. The shells' distinct trajectory from the south told of their origin. They were dual-purpose improved conventional munitions in artillery parlance. A clever little invention for killing. The missiles traveled to their destination and, with a time fuzes as triggers, kicked scores of bomblets out of the rear of each shell over the target. They worked as advertised. Like a string of loud fireworks, the bomblets exploded in and among the prisoners and their Marine custodians. There was little protection on the open, sandy plain. A forward observer attached to a neighboring Marine unit had seen the Iraqi prisoners and took them for a threat. The mistake was totally understandable in the paltry light and with the battlefield obscured by oily smoke. He made the call back to his battery which, in typical American artillery fashion, was on time and deadly accurate on target in response.

A short time later, after the fight wound down and some semblance of order was restored to our chaotic little world, we shuttled the American and Iraqi wounded off to a medical evacuation site. The Iraqi dead, however, briefly remained in our charge. Shredded by our friendly artillery while under the umbrella of our protection, they lay waiting for their final trip home. They had no names on their uniforms. They were the unknown of my war. We soon loaded them onto a five-ton truck and unceremoniously shipped them away leaving all of us wondering about their eventual fate.

From time to time, I recall that night and those eight Iraqi men. Were their bodies ever reunited with family? Were they ever honored for their sacrifice? Do Iraqis today pass by a cemetery and, seeing where they lie now, remember what they did for a cause they may or may not have believed in? Do they lie, like so many who wore the blue and the gray, under a marker that tells us nothing about who they were? I don't think I will ever know the answers. But, if they are interred in unmarked graves, I hope my words here provide some consolation to those that knew them and still yearn to know of their circumstances. They, perhaps, will remain nameless. But, to me and my Marine comrades who experienced their deaths firsthand, they never will be forgotten.

There is a Curse on this Ship

DURING our tenure at TBS, live fire and simulated combat exercises were part of the curriculum. The training was designed to be as realistic as possible. Included in the package, was battlefield first aid. It was just enough exposure to enable us to splint a broken limb, bandage a superficial wound, constrict the flow of blood from a ruptured artery or to be able to stabilize a victim of a wound that penetrated a lung. Anything else would have to wait until a corpsman or a doctor arrived. We were also herded into a classroom and treated to a slideshow of actual combat injuries. Slide after slide passed gruesomely by accompanied by the equally disturbing narrative of the instructor. After a string of too close, too bloody and gut wrenching views of what the violent impact of a bullet or shrapnel can do to a human body, the presentation began to take its toll on some of the 200 lieutenants in my class. More than a few put their heads down on their desks, unable to keep looking at the horror magnified on the screen. Some literally dropped out of their seats, woozy from near fainting and had to leave the room. A few of the weaker stomachs proceeded to the restroom to vomit up breakfast.

No matter how tough one thinks they are, nothing can prepare a person for the awful sight of mutilation of a fellow human. Unfortunately, as all members of the military keep in the back of their minds, that situation is a distinct possibility. All of us have grappled with mortality of a friend or family member whose time on earth has come to an end. It is different thing altogether to experience sudden, unexpected traumatic injury or death when one is not prepared. That was to be my fate.

ON a foggy day in 1989, typical of June in coastal San Diego, the gray bulk aircraft carrier, U.S.S. Constellation (CV-64), tied to the pier at North Island Naval Air Station in Coronado, California, was empty. Just returned from a long deployment to the western Pacific, Indian Ocean and Persian Gulf, she had discharged her carrier air wing. Three quarters of the crew were off the ship at home or on liberty while the duty section kept watch. All was quiet now. The past few months had been anything but restful. Plagued with a series of mishaps during that stretch, bad luck seemed to dog the ship since her keel was set down a generation ago. Today would be no different.

Begun in the late 1950s in the old Brooklyn Navy Yard, Connie, as many in her every changing ship's company affectionately called her, was a five deployment veteran of the Vietnam War. She was also a seasoned hand at the increasingly important western Pacific and Southeast Asian cruises which included the waters surrounding the Middle East and its strategically important oil reserves.

Connie, like all other American carriers in the twentieth century, was also a small city and a home to many sailors and Marines. Her cramped crew's quarters, mess halls and working spaces, while subject to a number of yard upgrades and repairs, were dingy and humid. In the dripping air of the Indian Ocean or Persian Gulf, Connie's ancient ventilation systems could barely pump breathable air to her remote nooks and crannies. Below, the heat given off by the oil-fired, steam boilers and machinery necessary to drive her four huge propellers, made things even less comfortable. But, myriad crews and air wings that served on her thought her a good ship despite the black cloud that hung over her.

The ship was launched in the shadow of death. Not fully completed in 1960, Connie's pre-commissioning construction crew accidentally kicked off a fire that burned for hours and killed fifty unlucky men, delaying her entry into America's ready arsenal for months. Future engineers and boatswain's mates that probed her lower spaces, vents and holding tanks swore that the voices of the shipyard dead haunted her dark and corroding bowels.

Later in her career, her deployments to Vietnam claimed more lives as at-sea provisioning, refueling and air operations took their toll. An aircraft carrier, at 1,100 feet long, sailing at night through rough and unfriendly seas while launching modern, expensive jet aircraft, is a place where peril lurks. The ship's normal routine consists of myriad moving people, parts and machines and each activity is equally dangerous. It is a miracle that sailors aren't killed more often aboard those floating cities.

I was introduced to Connie as a newly appointed executive officer of the Marine Detachment in

1987. Walking up the towering forward brow, dressed in ceremonial blues, I proudly saluted the colors flapping on the stern post and requested permission to board the ship. After my brief navy experience as a midshipman, I thought I'd never again board a naval vessel as part of ship's company. But, here I was. The officer of the deck greeted me as did the white-clad watch crew. The flak-jacketed Marine posted on the quarterdeck rendered a sharp salute. After I checked in, I met the ship's commanding officer and my new boss, the commanding officer of the detachment. He took me down below where I was introduced to the Marines with whom I would serve for the next two years.

PRIOR to departure on deployments, the navy requires that a ship go through days of refresher training. The tests ensure the crew is ready to complete the difficult tasks expected of it on the long trip away from home. One bright morning, Constellation departed San Diego for a week's exercises. Connie's reputation for ill fortune came along for the ride. A series of human missteps and negligence, along with faults inherent in miles of twisted piping, malfunctioning valves and broken gauges, led to a botched transfer of fuel. Spilling onto a red-hot boiler instead of into a holding tank, the resulting conflagration threatened the ship.

Twenty-one hours after the fire began the ship secured from general quarters and sailed back into San Diego. With the spaces in and around a main machinery room and part of the island gutted and useless, a stream of contractors and ship's company began the daunting task of refitting the ship for duty. It was a Herculean effort and reminiscent of the WWII repairs of the U.S.S. Yorktown. Yorktown had been heavily damaged at the battle of Coral Sea and made ready in Hawaii for service at the battle of Midway a few short weeks later.

NOW underway on that long awaited deployment, just off Baja California, an EA-6B Prowler, the electronic warfare version of the A-6 Intruder, along with its crew of four, mysteriously disappeared somewhere in the Pacific Ocean. To this date, nobody knows what happened to them. The Marine Detachment offered its color guard to the grieving squadron. A sharply dressed and razor sharp seven man squad fired a twenty-one gun salute out over the open ocean in memory of these lost aviators.

Not long after the loss of the EA-6B, an F-18 Hornet from our air wing, targeting an inert object on an empty Pacific range, inadvertently sent an anti-ship missile right through the bridge of a civilian tanker. The missile was carrying an inert warhead so the tanker was able to limp into Honolulu and tie up. Traveling in a taxi from Pearl Harbor, where Constellation had moored to replenish for our long Pacific cruise ahead, I and a few friends took a cab to Waikiki Beach. As we passed the Honolulu docks, the Indian tanker was visible, undergoing repairs. There, in the rising sun of an Oahu morning, we could see the towering, white painted bridge of the tanker punched by a neat hole.

Later on the cruise, the string of misfortune for the carrier and her crew continued. Off of Karachi, Pakistan, the Constellation entertained a motley looking bunch of sub-continental government officials including Asif Ali Zardari, the husband of Benazir Bhutto, the Prime Minister of Pakistan. In order to reinforce the impression among its guests of the power and might of the U.S. Navy, Constellation and its battle group staged a weapons demonstration and air show for the VIPs. A pair of A-6 Intruders, armed with 500 pound high explosive bombs and simulating an attack on a ground target skimmed by at a low altitude and released their ordnance. Through blatant error, the bombs dropped and exploded too close to the ship. Shards of metal shrapnel whizzed over the heads of the startled observers and rattled about the Constellation's island, radar masts and parked aircraft on the flight deck. Miraculously, no person was injured and only easily repaired damage was done to the ship and its equipment. The United States also barely avoided an embarrassing, potentially disastrous, political situation.

CONSTELLATION completed the remainder of her western Pacific, Indian Ocean and Persian Gulf tour and returned to the continental United States at Seattle, Washington. There over 1,000 eager relatives of Constellation's sailors embarked for the final leg of her voyage south to San Diego on a trip with a long and rich tradition. The navy calls it a "Tiger Cruise" and these junkets are intended to increase public awareness of what sailors do for their country. The Tigers were treated to good navy food and bunked below in tight berthing. They were given unfettered access to the ship's operations save for confidential spaces. They were also beneficiaries of a varied and entertaining series of demonstrations designed to wow civilians and place the navy in a good light. The air wing, naturally, was the top billed entertainment. Fighter jets, propeller aircraft and helicopters dancing in the sky motivated a dazzled young audience towards a life in the service as naval aviators. After the air show, the air wing departed the ship. Each squadron flew back to its home station somewhere up or down the West Coast.

Meanwhile, the Marine Detachment set up a weapons display on the fantail and allowed individual Tigers to fire M-16s and M-249 squad automatic weapons. Closely monitored by a watchful Marine, the Tigers blasted away at trash bags tossed over the fantail into the ship's wake.

The last night, before Connie pulled into San Diego, the detachment put on a live fire demonstration off the aft section of a nearly empty flight deck. As darkness fell on a June evening, the Marines engaged a fictional enemy with the firepower we had at our disposal including grenade launchers, machine guns, squad automatic weapons and M-16 rifles. With tracer rounds liberally sprinkled in, long trails of glowing red fire leapt from the muzzles, sped off the stern of the carrier and ricocheted off the glassy Pacific Ocean. At each end of the line of prone Marines, outfitted in full war gear, the three man M-60 machine gun crews traded eight round bursts with one another, crossing fire in the artificial kill zone far beyond the fantail. The senior enlisted platoon leader popped a red hand flare which arched up and fell gracefully back into water. The flare was a signal to all the Marines in the defensive posture that the imagined enemy had penetrated the position and it was time for the final protective fire. The Marines together let loose with everything available, producing a wall of lead that would mow down anyone or anything in front of the position. That last burst of ammunition, like the grand finale in a fireworks show, drew lots of oohs and aahs from the Tigers observing the spectacle. After the display, the Marines let the weapons cool and were ordered to ensure those weapons were safely cleared. Spent casings littering the Constellation's flight deck were cleaned up quickly so as avoid the hazard of fouling an engine of one of the few aircraft remaining aboard.

LATE in the morning of the following day, Constellation triumphantly sailed past the first sea buoy marking the entrance to the harbor at San Diego. Along her flight deck and every available rail, Marines and sailors, spic-and-span in dress uniform, manned the rails in an age old navy tradition for ships returning from sea. As the tugs nudged her against the quay wall, a loud cheer went up from the thousands of additional family and friends lining the busy pier. Eager, excited faces looked up at the towering ship seeking the familiar. Flowers, hugs, kisses and cheers were showered on the long absent and greatly missed crew as the two massive brows or gangways, ladders allowing access to and from the ship to the pier below, were lowered into place. The non-duty sections flooded ashore.

AFTER the bands stopped playing and the crowds dispersed, Constellation returned to the much slower routine of life in port. The Marine Detachment did as well. Relieved of the high pressure work of at sea security, the Marines fell back into the relatively humdrum work of guarding the entry points to the ship and other fairly mundane tasks. This included weapons maintenance and cleaning.

Below decks, in the Marine berthing space near the cage where all weapons were securely stored, two Marine lance corporals, Carl Johannson and Javier Flores, withdrew a squad automatic weapon for cleaning. The weapon had been used a few short hours ago in the Tiger Cruise demonstration and had only undergone a cursory and, as it turned out, unsatisfactory safety check prior to return to the caged armory.

The two men began to disassemble the weapon in a narrow, poorly lighted space between two bunks. Without checking that the weapon was safe, Johannson drew back the charging mechanism and let it slip forward. Inside the weapon, a 5.56 millimeter ball round sat waiting for a strike to its primer. Ignored and forgotten in the hustle and bustle of the Tiger Cruise demonstration, the oversight was a deadly remnant waiting to kill. The action of the bolt moving forward acted as designed and discharged the round into Flores' unprotected abdomen. The high velocity missile ravaged his liver, tearing a ragged hole as it exited his back. The bullet's fragments embedded themselves in a bulkhead behind. Carl screamed as Javier, draining blood, collapsed in front of him.

The Sergeant of the Guard, hearing the crack of the weapon, sprinted to the scene, pushed Carl out of the way and carried Javier to an open space in the berthing area to render first aid. There, with the skill of a professional, he stemmed the mess of blood pouring from the jagged holes in Flores' midsection and back. He then ordered his on duty guard members to summon ship's medical staff to the scene.

Sitting at my desk in a space nearby, I was startled when a white-faced and clearly disturbed Marine burst through the non-water tight door. He screamed to me that someone had been shot. I dialed the detachment commanding officer's four digit phone number and told him what little I knew. I then sprinted up the ladder and back down another leading to the scene. My first reaction was to clear the area around the wounded man, ensure all was being done to keep him alive and also secure the bunks and passageway where the incident had taken place.

Javier was conscious but in great pain. His blood stained the deck and nearby bulkhead but the rapid response of the Marine on duty had kept him conscious and his heart beating. I reassured Javier that help was on the way. The commanding officer arrived and gave equal comfort and as much care as could be mustered. The young man, pale from loss of blood, simply nodded and bravely waited.

Since the carrier's surgeon was ashore and unavailable, an ambulance was called and soon arrived at the foot of the forward brow. We placed Javier on a stretcher and he was whisked across the Coronado Bridge to Balboa Naval Hospital in San Diego to undergo surgery in an attempt to repair the damage.

After being anesthetized for his initial surgery, Javier never regained consciousness. The high velocity round had destroyed his liver and the trauma on the rest of his body too much for him to bear. The surgeon did all he could for him but was unable to keep him alive. As the days passed our visits to his bedside became more and more grim. We knew the end was near for him. We tried to talk to him, to encourage him to awaken from his coma. Nothing worked.

Despite the hopes and prayers of all his loyal friends and his mother's fervent appeals to a greater power, he was never going to come back to us. The face of the hospital commander who broke the news told us all we needed to know. There was no din of battle about him when he died. He was with those he loved and we all loved him. The medical orderlies began to disconnect his intravenous tubes and his artificial breathing equipment. It was quite a sight in that terrible room to see so many grown men, all supposedly rock hard Marines, crying their eyes out. The bad luck ship had seen another misfortune. Another life lost. Javier was gone. This time, however, it was I who had to watch him die.

IN the squalid alleys and backstreets of Olongapo City in the Philippines, before the United States closed its port facilities there, craftsman and artisans sweated in shabby and run down cottages and corrugated tin sheds to produce memorabilia for the sailors and Marines transiting through or stationed at the Subic Bay Naval Base. Overshadowed by the famous Magsaysay strip renowned for its jarringly loud night clubs, brothels and carefree sex, the black market trinket economy in town was a much less open and advertised commodity. The Filipinos, hunched over dimly lighted craft tables or lathes, were capable of producing the most elegant trophies, plaques, ship and aircraft models and any number of items later used to memorialize an event or reward past service to a unit. Filipino work hangs on countless squadron ready room bulkheads, Marine barracks walls or in many ship's wardrooms sprinkled throughout the Pacific Fleet. It was in one of these dank and noisy home factories that a banner was stitched together in honor of the Marines of U.S.S. Constellation.

Hand sewn and adorned with the Marines' emblem of the eagle, globe and anchor, the scarlet cloth with gold fringe told all who came by exactly who we were. Below the beloved and noble symbol of the Marines' glorious history was emblazoned a parsed stanza from Shakespeare's *Henry the Fifth*. The king cheered his soldiers on the eve of the battle of Agincourt. Henry reminded them that, despite their trials, they were the happy few. A band so closely knit that they were willing to shed blood for one another. They were, in both life and death, family.

I had asked a gentle and accommodating Filipina to sew it for me and compensated her handsomely. This was to be my gift to the Marines of the Constellation for all they did for me during my service on the ship. She kindly and expertly did as I asked.

As I detached from Constellation a couple of months after Javier's death, I shook hands with the Marines and said my goodbyes. There on the detachment master sergeant's door hung the banner. It was the last I saw of it.

U.S.S. Constellation is off the navy rolls. She is long out of service having been decommissioned in San Diego after forty-one years of service to America. Before her last crew member departed, I trust he, preferably a Marine, took the banner for safekeeping. I pray he treats it as more than just a souvenir. It should rightfully hang in a small town VFW post or local museum where it can be proudly displayed. It's got a history behind it. It represents all that it means to be a band of brothers. To be part of a group called Marines; united as one in duty, for Corps and for country. Symbols like that piece of cloth help us to keep close to our hearts the pride of service and poignant recollections of the fallen. With it, we keep close fond memories of fine men like Lance Corporal Flores who offered his young life in service on the sea.

Chapter 6

HEROES AND VILLAINS

"His emotions made him feel strange in the presence of men who talked excitedly of a prospective battle as of a drama they were about to witness, with nothing but eagerness and curiosity apparent in their faces. It was often that he suspected them to be liars."

– Stephen Crane –

❋ ❋ ❋ ❋

Hopeless

THE rate of desertion from both northern and southern Civil War armies is legend. Who wouldn't want to flee what was mostly a wretched existence? The lot of the soldier was many things but it was certainly not romantic. Boredom, bad food, disease and living out in the weather are sufficient reasons enough to pine for home. To then be tossed into terrifying combat which threatened injury or death cemented a desire to escape. Men and boys stole away in droves as soon as the chance presented itself and the threat of summary execution dissuaded few.

In most cases though, even the most rudimentary of leadership skills could have checked the flood. Involved and caring officers and non-commissioned officers pressing for better camp conditions, adequate food, functioning equipment and warm clothes could not have eliminated desertion altogether. That paternal care would, however, have reduced the numbers substantially. A greater and rarer talent was the individual mettle needed to keep men standing firm in the heat of battle. That took a lot more gumption than the aptitude needed to procure an army's supplies. The leader possessing such skills is born not made.

Such brave and resourceful captains were difficult to find in the Army of the Potomac. The political toadies, hired and promoted because of who they knew rather than what they knew, had limited capacity to lead these weary, hungry, wet and cold soldiers. They weren't war fighters, they were glory hounds. Their shortcomings in leadership were laid bare when the first shots were fired in battle.

THE lack of seasoned combat commanders was particularly acute in the beleaguered Eleventh Corps. Formed in mid-year 1862, the organization never really developed the coherence and esprit found in its sister units. The vacuum at its very top ensured it would stay that way. Heaven knows Washington and the army's headquarters staff tried desperately to fill the billet. The kind of man needed to solve their problems evaded them.

Thinking a like-minded and fluent Deutscher might do the trick, a German expatriate named Franz Sigel jumped to the fore as an obvious choice. Sigel, however, turned out to be the first errant stitch in an irregular and inept pattern of the Eleventh's leadership.

Sigel, a social reformer at heart, fled to the United States after the 1848 nationalist German movement, in which he played a small part. That failed coup was crushed by a wealthy and better equipped Prussian hammer. Unification of individual German states and a voice of the people in the country's affairs would have to wait.

In America, Sigel found a second home amongst a legion of like-minded, socially conscious Germans. Many discovered a demand for their martial training and experience in the Union army. A deft administrator, armed with the requisite abolitionist credentials and having honed the right political connections, Sigel caught notice of the right people - including Abraham Lincoln - and adroitly maneuvered himself into command of Eleventh Corps. His tepid combat record as a regimental and division commander was only secondarily considered.

At the head of the Eleventh Corps, his German roots and ability to recruit countrymen to the Union cause engendered a modicum of pride among the 12,000 or so under his charge. The slogan "I fights mit Sigel," the broken English rallying cry adopted by his troops, became a common refrain. The boast rang hollow. They mostly didn't fights mit anybody. Except for being engaged and taking heavy casualties at Second Manassas, the corps sat idle on Sigel's watch. The Eleventh, relegated to the army's reserve at Fredericksburg, twiddled thumbs in camp at Falmouth wintering over to the muddy spring of 1863.

Sigel kept busy, though. He was more than irritated at the relatively small size of his unit in comparison to the army's other, better manned corps. He complained often and loudly about its numbers and whined that its tactical role was nothing but an afterthought in the army's plans. Unable to convince the unsupportive General-in-Chief in Washington, Henry Halleck, to meet his demands to reinforce his corps, Sigel departed in a huff. The Eleventh's German loyalists were incensed. From there on it was only downhill for this body of men. Sigel, a figurehead at best, was the finest the Eleventh could have hoped for.

STILL relatively green and now in the unfamiliar hands of a stranger, the pious, dour O.O. Howard, the unmotivated Eleventh was primed for disaster. Howard was, in actuality, a brave officer who had lost an arm in the Peninsula Campaign. It was never his personal fortitude that came into question. His fault lay in his being sorely, fatally, out of touch with his people.

The corps' misery at Chancellorsville, as they were squeezed to the breaking in an untenable and terrifying vice as Stonewall Jackson's wild hordes sprinted headlong into their camps and scattered them, was the predictable result. As the Eleventh collapsed on the Army of the Potomac's right flank, the rest of the blue suited legions fell like dominoes. Howard's mystifying detachment from the fray didn't help.

The tarnished and slighted "Dutchmen" of his bedeviled corps became the whipping boys of the army. Half the regiments that comprised the corps were of Teutonic origin. Their struggle with the language of the new country combined with their dismal showing in early May in the underbrush near the Chancellorsville crossroads condemned them to ridicule and scorn from their fellows in the army. It was now expected of them to fail.

To no one's surprise, and admittedly only partially their fault, their Chancellorsville debacle was mirrored almost exactly on the first day's battle at Gettysburg. Pressed by Confederate forces on the western and northern ridges and fields outside town and without the benefit of supporting reinforcements or a coordinated battle plan, the star-crossed Eleventh Corps units threw down rifles and ceased to fight. They turned and ran, pouring back through the narrow streets in town in a scatter for their lives.

AMONG the fleeing rabble was another German revolutionary, the black bearded, cadaverous Alexander Schimmelpfennig. Except for a select group of Civil War historians and trivia buffs, nobody has ever heard of this guy. His historical anonymity is deserved. Schimmelpfennig wasn't a line soldier but rather a general officer and in command of a brigade in the Eleventh Corps' Third Division. While respected by fellow Germans in his brigade, Schimmelpfennig wasn't the inspirational rock needed to turn around a hopeless situation. But, then again, after the Union cavalry's John Buford and the infantry's John Reynolds had departed the scene, character on the Union side at McPherson's Ridge and along the Chambersburg Road had become a scarce commodity.

As the surviving Eleventh Corps units wedged themselves shoulder-to-shoulder in the narrow streets of town fleeing for their lives, Schimmelpfennig found himself cut off from his men and threatened with capture. So he did what any brave and resourceful leader would do to spark his men; he ducked into and cowered in a drainage culvert.

Later, after the town was solidly in Confederate hands, he took advantage of the cloak of darkness and sneaked into a nearby yard of a helpful Union loyalist. Instead of trying to creep back to Federal lines to take up the fight once again, he laid quite low, snacking on biscuits and sipping water while the battle raged around him. Succored by the sympathetic homeowner, he saw no need to risk capture and only blinkingly emerged only after the Confederates deserted the town.

Dirty and worn, his miraculous resurrection was a relief to his comrades who assumed his consumptive body lay among the rest of the brigade's dead somewhere near the Mummasburg Road. He may have received slaps on the back from his officers and the cheers of his men but the telling of his story did not go as well with the rest of the army. The press was equally harsh. Mercifully, he didn't have to put up with the ridicule for long. He contracted tuberculosis in his forty-first year and died in a sanatorium near Reading, Pennsylvania where he had gone to seek a cure.

The Eleventh Corps marched on. Under its bad luck badge of the crescent moon, it later did some good for the cause in the war for Tennessee. As hard as it tried, though, the Eleventh could never throw off the shackles of bad luck. It is remembered to this day for nothing else.

In Harm's Way

THERE were no Schimmelpfennigs riding on top of and inside four M109 155 millimeter self-propelled howitzers clanking along the barren, starlit Saudi Arabian – Kuwaiti border in the winter of 1991. The howitzers were prudently fish boned and liberally spaced on the flat desert sand as it made no sense to present an inviting target to Iraqi aircraft or a roving enemy armored reconnaissance team. It was early February, midway through the Coalition air campaign in which thousands of sorties softened up Iraqi command and control and Iraqi defensive positions prior to the ground invasion in the First Gulf War.

The winter skies over Saudi Arabia and Kuwait were crystal clear. Nature's myriad pinpricks provided ample light for the night vision goggles strapped on the heads of the Marines. Just across the border the ruins of their target smoldered. It had been a successful artillery raid and the Marines were satisfied with their work. Above them, in the sparkling night air, American and Coalition aircraft enjoyed the horizon to horizon visibility, using it to hammer pre-assigned targets or jump on unwary targets of opportunity.

The Marine artillery battery was equipped with modified self-propelled howitzers, legacies of the Vietnam War. It was the last remaining Marine unit using the rolling cannon and deployed to the Kuwait Theater of Operations. By this late date, most heavy Marine artillery units had been equipped with brand new humvees, better, heavier lift trucks and, most importantly, towed 155 millimeter howitzers. Those guns were lighter, much easier to airlift or ship than their self-propelled cousins. They were more simply maintained in the sand and crud of a desert environment and, with the aid of a good crew, could keep up with fast moving mobile infantry. However, this battalion, the Fifth of the Eleventh Marine Regiment, was going to fight this war with the gear it had on hand.

HAVING served in a M109 battery in that same battalion in two earlier career billets, I was familiar and faithful to the gun. Its big diesel engine, cramped crew cab, driver compartment, thin, cold to the touch armor and its pudgy 155 millimeter gun were old hand. It was the weapon I had been trained on at Officer Basic artillery training at Fort Sill. At that remote Oklahoma outpost, the place where both army and Marine officers learn to shoot cannon artillery, the M109 guns used for our training were in pristine condition, lovingly maintained by both the officers and enlisted men. They were required to move only slight distances to predetermined firing points and restricted in the size charge they could fire. Fort Sill ranges were just too close to civilization to risk an accident. On the grassy plains, the fifteen or so Marines in our class excelled. We took top honors in most of the individual subjects like gunnery, forward observation and a list of general military subjects as long as your arm. Jarheads, in the aggregate, took six of the top ten graduation spots. Despite our competence, the army did things right by us. As far as I was concerned, their hospitality and superior curriculum made it a pleasure to learn the trade in that environment. They even were kind enough to let the Marines have their own little headquarters on post and happily supported us as welcome guests.

On occasion, our hosts even took the time to put on a lively and entertaining weapons demonstration for us. They paraded out the arsenal of modern weapons which included stuff the Marine Corps only dreamed of having. Multiple Launch Rocket Systems, vehicle mounted lasers and Bradley fighting vehicles wowed the crowd. Army forward observers rode around in style. Marine forward observers humped with the grunts or, if they were lucky, got a ride with the infantry in the back of a five-ton truck. The army put the observer in a helicopter or a laser range finding equipped Bradley fighting vehicle. Nice work if one can get it!

As the performance approached its end, the army introduced their historical artillery demonstration team. To my surprise and pleasure, the team dragged out a Napoleon twelve pounder, a very common piece of direct fire artillery seen on any Civil War battlefield. The period dressed gunners jumped to the commands of the gun captain and blasted wooden and plastic targets with iron round shot and canister. Seeing just one gun in live action proved to me once again how very brave Civil War soldiers were to willingly place themselves anywhere near the business end of those things. Inviting oneself to danger that can cause injury to the body or can lead to death is irrational. Such a response is nothing less than suicidal. It runs counter to the overpoweringly strong ancestral trait that natural selection has instilled in human genetic code to perpetuate the gene, the individual and, by extension, the species. Yet, the actions of a few soldiers ignore millions of years of evolution. How can that be? Heroism must, therefore, run as deeply in our hereditary blueprint as the powerful urge to flee to safety. The "fight" part of the fight-or-flight response to a mortal threat takes hold more strongly in some. This, at least in my limited view of Darwinian survival, helps explain why we see heroes around us.

THE M109s returning from the Saudi-Kuwaiti border that night kicked up clouds of dust as they cut a new trail through the Saudi Desert. They had slid up to the predetermined firing positions, set up and sent rounds down range to great effect. After the last round, they had picked up their gear, turned around and rolled towards home with mission accomplished and without any counter battery fire. All that remained was to get to their previous position and get some well deserved sleep.

High above a pair of Marine A-6E Intruders carrying Mark-20 Rockeye Cluster Bombs circled the border area on the prowl for targets. They had miscalculated their airborne location thinking they were well inside a kill box over enemy territory in Kuwait. They weren't. They were over Saudi territory and anything below them should have been positively identified as friendly or enemy before being attacked. Spotting the dust trail the artillery unit's vehicles were kicking up, the

Marine aviators' pulses began to race. Wrongly assuming the artillery Marines were an Iraqi armored column, the pilots oriented their jets for attack.

MIGUEL Arroyo served as a section chief for one of the guns in the battery. I knew Miguel well from my days serving with this very battalion four years earlier. Miguel was in charge of a gun then as well. A veteran of artillery and the Marines, he tolerated young Marine lieutenants and that's about it. It took a while and a lot of work to convince him that I knew what I was doing. By the time I took over as battery executive officer, the officer responsible for the gun line when deployed or in the field, I think I finally gained his confidence. I knew he'd be a solid member of the battery's team of gun bunnies and would allow me and the other battery officers the flexibility to focus on other less experienced crews. When he wasn't down at the gun park tearing apart a howitzer breech or back at the barracks looking after his Marines, he'd be at the battery office keeping the officers and staff NCOs entertained. Guys like that, who keep on an even keel and maintain a sense of humor, are welcome additions to a military unit. He was also pretty active around the base and wouldn't take no for an answer when recruiting young Marines to play on the intramural softball team.

AT the battalion fire direction center, we tuned in to the play-by-play of the war overhead on the high frequency radios used by the air wing. We also kept abreast of the activity of other units via standard ground unit radio transmissions as our sister battalion's artillery raid progressed. It was kind of neat hearing the war being fought from the perspective of the few people keying the handsets in the combat units engaged. We were jealous of the Fifth Battalion guys because they were already in the fight while we were designated to hang back and wait around until the ground offensive began. After the raid was over, over-the-air conversations had quieted. There wasn't much to talk about as they moved back to their base of operations. Suddenly, the radios crackled to life. Fifth Battalion was calling for air medical evacuations. They were providing casualty information and their location and they needed a chopper – now! The Marine making the request was shouting.

OUT of the starry night sky, the A-6s roared in over their brother Marines and pickled off their bombs. Over the target, the casings surrounding the sub-munitions stripped away and the deadly cluster bombs spewed out like a shotgun blast. The anti-personnel and anti-armor bomblets rained down and popped all around the artillerymen. Protected only by the canvas on humvees or the thin armor shielding, the Marines were sitting ducks. They were in air defense formation but the decimated Iraqi air force was not expected to attack. They certainly didn't expect Marine flyers to ruin their day.

The Rockeye cluster bombs did their work. Two Marines were killed and three others, including Miguel Arroyo, were wounded. Standing exposed in the top hatch of the howitzer, he took a frontal blast to his body. Protected only by a flak jacket and helmet, shrapnel tore into his arm and shredded his face. Arroyo, already exposed outside the turret hatch, had jumped to serve the .50 caliber machine gun mounted beside him. He cranked the charging handle back and chambered a round and began firing at the attacking aircraft as the ordnance exploded all around. As the aircraft completed their attack, the column halted, Marines jumped to the assistance of the wounded and the frantic calls for help were broadcast out over the serene desert air. Miguel was dragged from the rear of the howitzer, broken and bleeding but conscious.

A few months later, after the armistice and our long awaited return to Twentynine Palms, some of the officers and enlisted men of Third Battalion were invited to the Fifth Battalion's Gulf War awards ceremony. We strolled over to their headquarters on a late spring day and stood in formation on the parade deck as the brave Marines in that unit were recognized for their valor in the war just ended. In the line of the honored, there stood Miguel. He had lost an eye in the friendly fire incident and his right arm was gone as well. After his battalion commander had pinned the Purple Heart to his chest and the ceremony had ended, I approached him, winding my way through the group of admirers who stuck around to give him their best. "Hi Staff Sergeant Arroyo," is all I could muster. He responded that it was good to see me and he sincerely appreciated me coming by to see the ceremony. All I could do was thank him for what he had done. I didn't know what else to say, it was all said before by many others. I shook his left hand and saluted him and left him to the line of others waiting for a chance to say some words.

Miguel could have minimized chance of injury by dropping down from his commander's hatch and hiding in that howitzer rumbling along in the night. The thin armor of the crew compartment would have provided a modicum of protection to him as it did the rest of his crew. Miguel Arroyo was a Marine. Instead of cowering, he did what his training had taught him to do. He jumped to the sound of the guns and returned fire even when all about was smoke and confusion. Miguel fought the urge of his inner self to run and hide. His years of experience and a focused mind overcame his instinctive desire to be scared and take flight. He put himself directly into harm's way. Miguel, like so many of his Civil War forebears, did what the Marines expected him to do on that starry, dark, horrible night.

❇ ❇ ❇ ❇

The Hero Stands Before Me

GREG Miller, a Marine captain, probably doesn't think he was a hero. In fact, if one asked any of the people who worked with him in Third Battalion's operations center, they would all agree that Greg was just an ordinary guy. He'd do the job and do it well and that was the extent of it. But Greg, like all heroes, came out of his shell when it really counted.

THE ground war portion of the First Gulf War had wound down and our battalion sat waiting for orders in a position near the Kuwait City airport. The operations center, of which Greg and I were part, took advantage of the down time to rearrange the watch schedule and get back to the less hectic peacetime rotation. Greg had the first watch of the night and so I settled down in my sleeping bag to grab some sleep. My temporary bed was next to one of the high backed humvees that were situated end-to-end with a canvas sheet tossed over the top to form our mobile operations unit. Inside the cramped space, Greg and his team monitored radios and kept in touch with our senior unit, Task Force Ripper, and the subordinate firing batteries sprinkled around our battalion position.

It was a cold night and I snuggled into my sleeping bag, stripped down to a pair of underwear.   My camouflage desert uniform, boots, socks and t-shirt were folded neatly and placed next to my sleeping bag near the humvee.

As I drifted off to sleep, through the thin canvas covering the operations center, I could hear Greg telling one of the Marines to refill the kerosene heater. We had picked one up in Saudi Arabia before the ground war and the Marines on watch would use it inside to keep warm in the late winter chill of the Saudi and Kuwaiti desert. Busy with the watch and rightfully expecting the Marine to take the heater outside and perform the task, Greg let his attention be diverted elsewhere.

The careless Marine opened a fuel can and began pouring kerosene into the nearly empty fuel tank of the still lighted, glowing portable heater. The fumes from the fuel ignited immediately. Jarred awake by the panicked shouts of several Marines under the canvas, I poked my head out of my sleeping back just as a flaming ball of the heater and fuel can were thrown out far from the tented structure. They landed on the desert floor and continued to erupt, lighting up the area around us. My stomach sank as the next sight appearing in front of me was of Greg Miller's body, fully engulfed, sprinting out from under the canvas.

The fire licked at his upper body and face and he was screaming in pain. I leaped to my feet as he fell to the ground before me. Combined with the moist sand at his feet, Greg's instinctive survival roll mercifully extinguished most of the flames. I threw my sleeping bag on him snuffing out the rest. I rolled him on to his back. His blackened arms, blistered and torn skin hung in grotesque strip as his arms shot into the air seeking relief.

As I tended to Greg, the remaining watch crew piled out of the flaming operations center, scattering in all directions. The canvas cover and plastic tarps over the humvees had ignited when Greg hefted the lighted bomb through a narrow opening leading out to the night. The forward motion he used to toss out the heater agitated its open fuel tank and splashed kerosene liberally over the operations center and his own two arms. Greg's quick thinking had prevented the heater from exploding in the shelter and killing or wounding the rest of the Marines nearby.

The two high backed humvees not only served as the operations center but they were also a temporary storage area for the battalion headquarters machine gun rounds, small arms ammunition, grenades for the M-16 mounted launchers and assorted flares and pyrotechnic signaling devices. The vehicles were ticking time bombs.

Seeing that Greg was no longer in immediate danger, I leaped into the front seat of one of the humvees in order to drive it out from under the canvas and prevent a further catastrophe. As I switched on the glow plug ignition switch, the strong arm of the battalion sergeant major, who himself had sped to the scene immediately after spotting the fire, grabbed me. He shouted to me that Marines were sleeping under the humvees. Moving the vehicle would crush bodies. Even though that practice was strictly forbidden for very obvious reasons and no human could be snoozing through this chaos, I had to believe him or risk killing a sleeping Marine. So, I jumped from the humvee and helped to move Greg away from the growing inferno.

A safe distance from the flames, Greg was tended to by the battalion medical staff. I could see him shivering and hear his teeth chattering as the burns and cold began to send his body into shock. The medical team did their best to comfort him and treat him and worked to evacuate him to a better equipped support hospital. He was soon on his way out of there to advance medical facilities, Germany and, eventually, home.

The night continued to go downhill. There I stood, in the freezing cold in my skivvies, as everything I owned went up in smoke. Cammies, flak jacket, saved letters from home, my gas mask and nuclear, biological and chemical protective gear and my nine millimeter sidearm were left close to the humvee and all melted to a lumpy crisp. Adding to the misery, the fire raging in the humvees began cooking off the ammunition and pyrotechnics in a loud, colorful and dangerous display. All of us fled to a safe distance and watched the fireworks. Nearby units panicked thinking our headquarters was under Iraqi attack. It took a few more hours and a lot of explaining over the radios to calm everybody down.

When sanity returned to our upside down world, I stood shaking my head in disbelief. A pair of Fruit of the Loom briefs was my sole worldly possession. A couple of sympathetic brother officers chipped in some spare cammies and boots and, covering my exposed skin, I managed to avoid hypothermia. I spent the night huddled under a borrowed poncho and poncho liner, fitfully trying to ward off the cold. It took some effort to clear my mind of the sight of Greg in flames.

BACK at Twentynine Palms, Greg met us when the busses transporting us from March Air Force Base and back up into the high desert drove through the front gates of our home station. They rolled to a stop and dropped us off in front of the headquarters building and barracks we hadn't seen in almost a year. Hundreds of family and friends were there to greet us along with Greg. His arms were bandaged and his face was smeared with anti-bacterial ointment. He was sullen and depressed having endured some painful surgeries to graft healthy skin on the badly burnt areas of his arms. He was also angry because his injury separated him from his comrades. I approached him and embraced him as carefully as I could.

We talked for a while and I gave my best wishes to his family attending with him. As he moved on to greet others, I remained where I was, awestruck and speechless; humble and appreciative of being in the presence of a hero.

Greg wasn't the favorite of the higher ups in the battalion staff. His work was good, his intentions pure and the Marines really enjoyed working for him. But he wasn't going to go out of his way to kiss somebody's butt. As a result, nobody bothered to write this guy up for an award. I guess they figured that it was his fault that the whole thing happened on his watch. One would assume that sacrificing one's own safety and having incurred a traumatic injury in the act of preventing the death or maiming of a couple of Marines would come up to the level of commendation in a rational person's eyes. In the pot of medals tossed around to people doing their jobs, I would have thought one could be found to acknowledge an intrepid deed. In making that assumption, I couldn't have been more wrong.

✳ ✳ ✳ ✳

Walk for a Moment in His Shoes

FOR every hero who unflinchingly stood fast as bombs dropped around him or incurred physical injury to prevent the same to others, there are dozens more not up to the challenge. So it was at Gettysburg. Each of that battle's icons, faces emblazoned on a bronze or stone monument, has as his opposite a villain, doomed to infamy by the slings and arrows of historians and arm chair buffs. In any discussion of Gettysburg, on the winner's side anyway, the names of John Buford, Winfield Scott Hancock and Joshua Chamberlain spring into conversation as saviors of that day. Their heroics are indeed memorable and have become the stuff of legend. The names are even more endearing to casual students of the battle after Michael Shaara released his popular novel *The Killer Angels.* That 1974 fictional account brought these characters to life. General Dan Sickles, the notorious leader of the army's Third Corps, is barred from their august company.

DANIEL Edgar Sickles was no stranger to controversy. He was one of those rare souls that simply could not mind his own business and stay out of the public eye. In one of the more sensational affairs of the era, he shot dead his wife's lover in broad daylight in the capital's Lafayette Square in full view of the Executive

Mansion. At his trial for murder, the jury acquitted him, wholeheartedly accepting the arguments of Sickles' counsel, future Secretary of War Edwin Stanton. Sickles had been temporarily insane when he pulled the trigger.

As an elected New York State official he was involved in several squalid incidents including bringing a known prostitute into the Assembly chamber. While that may not even raise eyebrows today, ante-bellum American morality held elected representatives to a different standard.

Sickles, before he ever donned a uniform, proved himself an extraordinary personality. After his military career was abruptly ended by a cannonball at Gettysburg, he kept in the spotlight. He spent his remaining working days self-aggrandizing his wartime performance and belittling the voices he felt had wronged him in the past. Queerly, he made it a habit to visit the bones of a shattered leg, donating the personal memento to the Army Medical Museum. If the macabre intrigues, one can gaze upon the fractured skeletal remnants archived at the National Museum of Health and Medicine on the campus of the Walter Reed Army Medical Center in D.C. General Sickles, a glutton for attention, certainly would not mind.

SICKLES' contentious tale at Gettysburg centers on a feature on which countless military engagements have turned – the battlefield's terrain. As one heads down Cemetery Ridge towards Big and Little Round Tops, one soon arrives at the position in the Army of the Potomac's line assigned to his Third Corps. The Tammany politician and womanizer turned soldier was tasked with tying his unit in with Hancock's Second Corps placed neatly along prominent Cemetery Ridge to his right. As for Sickles' left flank, General Meade was less clear. Obscurely, the army commander told him to hinge his corps with ". . . Round Top, [and] if it was practicable to occupy it."

Apparently, Dan Sickles didn't find such a move in the least bit practicable. Further, he ignored his orders to link with General Hancock's men. Instead, after riding over where he needed to go, looking around and thinking about it for a short time, he pushed his corps far forward onto higher ground near the Emmitsburg Road ahead of him. Here the controversy begins. To this day, it remains subservient only to the fuss created by Robert Lee's decision to attack the Union army's center on the third day.

A number of pseudo-strategists have trudged around the salient formed by Sickles' brazen move of the Third Corps on the second day at Gettysburg. They are judge, jury and executioners all. I am one too, but I lean a bit towards exonerating the accused. I cannot help but be captured and enmeshed in the debate. It intrigues me to find more out about it.

When he and his men reached the Emmitsburg Road, the corps was thrown out in a line roughly paralleling it and angling back on both sides in a feeble attempt to connect back to the rest of the army's lines. He was a boil on the Union army's skin waiting to be popped by a Confederate lance. His troops occupied ground in and around the Trostle Farm, the Peach Orchard and the Wheat Field; all places now firmly cemented in Gettysburg lore. Sickles also positioned men near the rocks of Devil's Den and the swales and hollows in the western shadow of the Round Tops. In doing so, his flanks, as they say in military parlance, were quite exposed and waving like laundry in the wind.

Sickles, for all his personal faults and inexperience as a military professional, was certainly not ignorant of the obvious. His assigned ground, the patch of land on the southern fringe of Cemetery Ridge, drops noticeably before the ridge rises a bit and merges with the northern upslope of Little Round Top. Standing there, it's as if one is in a hole. Even a novice cannot help but empathize with Sickles' decision to move his corps to the west to a better vantage point. In essence, he could not see a darn thing in front of him except the slow rise up to the intermediate ridgeline carrying the Emmitsburg Road on an oblique angle to his front. Staying where he was would blind him to the disposition of the enemy. He would only discover their true intentions when they were arrayed directly to his front with weapons charged and bayonets flashing. His was an unenviable position in which to be.

Sickles' detractors delve into a library of evidence to back up their claims of his misconduct. If he had lined his corps along the low ridge as ordered, it is true that Winfield Hancock's Second Corps was immediately to his north with supports if necessary. It is also a fact that it was made explicit to him by George Meade to connect with Hancock on his unit's left. Further, it is indisputable that when Sickles leaped forward from the main Union line, he left Little Round Top unoccupied and open to Confederate capture.

One does not need to be an expert military topographer to observe how advantageous a position Little Round Top was to the Union army. We know Sickles saw it differently. Despite Meade's discretionary instructions to Sickles about those heights, leaving Little Round Top unoccupied was an undisputed tactical error. Higher ground always lends the advantage to those wise enough to occupy it. Staff officers serving Meade later repaired Sickles' blunder by rushing troops and artillery to the top of that later sanctified hill. There, those rapidly deployed regiments, along with a few timely delivered pieces of artillery, engaged in a dramatic and bloody defense that prevented Confederate flanking of the Union left. Reinforcements also forestalled a general panic. There would be no repeat of first day's Union debacle.

Sickles judged, however, that his newly created salient was within his operational flexibility. As commander on the ground, he determined it was the best course of action and stayed faithful to the mission. In doing so, he set the stage for critics to pick apart his apparently faulty judgment, all with the benefit of hindsight.

Most of his detractors, lobbed editorial comments, safely ensconced in newspaper offices, cozy studies or anywhere other than that man-made hell that was the late afternoon of the second of July. Most also fail to pay attention to the opinions of attacking Confederates who, upon their move to flank the Union army, were quite surprised and displeased at the unexpected strength of a Federal line of battle so far to the front.

Sickles placed his Third Corps in a position which inevitably had it take the brunt of concentrated Confederate attacks that entire afternoon. His men gave as good as they got. Both his corps and those unfortunate to be part of the Confederate assault were bled dry. Say what one wishes about Dan Sickles but there was no doubt he was, above anything else, a fighter. This man was not afraid to set his men alongside those of the enemy. At his headquarters near Trostle's barn, surrounded by staff and barking orders, he stuck to his ground only leaving after suffering a horrific injury. A Confederate solid shot, which he and those around him could see skipping across the field towards them, tore into him and left his shattered right leg hanging by a few tendons and ribbons of skin. He was helped off his horse, placed on a stretcher and could be seen carted off the field reportedly puffing on a cigar en route to a field hospital and a fairly straightforward amputation. A surgeon only had to clip a few tendons and remnants of skin to complete the job that Confederate artillery had begun. Tidying up by sewing a flap of skin over the stump and Sickles was a new man.

It can be awfully fulfilling to malign an historical figure like Sickles using reams of paper evidence gleaned from many sources. Historians take great pains to prove his actions were detrimental to the defensive posture of the Union army deployed on Cemetery Ridge but they rely too on hearsay and bias. If by some sleight of hand or magic trick, however, one could be whisked to stand in Sickles' boots that day, it is interesting to speculate how many detractors would change their minds. He, like the soldiers and officers around him, was tired and sore from days in the saddle on long marches and certainly both hungry and thirsty. While he would be reluctant to admit it, he was probably apprehensive at intelligence of Confederate troops massing in the woods in front of his corps' position. Sickles had to ride the breadth of his line or back to Meade's headquarters or to other places on the battlefield simply to keep informed about the enemy situation, the deployment of supporting units including artillery and status of the infantry of his corps. The ground he was assigned to defend was new to him and his orders, clearly, allowed him some choice as to his corps' deployment. So he made the call and advanced the timeline for that day's battle. His decision, his personal sacrifice and the lives of the members of the Third Corps who fell in the salient, preserved the fighting strength of the Second Army Corps. That vaunted unit would sorely need all it had for the test at the Union line's center coming the following day.

THERE is no monumental likeness to remind us of General Sickles at Gettysburg. No equestrian statue, no oversized bronze sculpture displaying a brooding or contemplative pose. On the site where Sickles' leg was pulverized by a Confederate shell sits a low stone pile topped off with the diamond badge of his beloved Third Corps. In other less conspicuous places around the battlefield are other more subtle reminders that Sickles played a part in this momentous event. These tokens of remembrance are just part of his legacy there.

As James Hessler tells us in his definitive book entitled *Sickles at Gettysburg,* Sickles did much to give us the Gettysburg we see today. As a member of Congress and head of the New York State Monuments Commission, he worked tirelessly for establishment of the National Park and the long-term preservation of the battlefield grounds. He also was instrumental in bringing most of the structures erected to the memory of the soldiers and units of the Excelsior State to the field. Thus, his name and memory, despite not being sanctified in the form of a personal statue, are kept in our minds by the obelisks, castles, slabs and markers appearing across the battlefield on behalf of those who fought for the great state of New York.

Hessler's narrative relates an often repeated, and some say apocryphal, tale about a fattened and graying Sickles visiting Gettysburg some time after the guns were silent and the smoke had cleared. When pressed as to where his likeness could be seen on the vast field he remarked nonchalantly that the "whole park was his monument."

It certainly is.

✳ ✳ ✳ ✳

Saving the Day

ON a map, the physical boundaries of the city of Rochester trace out a cockeyed water drop that appears to hang down from the southern shore of Lake Ontario. The slender stem of the drop is composed of narrow strips of city owned land paralleling both sides of the terminal course of the Genesee River as it flows into the lake. At the very tip of that stem, dramatically spotlighted at night, a 900 foot drawbridge spans the river connecting the Rochester neighborhood of Charlotte to the town of Irondequoit. As a replacement for a long deteriorating, rotting lift bridge with a history of congestion and maintenance problems, the new bridge has palliated heavy traffic and improved the aesthetics of the surrounding area. The bridge is named after Colonel Patrick O'Rorke, the young officer who had, as an infant, unknowingly adopted Rochester as his new home.

OUT of West Point and promoted to colonel, O'Rorke led the 140th New York Volunteer Infantry Regiment made up of soldiers that hailed from the Genesee Valley. For a brief time at Chancellorsville, he was advanced and took over the entire brigade of which that regiment was part. After the Army of the Potomac went through a major reorganization after Chancellorsville, O'Rorke was sent back to lead his New Yorkers on the march to Gettysburg. It wasn't long before he and his men were set up to the east of the battlefield, in the shadow of the humps of the Round Tops as part of the Fifth Corps reserve.

While the fight in front of the Union line at the Trostle farmstead, the Wheat Field, the Peach Orchard, Houck's Ridge and Devil's Den raged, O'Rorke and his men sat at the ready. As the afternoon of the second of July wore on, the colonel and his nervous 140th New York were directed to gather their gear and advance to support the collapsing front of General Sickles' Third Corps. Moving forward, but at the tail end of his brigade's line of march, O'Rorke was abreast of the slope of Little Round Top when General Warren, Meade's Chief of Engineers, galloped up to him. He urgently requested Paddy's regiment detour and provide assistance to cover an open area on the hill above. Paddy, a good soldier, hesitated. He had received alternative orders. The senior Warren assured him he would take responsibility. Satisfied, O'Rorke turned to his men and ordered them up the wooded rear slope.

As the sun began to set, the 140th broke out of the trees on top of the hill. In front and below them, the boys of the 140th gaped at the seething mass of Rebels in the valley below. A sizeable portion of the attackers were scaling the front of Little Round Top and were in and amongst the boulders. The massive rocks provided superb cover. O'Rorke, taking stock of the dire situation developing, acted spontaneously and directed his men to charge the Confederates bounding up and around the rocks in front. Paddy showed them the way. Before he had a chance to control his troops and form them into line of battle, a Confederate minie ball to the neck cut young

O'Rorke's life short. The press of the fresh blue troops on the hill broke the Confederate advance. O'Rorke and his 140th New York Volunteers had plugged a gaping hole in the Union left and prevented Rebel occupation of Little Round Top's crest.

JOSHUA Chamberlain and his 20th Maine, positioned at the very end of the Union line on Little Round Top, usually get the credit for saving General Meade's and the Army of the Potomac's reputation that day. Historians don't unanimously agree with that assessment but quite a few who have read Michael Shaara's novel *The Killer Angels,* and its 1993 cinematic interpretation *Gettysburg,* are convinced. After Gettysburg, Chamberlain lived a long and storied life. O'Rorke died on the field. While Chamberlain was no self-aggrandizer, live people are far advantaged over the dead in neatly tying up their personal legacies. Chamberlain not only survived the Civil War, he lasted well into the twentieth century. He died in 1914, succumbing, it is believed, to a war wound received at the siege of Petersburg fifty years earlier.

His post-war life was filled to the brim. Among other endeavors, he penned his exciting life's story in his reminiscences. Professionally, he served as Governor of Maine and also as President of Bowdoin College. He was ever present in front of crowds, speaking about the war, his combat service and the meaning of the Civil War to an eager and attentive nation. It didn't hurt his reputation one bit that he was awarded the Medal of Honor thirty years after the fight on Little Round Top. His commemorative speeches at Gettysburg and elsewhere as a leader in the Union Civil War veterans' organization known as the Grand Army of the Republic, kept him in the public eye.

WITH hardly an opportunity to excel on the speaking circuit or ink his autobiography, Patrick O'Rorke's legacy had no chance against Chamberlain's longevity. But Paddy did outlive Chamberlain in a way. Take a trip up Little Round Top the next time at Gettysburg. Whether one rides up on a tour bus, drives her own car, rides a bike or walks from town, it's a sight well worth the effort.

As one mounts a short rise, breaks out of the trees and steps out on to the front face of the bouldered slope, the strategic importance of the position immediately becomes clear. It is apparent from standing where O'Rorke and his 140th New Yorkers did what defense of this fairly confined space meant to the entire Army of the Potomac. From there one can see all the way up the sinuous line of Cemetery Ridge with the spires of the town in the distant background. A sizeable Confederate force on the slope accompanied by several batteries of artillery would have most assuredly changed the battle's outcome. One can easily picture the Federal army rolling up and collapsing if O'Rorke's desperate charge had failed and the Confederates had indeed swept the high ground.

There is one last quirky fact. It gives O'Rorke a leg up or, if one prefers, a nose up in the minds of modern tourists. At the point at which the 140th New York Volunteer Infantry battled on Little Road Top, there sits a monument dedicated to their valor and their commander's sacrifice. A bronze profile of Paddy's upper body projects outward on the side facing Devil's Den and the valley below Little Round Top. The monument's designer molded a prominent nose for Paddy which sticks out noticeably from the flat stone surface. That anatomical protuberance shines brilliantly while his beard, neck and uniformed torso remain tarnished and subdued. It is said that good luck goes with anyone who rubs Paddy's nose. Despite requests from the Park Service urging restraint, thousands of camera carrying scofflaws have contributed further to his nose's luster. Having it on his face certainly didn't help its original bearer on that summery Thursday in July long ago. So, who knows if the bronze representation brings a fairer outlook to the countless who buff it each year? Aside from risking an unlikely summons for vandalism from the National Park Police, it certainly can't hurt.

O'RORKE'S body was transported back to Rochester after the battle. When ceremony and remembrances had echoed away, his remains were lowered in the ground in a cemetery close to the center city. Not too long after he was interred, the cemetery filled. As the years passed it was no longer visited and fell into disrepair. Rochester, however, did not forget him.

Recognizing his contribution to the preservation of the Union, a group of local supporters had the coffin dug up from its weed choked surroundings. His body was moved to its permanent resting place in the expanse of Holy Sepulchre Cemetery on Lake Avenue just a few short blocks from the bridge which now bears his name.

Of Paddy O'Rorke, nothing is left but the legend, his grave marker and a monument on Little Round Top. Less importantly, his sobriquet and youthful image are scripted on a pub sign hanging outside a cozy tavern not far from where he died. Much farther north, that same name adorns a lift bridge's bastions in his adopted city. In his Rochester, he lies at peace. But next to the well worn narrow trails on a bolder strewn hump near Gettysburg, on the ground where he fell, the hero's nose lives on.

Epilogue

"It's a beautiful day. Don't let it get away."

– U2 –

❋ ❋ ❋ ❋

Gettysburg Sun

ON Wednesday, March 19, 2008 it rained in Gettysburg. In fact, it poured down in buckets. The town's fish wrapper, *The Gettysburg Times,* reported that the deluge lasted for hours, inundating low areas, turning creeks into rivers and slowing traffic on flooded streets. Outside of town, up on Oak Hill, the sheets of water drowned the gas lit flame flickering on top of the Eternal Light Peace Memorial. Its beacon was intended to shine forever. But, even the best efforts of man could not stand against the inexorable forces of nature.

Seventy years prior, in front of a huge crowd, that same flame was lighted for the first time after a speech of dedication by Franklin Roosevelt. The president had come to Gettysburg to preside over the seventy-fifth anniversary festivities commemorating the battle. Alongside the Civil War veterans in attendance, the Peace Memorial's public unveiling was a highlight of the event. The forty-seven foot tall limestone shaft set upon a base of granite was permanently placed on the slight rise of the hill which had come into prominence during the fight on the battle's first day. The stone from which it was chiseled had been quarried from rock deposits deep in the ground both north and south of the Mason-Dixon Line. It was a symbolic gesture to a once divided and now united America.

At that same 1938 remembrance, 1,800 or so Civil War veterans came by car and rail to be honored at the event. Twenty-five of those grizzled nonagenarians had actually fought on the ground on which the commemoration took place. A few were wheeled about in chairs and some could barely stand. A couple of hale and hearty survivors, all graying and most sporting whiskers reminiscent of their youthful days in another time, appeared in tip top shape and gamely refused the valet services of the boy scouts assigned to assist them. Whether vigorous or sickly, at the tail end of their earthly existence, these men absorbed the exaltation and praise heaped on them by the hundreds of thousands of humbled citizens in attendance. But, much more of life trailed behind these icons than stood ahead of them. It would not be long before nature also doused the living flames of these heroes. Their voices, relaying personal recollections of the battle in aged and croaking whispers, were silenced. Their inevitable deaths were surely a great loss to relatives but equally so to the countless, curious who yearned to revel in their stories. The masses never tired of hearing them time and again. The seventy-fifth anniversary gathering presented the opportunity for strangers, those desiring the simple pleasure of understanding the very essence of the Civil War, to look into the very same eyes which gazed at Pickett's disaster or Hancock's splendor. It would be the final chance to shake a hand that held a rifle or a sword and wielded it in anger on the field. It would be the last time to touch a lone figure who, himself, personified all that was Gettysburg.

IN July of 2013, the Gettysburg sesquicentennial will be upon us. In the scheme of all things related to the battle, it means absolutely no more or no less than the 149th anniversary. But, if the rounder, neater package of years draws visitors and breeds a new generation of youth who become enthralled with this place then so be it. Anticipating the surge in new interest along with the steadier crop of the always faithful, the Gettysburg Convention and Visitors Bureau has put a link on their website devoted to the event. Also, together with the Adams County Historical Society, the National Park Service and a few select individuals, they've also invested the time and money to sponsor a second Internet advertisement called *150th Gettysburg.* Both websites are up and running and posting information on scores of upcoming reenactments, speeches and public tributes along with weblogs and updates. They also highlight other events coinciding with the 150th anniversary celebrations of the larger Civil War itself.

The 150th anniversary of the battle seems a good excuse as any for dedicated, motivated reenactors to make some noise. The Gettysburg

Anniversary Committee is committed to ensure that is so. A blockbuster staged battle is tentatively scheduled for the fourth through the seventh of July. Several thousand diehards in full regalia will be here for that along with thousands more who can think of nothing better to do than watch the pageantry and smoke of what will be a memorable display.

The streets of this tiny town will be far more crowded than during a normal July week. The hotels and motels in the borough and in surrounding areas will be booked. The hard working people running the shops and restaurants will be tasked to the very limits of equanimity. The multitude, descending like biblical locusts, will strain even the most patient among them. Those good people, I am confident, will meet the challenge.

But, I won't be there. My psyche demands space; some elbow room as I move around my adopted second home in this miniscule, lovely southern Pennsylvania town. While I'd like to think I'm special, the townspeople, Park Service officials and other visitors surely won't miss me. They'll have plenty to keep them busy. Besides, there will be many more times for me to get back and I'll do so. I will wait until the temperatures are more forgiving, the sun is lower in the sky and the press of humanity ebbs. But, for those that go to the 150th and are able to survive the crowds, the event should be like nothing they've seen before.

BY mid-November the skies over Rochester are curtained and perpetually gloomy. Sheathed in a stratus cloud layer whose pewter blandness melds indistinguishably with the gray and white landscape below, the northern Lake Ontario shoreline is bereft of sunshine. Combined with the shorter days at this northern latitude, seasonal affective disorder takes hold of many and wraps them in despair. The housebound haters of bitter cold, snow and outdoor winter sports, pine for the return of the sun. Those with the means and whose patience is at an end, give up altogether and jet south or west to fairer winter climes. The rest, veterans of the lake shadow overcast, agonize for more temperate weather.

Spring takes its time but does eventually come and, shaking off winter blues, Rochesterians face towards the sun, letting its bright face warm faces and bodies and thaw chilled psyches. Spring is short in the north country. It does not dawdle, jumping right into the summer. Frustratingly, that season brings its own discomfort in the form of heat and humidity. Like spring, the passage of days from Memorial Day to Labor Day seems equally brief. But, at summer's conclusion, the stage is set for the northeastern seasonal prime time. Usually on the heels of a strong weather front, dirty and humid air is swept aside, dewpoints drop and the sun hangs over the eastern seaboard like a sparkling gem. This golden weather is predictable and welcome as summer turns to September and the days shorten approaching the autumnal equinox. As with a holy day set by the course of an astronomical body's appearance in the heavens, we time our trip south to coincide with the distinctly fine weather lucky easterners enjoy this time of year.

THE same sun over Gettysburg was at work the week of September 11, 2001. The clear skies and unlimited visibility had allowed al Qaeda terrorists to navigate their flying bombs south along the broad course of the Hudson River down to the southern tip of Manhattan. They also had little trouble picking out the Pentagon among the jumble of buildings in urban Washington. If the day had been cloudy and damp, their plot would have been foiled.

Having already planned our annual journey to our home away from home, we stayed the course. Despite the wall-to-wall news coverage and the real uncertainty about what other violent surprises al Qaeda had up its sleeves, midday Friday of that week my brother and I pointed the car to Route 15 and set off to Gettysburg. The sky, as it was on that infamous Tuesday, was of the purest blue. The sun, burning high in the southern sky, was bright and warming. The air was desert dry and one could see clearly for miles. Fall, arriving a few days hence, stayed hidden. Just a hint of color spotted the broadleaf trees on the higher elevations of the Allegheny Plateau. From our point of origin in Rochester, to the high spot on Route 15 and all the way to Gettysburg, not a cloud dared show its face. All along the way, the road looked more perfect and inviting than it ever had. As it narrowed and the speed limit slowed us through the small Pennsylvania towns and boroughs we have come to know, a strange and wonderful sight began to appear.

People, literally thousands of them, crowded by the side of the road. On sidewalks, grassy medians, hillsides and parking lots, in lawn chairs or standing or sitting cross-legged, they spontaneously came out in remembrance of those who died during the attacks of the Tuesday past. On those narrow lawns and sidewalks now so close to busy Route 15, in front of row houses and shuttered apartments, people who normally kept their distance from the road, stood proudly by it. Holding American flags, yellow ribbons and signs telling all that we can never forget, they waved and cheered and begged us to honk our horn if we supported America. We honked quite a bit.

THE sun, far past the meridian and dipping now towards the southwestern horizon, cast brightly in the passenger side windows as we motored through Dillsburg. It followed us the rest of the way down to Gettysburg and as we passed through town and out to the park to Cemetery Ridge. There we stopped at a familiar place; the High Water Mark. Perhaps, it was the very parking slot at which I had stopped some twenty-seven years earlier on my way to the start of my Marine Corps career. It was later in the day this time. Much past the time and far cooler than when I had diverted to Gettysburg on that long ago, steamy June day.

Then, I had listened to a guide tell a tired and sweating group about Longstreet's attack and how his obedient soldiers had failed to get past where we stood now. Knowing then only what I had read about war, I tried to imagine what it would be like to be in their shoes. Now, I knew a bit more. I felt their despair. More than a quarter century later, I had gained a new perspective of battle from what my own eyes had seen. My sense of what the men in blue and gray had gone through was sharpened by personal experiences. I was able to better appreciate what it took to overcome the crushing anxiety that took hold inside these unlucky men.

WE moved from the park road and over to sit on a flat stone. Its smooth surface stuck up from the dry grass and bare patches of dirt in front of the Copse of Trees. It was quiet there. Most of the wayfarers milling about the High Water Mark had let the dropping sun chase them back into town. The sun was gone now. The western sky over South Mountain glowed orange for a time and then settled back to a dusky blue. Transcontinental flights, allowed back in the sky after the government had grounded the fleet in the wake of the attacks, traced east-west contrails high above. The powder white lines grabbed and reflected the rays of the disappearing sun. The Confederate states' monuments on distant Seminary Ridge disappeared in the darkening shadows.

WE talked not about the battle of Gettysburg but about what had happened that week. Another war, this one like no other before it, had begun. Once again, Americans would fight. We did not know it then but this war would continue longer than all the others fought by Americans before. It would take place in far away tribal Anbar Province, high on a frigid, dry ridgeline in the Hindu Kush or in clandestine operations centers hidden deep within the national bureaucracy. This was to be my unborn son's war and the war of the children he will later bear. It will remain subdued at times and flare up at others, kindling new fears and familiar outrage. It will take no predictable shape or form. There will be no waves of flag carrying zealots in neat rows marching across fields. No mounted horseman or cannons set hub-to-hub. The laws of armed combat will be difficult to apply. This will be a war of the night, of stealth; a calculated chess game pitting coldly efficient technology against primitive hate. This is to be a fight for the mind first and only, secondarily, brute force against a body. At its conclusion, whenever that far off day may be, there will be no high water mark, no stone monument to a valiant leader, no post-war tourist havens lined with shops catering to the curious; shelves overflowing with cheap remembrances. The only similarities to wars of our past would be the hate and the killing.

THE guns will eventually be silent. They always grow quiet when humans become exhausted and sickened by what they have done. Millions of eyes will strain to the future to see that end. Will it ever come? Someday. Until then the war goes on. The dead are offered trite and soon forgotten remembrances in hometown newspapers. The pictures of the innocent faces are broadcast; flashing by on a computer or flat screen accompanied by silent platitudes. No words can, or ever will, assuage the pain. The only comfort the families of the dead have for now is to take the painfully familiar exit from the dismal and afflicted road they travel and arrive at a hushed and unwelcoming respite. A lamentable sanctuary. A quiet place where white rectangles are arrayed, side-by-side, nearly touching, in the fresh loam and immaculate gardens of graveyards.

If you are on the road from Rochester to Gettysburg and traveling on Route 15, here are some of my favorite places to stop:

* *Dinosaur BBQ.* 99 Court Street, Rochester. Not exactly on Route 15 but a wedge shot from it. Superb food and great atmosphere in the old L.V.R.R. station.

* *Mount Hope Cemetery.* 1133 Mount Hope Ave., Rochester. A gorgeous Victorian sanctuary.

* *Bath National Cemetery.* San Juan Ave., Bath, NY. Among other famous occupants, visit the grave of Private R.K. Snedon whose Civil War sketches and remembrances are fascinating.

* *Keystone Tioga Welcome Center.* Route 15, Tioga, PA. Welcome to PA! Enjoy the view!

* *Fry Bros. Turkey Ranch.* 19919 Route 15, Trout Run, PA. Turkey, mashed potatoes, stuffing, gravy, cranberry sauce . . . c'mon!

* *Clyde Peeling's Reptiland.* 18628 Route 15, Allenwood, PA. Kids will love it!

* *Peter J. McGovern Little League Museum and Hall of Excellence.* 525 Route 15, So. Williamsport, PA.

* *Horseshoe Bar*, Route 15, New Buffalo, PA. Street number? We don't need no stinkin' street number. Watch for the dragon! You can't miss it.

Acknowledgments

My sincere thanks to Carol Lavigne, Craig Kelley, John Messenger, Judy Messenger and John Kyle. Each reviewed early versions of this memoir and provided helpful feedback which made it better. I would also like to thank my wife Jill and son Jack who tolerated my rudeness as I disappeared on occasion when engaged in writing. They stayed attentive while suffering my incessant lecturing during the five hour drives to Gettysburg. They patiently and energetically tagged along as I walked in the footsteps of soldiers of long ago.

About the Author

John Thomas ("J.T.") Ambrosi was born in Rochester, New York. He studied at the University of Rochester, focusing on history and public policy. After a hitch as a U.S. Marine, including service in the First Gulf War, he helped found what was to become a Fortune 1000 company. In 2011, J.T. left the corporate world and began consulting on policy matters, specializing in telecommunications. In his spare time, he writes a semi-weekly blog for Messenger Post Media entitled Wren Field Rambling. He lives in the idyllic Erie Canal town of Pittsford, New York along with his wife Jill, son Jack and a puppy named C.J.

CPSIA information can be obtained
at www.ICGtesting.com
Printed in the USA
BVHW091138240121
598598BV00024B/2161